CROSS-LEVEL INFERENCE

CROSS-LEVEL
INFERENCE

Christopher H. Achen and
W. Phillips Shively

THE UNIVERSITY OF CHICAGO PRESS
Chicago and London

Christopher H. Achen is professor of political science at the
University of Michigan. W. Phillips Shively is professor of
political science at the University of Minnesota.

The University of Chicago Press, Chicago 60637
The University of Chicago Press, Ltd., London
© 1995 by The University of Chicago
All rights reserved. Published 1995
Printed in the United States of America

04 03 02 01 00 99 98 97 96 95   1 2 3 4 5

ISBN (cloth): 0-226-00219-5
ISBN (paper): 0-226-00220-9

Library of Congress Cataloging-in-Publication Data

Achen, Christopher H.
    Cross-level inference / Christopher H. Achen and
W. Phillips Shively.
        p.   cm.
    Includes bibliographical references and index.
    ISBN 0-226-00219-5. — ISBN 0-226-00220-9 (pbk.)
    1. Political science—Methodology.   2. Political statis-
tics.   3. Probabilities.   I. Shively, W. Phillips, 1942–   .
II. Title.
JA71.A26   1995
320'.01—dc20   94-22590
                                                  CIP

For my mother, Louise Prom,
my stepfather, Walter Prom,
and in memory of my father, Clarence Achen
— C. A.

For Barbara, with love.
— W. P. S.

CONTENTS

PREFACE

In preparing this book, we have benefited from the advice of many colleagues and friends. John E. Jackson, Gary King, and Charles Franklin read a preliminary version of the entire manuscript, giving us detailed and searching comments and saving us from many errors and omissions. Our gratitude is perhaps best expressed by saying that we have tried to respond to the challenges they raised, and that in consequence, nearly half the book will be new to them.

James Alt, Larry Bartels, Henry Brady, Lutz Erbring, Joseph Houska, Michael Goldstein, Henry Heitowit, J. Morgan Kousser, John L. McCarthy, Walter Mebane, Bradley Palmquist, David Prindle, Douglas Rivers, Steven Rosenstone, and especially J. Merrill Shanks all made helpful comments and suggestions at various stages of our thinking. We are grateful to them. Rumi Price coded the ecological data and carried out the calculations in the first part of chapter 7, and we are indebted to her for the exceptional precision and responsibility she brought to the task. Mary Ellen Otis prepared portions of the manuscript with skill and enthusiasm.

We would also like to thank John Tryneski and Diana Gillooly of the University of Chicago Press for their help and their patience.

The authors also express their appreciation for research support of this project from the Survey Research Center at the University of California, Berkeley, the Center for Political Studies, Institute for Social Research, at the University of Michigan, and the College of Liberal Arts of the University of Minnesota.

The survey data used in chapter 7 were supplied by the Inter-

University Consortium for Social and Political Research of the Center for Political Studies, Institute for Social Research, University of Michigan. The responsibility for analysis and conclusions remains our own.

Finally, we thank our families for their support throughout the writing of this book.

ONE

CROSS-LEVEL INFERENCE

By their nature, the social sciences deal with concepts and observations at different levels of aggregation. Economists model both individual consumer demand and aggregate demand; sociologists theorize about individuals, families, social classes, and communities; political scientists seek to explain the political activities of individuals, political parties, bureaucracies, and nation-states, all embedded in the international system. Since a family of variables across varying levels of analysis are closely and directly related, yet may operate quite differently from one another at their respective levels of analysis, examination of members of the same family, across levels, can enrich understanding. But working at varied levels of aggregation can also lead to tribulation, especially if the fundamental behavioral processes take place on one level while the relevant substantive implications or the available data occur on another. In such cases, we must infer relationships at one level from theory or data on a different level; doing so constitutes the problem of "cross-level inference."

AN EXAMPLE

Cross-level analysis is deceptively difficult. Logical contradictions may afflict even the smoothest-seeming translations between levels. For example, consider Michels's well-known "iron law of oligarchy." To paraphrase his theory, Michels (1949) concluded from an analysis of the German Social Democratic party that radical social change is impossible. He stated the dilemma thus: In order for the unprivileged in society to work any change on their own behalf, it is necessary for them to combine and organize. Individually, they are no match for the more privileged members of society—their bosses, their landlords, their priests—but if they combine in an organized movement, they can wield political power and effect change. However, in organizing they must develop a specialized leadership group and give over the direction of the movement to that group. Over time the leadership will take on the characteristics of the old privileged class, and in the end nothing will have changed.

Note that Michels's analysis is conducted solely at the level of the individual political party. His book, in fact, is a critical history of the Social Democratic party of Germany. If his theory is extended to the level of party system (a higher level of aggregation) a distinctly different theory emerges, with a less pessimistic conclusion.

Every state has a system of political parties, the set of all parties actively seeking power. To say with Michels that any party, from the moment of its organization, moves steadily toward caution and conservatism is not to say that party *systems* will necessarily be cautious and conservative. How does this work? Let us draw an analogy from the characteristic of demographics that populations maintain youth, even though no individual can maintain perpetual youth. In a sense, Michels's complaint that radical change is impossible because a political party cannot remain radical for long is parallel to a complaint that youth is impossible because a person cannot remain young for long. Radicalism may not be possible in the long run for any individual party, but it may be possible for a party system, if parties regularly disappear and are replaced by new, fresh parties. At the system level, then, it is by no means impossible for parties to maintain a strong capacity for radical change.

This illustrates the theoretical disjunction across levels of aggregation of what may look like a straightforwardly single process. While Michels may have been right at the level of the individual party, he was wrong at the level of the system of parties.

THE THEME OF THIS BOOK

Theoretical disjunction poses two kinds of problems for social analysis. One problem is that of *theoretical consistency*. Hypotheses valid at the microlevel often have readily apparent and intuitively plausible macrolevel analogues, and yet the macropropositions may be shown to be incoherent nonsense (Green 1964). Avoiding false analogies across levels is obviously a prerequisite, not only to statistical inferences from one level to another, but simply to theoretical coherence. Thus theoretical consistency in aggregation is of fundamental importance to the social sciences. We discuss it further in appendix A to this chapter.

Most of the literature on aggregation has been concerned, however, not with theoretical consistency but with *statistical issues*—"cross-level inference" or "aggregation bias" or "ecological inference." Here the concern is typically with using macrolevel data to infer microlevel relationships. It is this problem that has brought most scholars' attention to varied levels of aggregation, and most previous work has focused on it.

W. S. Robinson (1950) was the first to bring the problem to general attention. Robinson noted that aggregate statistical findings would not necessarily mirror the individual-level relationships underlying them. In his best-known example, he showed that states with more foreign-born residents tended to have more residents literate in English. A scholar using only aggregate data would have concluded that the foreign-born were unusually literate in English. However, individual-level census data showed that just the reverse was true: foreign-born residents were less literate in English than native-born Americans. Thus even the sign of the aggregate-level relationship was wrong. Robinson concluded that we should avoid using aggregate-level correlations to draw conclusions about otherwise unobservable individual-level relationships; he called this the "fallacy of ecological correlation." Later scholars have ameliorated Robinson's pessimistic conclusion slightly, but never to a full degree of satisfaction.

This book, too, addresses primarily the statistical problem of cross-level inference rather than the problem of theoretical consistency. In large part, we take the substantive model as given and concentrate on estimating its parameters. Most of the statistical models discussed are sufficiently modest that the full complexities of cross-level consistency are sidestepped. Even in these restricted cases, however, the statistical and theoretical issues are sufficiently intertwined that we are virtually always forced to explicitly derive macrolevel models from their microlevel counterparts before statistical work can begin. In that sense, there is no escaping the need to demonstrate theoretical consistency across levels.

To state the general theme of this chapter and this book before we get into the details:

Cross-level inference is a problem of statistical underidentification, that is, a problem of insufficient information (Richmond 1976). Data gathered at the macrolevel do not allow us to definitely determine the process at work among the same variables at the microlevel unless—as is almost never the case—we have complete knowledge of the process of aggregation itself. As is usual in cases of underidentification, the solution is to add additional assumptions or external information to effect closure.

Cross-level analyses are complex, and the added assumptions or information are often very demanding of theoretic agility and contextual knowledge. In consequence, too many practitioners try to evade the problem, or else attack it with conventional but inflexible sets of assumptions that are inappropriate for the data. Even some recent and relatively sophisticated models fall into this trap.

We argue for greater flexibility and offer in the chapters that follow several alternative ways to approach cross-level inference. These are by no means the last word. Some are relatively informal, others are approximations, still others are narrow in applicability. Nearly all stand in need of additional theoretical development. While we hope and believe that each will prove useful in its own right, more important to us is the hope that our critique of contemporary practices, and the alternatives we offer as examples of what might be done, will encourage flexibility and experimentation by others in their cross-level work.

THE PROBLEM OF CROSS-LEVEL INFERENCE

For reasons of cost or availability, theories and descriptions referring to one level of aggregation are frequently testable only with data from another level. The most common variety of cross-level analysis encountered in the political science and sociological literature is "ecological inference"—the use of aggregate data to study the behavior of individuals. Thus county measurements of air quality and cancer rates are correlated to assess the effect of air pollution on personal health (e.g., Lave and Seskin 1977); murder rates are correlated with execution rates to estimate the effect of capital punishment (e.g., Bowers 1974); and the movements of aggregate demand over time are examined as guides to the behavior of consumers (e.g., Deaton and Muellbauer 1980, chap. 3).

These examples are typical of ecological inference in that data from groups (counties, constituencies, or nations) are used to infer the behavior of individuals in them (medical patients, voters, or consumers). In certain cases, no other approach is possible: for example, if social scientists want to know whether Weimar voters chose Hitler out of ignorance or out of conviction, survey research is not an available tool, since opinion surveys did not come into use until a decade later. Thus ecological inference is often inescapable.

HISTORY OF THE PROBLEM OF ECOLOGICAL INFERENCE

Modern attention to the problem of ecological inference dates to Robinson (1950). However, aggregate data analysis has an earlier history which is instructive. The Second World War marks a great divide in the social sciences in many ways, but perhaps in no other way is that divide more sharp than in the collapse of aggregate data analysis after the war and its replacement by individual survey analysis as the dominant method of quantitative social research.

The great tool of quantitative research in the nineteenth century and the first half of the twentieth century was aggregate data analysis. In France and Germany, the leading social scientific communities of that era, slightly different traditions developed.

The French especially developed social cartography, as exemplified in André Siegfried's (1913) pioneering study of the political sociology of western France. Perhaps one reason for the French cartographic tradition was their emphasis, at least with regard to political analysis, on questions of continuity and change. These are readily addressed through comparisons of maps over time, as in the work of Goguel (1951). The cartographic tradition, of course, was merely a major theme of French social analysis; the great master Durkheim used aggregate analysis of a different sort in his *Suicide* (1897), comparing suicide rates among varied groups in the population.

While the French emphasized comparisons of groups and regions, the Germans leaned more to cross-level inference, in which aggregated data are used to address what are unambiguously questions of individuals' behavior. This may have been due to Germans' fascination with the class base of political parties' support, a research question which pulled them toward cross-level inference. Examples are Blank's (1905) estimation of the logical minimum number of bourgeois voters who must have voted for the Social Democrats in order to have produced observed outcomes (he estimated that, as early as 1893, at least one-fourth of the SPD vote was bourgeois) and Tönnies's (1924) correlation of the party vote across two elections in Kiel. A remarkable addition is Bernstein's (1932) exposition of the problem of ecological inference, which anticipated what would only be worked out by Robinson and Goodman across the 1950s in the United States. Bernstein's article,

TABLE 1 Ogburn and Goltra's 1919 Regression and Correlation Results: Regression Equations, Correlation Coefficients, and Partial Correlation Coefficients

Measure Number	Title of Measure	Regression Equations	r_{xy}	$r_{xy \cdot z}$
1.	Noncitizen immigrants disenfranchised	$X = 68.07 + 0.35Y + 0.07Z$	+0.52	+0.47
2.	Creating office of lieutenant-governor	$X = 19.69 - 0.05Y + 0.23Z$	-0.03	-0.06
3.	Consolidating Portland and Multnomah County	$X = 45.18 + 0.18Y - 0.01Z$	+0.18	+0.18
4.	State credit for irrigation and development	$X = 48.66 - 0.38Y - 0.17Z$	-0.50	-0.45
5.	Classification of property for taxation	$X = 42.09 + 0.04Y - 0.15Z$	-0.03	+0.05
6.	To establish state normal school at Ashland	$X = 48.54 + 0.09Y - 0.27Z$	+0.01	+0.11
7.	To provide method of merging towns	$X = 65.97 + 0.29Y + 0.01Z$	+0.33	+0.32
8.	To increase pay of legislature	$X = 27.02 - 0.14Y - 0.02Z$	-0.24	-0.22
9.	Universal eight-hour day	$X = 89.94 - 0.55Y - 0.82Z$	-0.53	-0.47
10.	Eight-hour day for women	$X = 118.94 - 0.33Y - 1.07Z$	-0.41	-0.30
11.	Nonpartisan judiciary	$X = 49.64 - 0.02Y - 0.01Z$	-0.12	-0.02
12.	$1500 tax exemption (single tax)	$X = 96.32 - 0.05Y - 1.13Z$	-0.27	-0.06
13.	Public docks and water frontage	$X = 88.12 - 0.18Y - 0.83Z$	-0.34	-0.20
14.	Prohibition	$X = 31.54 + 0.78Y - 0.28Z$	+0.46	+0.49
15.	Abolition of death penalty	$X = 73.33 + 0.00Y - 0.59Z$	-0.16	-0.01
16.	Single tax heavily graduated	$X = 82.55 - 0.22Y - 0.87Z$	-0.36	-0.22
17.	Consolidation of corporation and insurance departments	$X = 54.63 - 0.27Y - 0.63Z$	-0.40	-0.31
18.	Cheaper dentistry (Painless Parker bill)	$X = 100.66 - 0.46Y - 0.77Z$	-0.47	-0.39
19.	County officers' terms made longer	$X = 29.89 + 0.22Y + 0.14Z$	+0.36	+0.29
20.	Creating tax code commission	$X = 17.03 + 0.04Y + 0.11Z$	+0.11	+0.05
21.	Abolishing Desert Land Board	$X = 36.40 - 0.32Y - 0.17Z$	-0.54	-0.49
22.	Proportional representation	$X = 66.62 - 0.32Y - 0.63Z$	-0.44	-0.35
23.	Abolition of state senate	$X = 79.98 - 0.33Y - 0.84Z$	-0.38	-0.25
24.	Department of industry for unemployed	$X = 80.36 - 0.41Y - 0.85Z$	-0.47	-0.40
25.	Primary election of delegates for nominating primary	$X = 20.44 - 0.28Y - 0.08Z$	-0.43	-0.45
26.	$300 tax exemption and two-thirds vote to amend	$X = 40.36 - 0.33Y - 0.15Z$	-0.50	-0.45

Note: X = percentage of voters in favor of measure, by precinct; Y = percentage of those voting that are women, by precinct; and Z = degree of conservatism, by precinct.

which was overlooked in the general collapse of German social science at the rise of Hitler, is included as appendix B to this chapter.

In the United States, too, as quantitative social science developed in the early twentieth century, political analysis depended heavily on aggregate data. (See Gow 1985, on which these paragraphs are based.) Perhaps the earliest American example occurs in Arthur Bentley's *Process of Government,* well known for its contribution to "group theory," which contains a brief reference to his cross-plots of one set of Chicago election precinct outcomes against another (Bentley 1908, p. 498).

Much of the subsequent aggregate work developed in connection with the "Chicago schools" of sociology and political science. The first substantial analyses were carried out by Chicago sociologist William F. Ogburn and his associates. In 1916, Ogburn and Peterson published a study of social-class effects on the vote using precinct returns from Portland, Oregon, and judgmental coding of the social class of each precinct; they used cross-tabular methods. And in 1919, Ogburn and Goltra studied an early version of the "gender gap" with Portland data. The methods were ecological correlation and regression; a table from their article is reproduced here as table 1. According to Gow (1985, p. 7), this article marks the first appearance of regression techniques in a political science journal. However the precise connection between the aggregate coefficient estimates and the behavior of individuals was not understood until Miller's (1952) and Goodman's (1953) work.

The first ecological factor analysis was apparently done by Harold Gosnell (1937), who had learned the technique from his Chicago colleague L. L. Thurstone. Like ecological regressions done at this time, the relation to individual-level parameters was not grasped. Similarly, Key's *Southern Politics* (1949) relied heavily on cartographic evidence and on scattergrams of aggregate data to explore the nature of party factions in the South.

Over the decade following the Second World War, survey methodology swept the social sciences. The new tool obviously improved scholars' work and broadened the range of what they could do, but its rapid dominance also carried costs. In many ways its victory was *too* complete, and the social sciences are only now working their way back to positions of greater balance.

One cost of the victory of survey analysis was that the availability of survey research magnified the already pronounced American emphasis on individuals and on individualistic explanations of behavior. For four decades scholars have underemphasized the effect of communities and of group and organizational structures on social processes. One result of this shift is that the role of context in our research has degenerated from work in which context is intimately involved in broader analysis, as in Key's work, to a large literature of "contextual" studies, most of which have taken as their research problem variants on the nearly trivial question of whether "context" does or does not have any effect at all.

Another cost of the victory of survey research is that analysis and the development of theory shifted away from processes which work themselves out slowly over time, and which are thus difficult to capture in a "snapshot" survey. A good example of this is provided by companion articles published by Key (1955, 1959). "A Theory of Critical Elections" (1955) described a process of rapid electoral change, using the examples of the shift to the New Deal and the presidential election of 1896. This article spawned a large literature on electoral realignment. "Secular Realignment and the Party System" (1959), however, described equally important processes of slower electoral change spanning 20 or 30 years; it was nearly ignored and had few offspring. The first article dealt with questions which could be conveniently studied by survey research, while the second did not.

A final result of the hegemony of survey research was that for a couple of decades impressive quantitative historical work remained somewhat neglected by the broader social sciences. A good example is Ruth Silva's (1962) fine study of the 1928 American election.

In an interesting way, the "problem" of cross-level inference appears to have arisen simultaneously with this shift to survey research. The problem is a genuine one, of course, and forms the subject of this book. What is interesting is that this problem was noted at least three times in the early twentieth century (Ogburn and Peterson 1916; Bernstein 1932; Gehlke and Biehl 1934), but was ignored. Bernstein, in particular, translated in appendix B, reads almost exactly like the later literature of Robinson and Goodman. A cynic might conclude that social scientists tend to ignore logical problems and contradictions in their methods if they do not see anything to be done about them.

In contrast, when W. S. Robinson rediscovered the problem in 1950, at a time when survey research was emerging as an alternative to aggregate data analysis, his article fit researchers' predispositions and had an enormous impact.

Despite the difficulty of drawing firm conclusions from it, however, cross-level inference continues to be an important research strategy for the simple reason that there are many research problems for which it is inescapably necessary. Today, cross-level inference is especially prevalent in historical research, for the obvious reason that individual-level

mates. The most popular of these is the assumption that p_j and q_j are each constant across districts, or at least that any variation in them may be absorbed into a well-behaved disturbance term (Goodman 1953, 1959). Following Goodman (1959, p. 612), researchers conventionally assume that for all j

$$(3a) \qquad E(p_j|X_j) = p$$

and

$$(3b) \qquad E(q_j|X_j) = q.$$

This postulate permits estimation of the individual-level parameters by ordinary regression. Thus, rearranging terms in equation (1),

$$(4) \qquad Y_j = q_j + (p_j - q_j)X_j \quad (j = 1, \ldots, m)$$
$$= q + (p - q)X_j + U_j,$$

where $U_j = q_j - q + (p_j - p - q_j + q)X_j$.

Equation (4) has the form of a bivariate regression equation, with intercept q and slope $p - q$. In addition, by equations (3a) and (3b), we have $E(u_j) = 0$ and $E(X_j u_j) = 0$ for all j. Hence, so long as there is some variation in X, all the conditions needed for ordinary least squares (OLS) estimates to be unbiased are fulfilled. Using the district-level percentages as observations, we can regress the percentage for Hitler on the percentage Catholic, and under the assumptions of equations (3a) and (3b) the intercept q will estimate the vote for Hitler among non-Catholics, while the sum of the intercept q and slope $p - q$ will estimate p, the vote for Hitler among Catholics. This technique is known as Goodman "ecological regression," and we discuss it and its many extensions in the following chapter.

Here we simply note that the identifying conditions imposed by conventional ecological regression are very strong. They require that the expected transition rates be statistically unrelated to the aggregate independent variable. In a regression of vote on social class, for example, these conditions require that working-class voters in prosperous districts are just as likely to remain loyal to left-wing parties as are working-class voters in very poor districts. Assumptions of that sort are always dubious, and they are not easily tested. If the assumptions are in error, ecological regression may seriously mislead (see chap. 3).

The Goodman assumptions are not the only possible postulates that imply a linear regression format for studying group voting patterns with aggregate data. As Klein et al. (1991), Freedman et al. (1991), and

Klein and Freedman (1993) have recently emphasized, one may arrive at ecological regression via another route, the "neighborhood model." Returning to the vote for the Nazis, imagine that Catholics and non-Catholics vote for Hitler in precisely the same proportion p_j in any given district, but that the proportion varies across districts. In particular, suppose that, in expectation, the proportion voting Nazi varies linearly with the proportion Catholics. Again letting Y_j be the Nazi vote in constituency j and X_j the proportion Catholic, we have, in parallel with equation (4) above,

$$(5) \qquad y_j = p_j X_j + p_j (1 - X_j) + U_j \quad (j = 1, \ldots, m),$$

where $p_j = a + bX_j$. Here a and b are constants and u_j is a disturbance term. Substituting into equation (5) gives

$$(6) \qquad\qquad Y_j = a + bX_j + U_j,$$

which is a linear regression setup just like equation (4). In other words, the Goodman model and the neighborhood model are empirically indistinguishable: Both imply a linear regression of Y_j on X_j.

The interpretation of the coefficients in the two models is radically different, however. In the conventional Goodman setup, the Catholic vote for the Nazis would be given by the sum of the slope and intercept, namely, $p = a + b$. In the neighborhood model, on the other hand, the value of p would be the value of $a + bX_j$ averaged over all Catholic voters. In the case of equal-sized districts, if $\bar{X}$ is the mean of the X_j, then it turns out that $p = a + b(\Sigma X_j^2/m)/\bar{X}$. Similarly, in the Goodman model, the non-Catholic vote for the Nazis, q, is found by setting $q = a$. In the neighborhood model, by contrast, since Catholics and non-Catholics in each district vote alike, q is just the value of $a + bX_j$ averaged over all non-Catholics, which turns out to imply that $q = a + b(1 - \Sigma X_j^2/m)/(1 - \bar{X})$.

Because each x_j is a proportion and thus falls between zero and unity, it is not hard to show that the neighborhood model necessarily estimates p to be smaller and q larger than in the Goodman regression. Thus Catholics and non-Catholics (or any other division of the population) will appear to be less polarized politically under the neighborhood model. It is perhaps no accident that plaintiffs in voting rights cases, who are required to demonstrate polarized voting, have often favored Goodman's method, while defendants have had recourse to the neighborhood model. (See the debate in the references cited above, notably Freedman et al. 1991 and Grofman 1991.)

The Goodman setup and the neighborhood model are not equal

competitors, of course. As a model of how people vote, the neighborhood model is simply bad science. Whatever its uses as a courtroom debating point, its assumptions have been discredited by survey research for half a century.[1] But the conceptual point it raises is an important one. For too long, scholars have proceeded as if linear ecological regression under Goodman's interpretation had an inherent a priori superiority over all possible alternatives. The neighborhood model reminds us that the Goodman assumptions, whatever their initial plausibility or aesthetic appeal, are but one choice from many possibilities. In the end, neither linearity nor Goodman's identifying conditions have any special claim on our affections, unless they can show empirical success. These data analytic issues are crucial; see chapters 5 and 6.

Indeed, Goodman's approach has encountered serious difficulties in practice. In particular, it has shown a tendency to produce logically impossible estimates: for example, 130% of the non-Catholics voting for Hitler, or -20% of the Catholics. It is in this form that most social scientists have encountered the problem of ecological inference; it is another version of Robinson's "ecological fallacy." Apparently, the assumptions of equations (3a) and (3b) are often unfulfilled in practice.

BLALOCK'S URN MODEL

An alternative way to visualize the problem of ecological inference is the "urn model" of Blalock (1961, chap 4; it is also presented well in Hannan 1991). Blalock showed that we may think of geographic aggregations as samples drawn from the total population by historical processes such as migration and demographic transition. That is, we may think of history as having constructed geographic districts by drawing individuals from the national pool and placing them in districts. This assignment process might take place in several different ways, depending on its relationship to the substantive process the investigator wishes to explain.

Suppose that the substantive process at work in the ith individual in

1. This is not to say that the neighborhood model is never superior to the Goodman model, no matter how poorly specified the latter may be. In particular, when no controls for partisanship or past votes are introduced, Goodman's version of ecological regression will tend to overestimate p and underestimate q (see chap. 3). The neighborhood model reduces p and raises q relative to Goodman, so that with luck, it may come out nearer the truth. Examples appear in Freedman et al. (1991). But of course, the more appropriate course of action is to allow explicitly for p and q to vary with partisanship or prior votes (see chaps. 5, 6, and 7).

constituency j is given by $y_i = f(x_i, u_i)$, $i = 1, \ldots, n$, where y_i is the vector of scores on the dependent variable, x_i the vector of scores on the independent variables, and u_i the disturbance term. We now wish to characterize how individuals obeying this process might be assigned to districts. In reality, assignments take place sequentially, and individuals can take account of prior assignments of other people in deciding where they wish to live. For present purposes, however, it is simpler and equally satisfactory to treat all assignments as simultaneous, so that the probability of living in a particular district depends only on the individual's own scores on the independent and dependent variables. Correlations between aggregate variables and individual assignments are easily induced with this setup, as the example below demonstrates.

For notation, let $p_i(j|Z_i)$ be the probability that individual i is assigned to constituency j, conditional on the person's scores on some other variables Z_i. Then we may define the following types of assignment of individuals to districts for all i, j:

1. Independent assignment: $p_i(j|y_i, x_i) = p(j)$. In this case, each individual has the same chance as any other individual of entering a particular district. This is the strong form of "random assignment to districts."
2. Conditionally independent assignment (Blalock's "assignment along the independent variables"): $p_i(j|y_i, x_i) = p(j|x_i)$. In this case, individuals may vary in their probability of assignment to a particular district, but as a function of the exogenous variables only. Obviously, condition 1 is a special case of condition 2.
3. Conditionally dependent assignment (Blalock's "assignment along the dependent variable"): $p_i(j|y_i, x_i) \neq p(j|x_i)$. This case holds when condition 2 fails: Assignment depends on the dependent variable, even after conditioning on the independent variables.

The strong form of random assignment, condition 1, is obviously enough to guarantee successful aggregate inference, but it is stronger than necessary. Successful aggregation requires only condition 2, that assignment to districts be conditionally independent. When the substantive process is represented by a linear regression equation, for example, so that $y_i = x_i\beta + u_i$, conditional independence is equivalent to requiring that x_i may influence the probability that individual i is assigned to district j, but the disturbance term u_i may not. In this sense, the aggregation process must be statistically "ignorable." When this condition fails, as in condition 3, aggregate regression is biased. In the

TABLE 2 The Population

	Working Class	Middle Class	Total
Republican	30,000	90,000	120,000
Democrat	120,000	60,000	180,000
Total	150,000	150,000	300,000

ecological regression case, conditionally dependent assignment causes the failure of the Goodman assumptions that the district transition rates p_j and q_j are mean independent of X_j.[2]

Tables 3 and 4 display a simulated example. Given a population whose individuals are distributed as shown in table 2, the individuals are divided into three aggregate units. First, let us aggregate them by class, constructing our districts by locating working-class individuals in district A with probability .1, in district B with probability .3, and in district C with probability .6; middle-class individuals are located in district A with probability .5, in district B with probability .4, and in district C with probability .1. Location does not depend on party, except indirectly through the fact that workers tend to be Democrats and the middle class tend to be Republicans; thus, this is conditionally independent assignment. Table 3 displays the expected values of the cells of districts A, B, and C under this sort of grouping. We note from table 2 that the probability that a worker will be a Republican is $30,000/150,000 = .2$; similarly the probability that a member of the middle class is a Republican is .6, the probability that a worker is a Democrat is .8, and the probability that a member of the middle class is a Democrat is .4. In district A, for instance, the expected number of workers (given a probability of .1 that a worker locates in district A) is 15,000, and the expected number of workers that are Republicans (the upper-left call of the table) is $.2 \times 15,000 = 3,000$.

We see from the table that, although the expected proportion work-

2. Beyond aggregation effects, "contextual" interaction can also cause the Goodman assumptions to be violated. This will occur if, once aggregation is completed and the distribution of the individual-level independent variable by district is thus set, individuals act on each other to change their values of p and q. (Obviously, "completed" and "set" are a bit metaphorical here; both aggregation and interaction are continuous processes.) For instance, in a district that is heavily working class, frequent contact of working-class voters with each other might reinforce their loyalty to the Socialist party and lead to a higher level of p (the probability that workers will vote Socialist) in that district. See below, chapter 9, for a more detailed discussion.

TABLE 3 Effects of Aggregation along the Independent Variable:
Expected Frequencies

	District A		
	Proportion Working Class	Proportion Middle Class	Total
Proportion Republican	3,000	45,000	48,000
Proportion Democrat	12,000	30,000	42,000
Total	15,000	75,000	90,000

E(Proportion working class) = 15,000/90,000 = .17
$E(p)$ = 3,000/15,000 = .20

	District B		
	Proportion Working Class	Proportion Middle Class	Total
Proportion Republican	9,000	36,000	45,000
Proportion Democrat	36,000	24,000	60,000
Total	45,000	60,000	105,000

E(Proportion working class) = 45,000/105,000 = .43
$E(p)$ = 9,000/45,000 = .20

	District C		
	Proportion Working Class	Proportion Middle Class	Total
Proportion Republican	18,000	9,000	27,000
Proportion Democrat	72,000	6,000	78,000
Total	90,000	15,000	105,000

E(Proportion working class) = 90,000/105,000 = .86
$E(p)$ = 18,000/90,000 = .20

ing-class varies from .17 to .86, the expected value of p is a constant. Here it is true, as required by the Goodman assumptions, that p is uncorrelated with the aggregate independent variable (in this case, proportion working-class). Ecological inference via regression would yield unbiased estimates.

Contrast the effects of conditionally dependent aggregation in table 4: Districts are constructed as in table 3, except that individuals are now located in districts on the basis of their party.[3] In contrast to table 3, as E(Proportion working-class) decreases across districts,

---

3. Republicans are located in district A with probability .1, in district B with probability .3, and in district C with probability .6; Democrats are located in district A with probability .5, in district B with probability .4, and in district C with probability .1.

TABLE 4 Effects of Aggregation by the Disturbance Term: Expected Frequencies

	District A		
	Proportion Working Class	Proportion Middle Class	Total
Proportion Republican	3,000	9,000	12,000
Proportion Democrat	60,000	30,000	90,000
Total	63,000	39,000	102,000
	E(Proportion working class) = 63,000/102,000 = .62		
	$E(p)$ = 3,000/63,000 = .05		

	District B		
	Proportion Working Class	Proportion Middle Class	Total
Proportion Republican	9,000	27,000	36,000
Proportion Democrat	48,000	24,000	72,000
Total	57,000	51,000	108,000
	E(Proportion working class) = 57,000/108,000 = .43		
	$E(p)$ = 9,000/57,000 = .16		

	District C		
	Proportion Working Class	Proportion Middle Class	Total
Proportion Republican	18,000	54,000	72,000
Proportion Democrat	12,000	6,000	18,000
Total	30,000	60,000	90,000
	E(Proportion working class) = 30,000/90,000 = .33		
	$E(p)$ = 18,000/30,000 = .60		

$E(p)$ systematically increases. Now p will be correlated with the aggregate independent variable, and the Goodman assumptions will be violated.[4]

In practice, individuals come to be located in districts through a multiplicity of processes—transportation links, location through their

---

4. It is clear enough what is going on here. When the number of workers in a district is set by drawing workers for placement in the district, approximately 20% of those workers will be Republicans each time, and p (the probability that a worker is a Republican) will vary randomly from district to district around its expected value of .2. Thus, p will not be correlated with the aggregate independent variable. When the number of workers is a result of drawings of Democrats and Republicans, however, the proportion of workers that are Republicans is a function of how many Republicans were drawn in the first place. The higher the proportion of Republicans by district, the higher p will be; and since proportion Republican and proportion worker are related at the aggregate level, p will be correlated with proportion worker, the aggregate independent variable.

jobs, preference for certain types of housing, concern for schools, ethnic preferences, historic patterns of migration in earlier generations, and so forth—some of which almost surely will be correlated with the dependent variable even after the typical garden-variety independent variables are controlled. Then assumptions (3a) and (3b) are violated, and ecological bias results. It is this effect that causes Robinson's correlations to reverse sign and Goodman's regression estimates to stray from their true values.

Blalock's interpretation of the problem does not tell us anything about estimation beyond what Goodman had already done, but it does emphasize for us how daunting the Goodman assumptions are. Unless we can statistically control for all of the historical and individual processes of migration and settlement that have placed individuals in aggregated districts, that is, unless we can model the substantive process so well that location itself has no additional predictive power, bias will be induced in the ecological regression estimates. Thus, while Goodman's model has been widely adopted, investigators have lived with it in unease.

EVASION OF THE PROBLEM THROUGH A "SOCIAL FACTS" ARGUMENT

In an attempt to sidestep the problem of ecological inference, some investigators have taken refuge in a claim that they are not inferring individual behavior at all, but are studying "social facts" on aggregated groups. Now social facts are well worth studying, but not all grouped data are social facts.

At least since Durkheim, social scientists have been aware that social life exhibits emergent properties not visible at the individual level. Thus business firms and political parties are each collections of individuals, but for many purposes it is more convenient to explain their behavior as if they were unitary actors. As such, they may have talents and capacities beyond those of any individual: for example, they may behave as if they had long-term interests which survive the complete turnover of their personnel. Moreover, their interactions (markets or party systems) may have properties qualitatively different from those of individuals. These properties emerge only at the group level.

Social scientists are agreed that social facts are somehow central to their work. Though social facts may be approached in a variety of ways (see chap. 9, on contextual analysis), a tradition favored especially by sociologists is that of "holistic" explanation. On this view, social facts constitute an explanatory realm of their own, and reductionist accounts are excluded. Thus a crowd of 12 people is said to have 13 personalities (Le Bon 1897), and the thirteenth is not derivable from the other 12.

In the ecological inference context, the holistic perspective has been employed primarily as an escape from Robinson's critique of ecological inference. Ecological inference is said to consist of explaining the behavior, not of individuals, but of aggregate units—counties, constituencies, or states (e.g., Brown 1982, 1988; Marks and Burbank 1990). Thus the ensuing differences between the individual-level and aggregate-level results are no surprise: they refer to different aspects of reality. The individual data describe the behavior of individuals; the aggregate data describe the behavior of social aggregates. Since many new properties emerge at the aggregate level, naturally the results from the two levels differ. From the holistic viewpoint, all efforts to "solve" the ecological inference problem result from a naive view of social life. So long as there are social facts, there will be a difference between individual- and aggregate-level analysis, and *vive la différence.*

Unfortunately, this sweeping dismissal of the ecological inference problem will not withstand close scrutiny. The aggregate units ordinarily encountered in ecological inference lack the characteristics of unitary social actors. For example, they may be census enumeration tracts, voter precincts, or mosquito abatement districts—social units whose boundaries are unknown to the voters, whose correspondence to natural social groupings may be negligible, and whose impact on the social world is confined to a handful of nonresident clerks in a dusty and distant office

Even when the units of aggregation are more meaningful politically, such as counties or states, the holistic argument has little purchase. For it is not enough to claim that for *some* purposes, counties and states may plausibly be treated in unitary fashion; this must be true with respect to *the behavior at issue,* for example, voting. There must be forces at work within each country, such as a central hierarchical leadership or a system of strong norms and roles, which direct county voting along certain lines regardless of voters' private preferences. There have been American cities or counties that could be described this way, but their numbers have been exceedingly few.

Even here at its strongest, then, the holistic argument depends upon generally inaccurate empirical presuppositions about voter behavior in natural political units. Indeed, the effort has rarely been made to construct a theoretical or empirical base for the holistic approach, to identify the appropriate units of aggregation where the relevant assumptions might hold, and to collect suitable data. The holistic assumptions are often used, but rarely stated and even less often verified. In practice they are all too conveniently applied to whatever unit of aggregation appears in the data set. All discussion of the ecological fallacy is sidestepped. The result is not sociology but metaphysics.[5]

CONCLUSION

In contrast to the hopes of many, we do not think of cross-level inference as a problem that has a single solution. It is a problem of theoretical underspecification which can be addressed in numerous ways, some better and some worse for a particular question. The aggregate marginals give us only a set of logical bounds of impossibility around the true individual-level parameters—the bounds described in connection with equation (2) above. *How we then locate our estimate of the parameters within those bounds depends solely on prior assumptions, that is, on the story we choose to tell about the data.* Goodman ecological regression, for example, uses an assumption of constant expected probabilities across districts, summarized in equations (3a) and (3b) above. But other assumptions, often more appropriate, are available as well. The choice of approach, and the fruitful use of *any* approach, requires of the investigator substantive knowledge and theoretic artistry, directed to the particular features of the problem at hand.

The next chapter sets out in detail Goodman ecological regression, the standard approach to aggregate data analysis, along with some recent extensions of it. Chapters 3 and 4 show why this model so often fails. Subsequent chapters then offer a variety of alternative approaches, based on varying sorts of assumptions, with demonstrations of how they may improve on ecological regression.

---

5. There are, of course, truly aggregate-level questions which are not reducible to the individual level and for which aggregate-level analysis is obviously the appropriate mode. Such questions would include whether inequality of incomes (for nations) engenders revolution, or whether the independence of central banks reduces inflation. Readers will have no difficulty in recognizing them. Our concern is not with these but with aggregations of individuals who are defined for convenience as groups even though they do not act as groups.

APPENDIX A

Cross-Level Theory and the Macroconsistency Problem

In the Michels example, the presence of multiple levels of analysis enriched our understanding without imposing any burdens. Distinct explanations at different levels coexisted nicely, and no logical contradiction was involved in adhering to both of them. Sometimes, too, a single theory integrates well across levels, a straightforward case of cross-level theory. More often, however, a theory is credible only at one level (usually the individual level), but for purposes of theoretical development or data analysis, scholars choose to work with the relationship at another level (usually the aggregate version) which is more convenient or serves more relevant purposes, but has no clear theoretical standing. In that case, micro- and macrotheories exist side by side in an uneasy relationship, with one or both incomplete or unsatisfactory in light of the other.

Too often, researchers working at the macrolevel simply assume a macrorelationship similar to the one they believe operates at the theoretically meaningful microlevel. No attempt is made to derive the one from the other. Unfortunately, the subtleties of aggregation are such that, all too often when the derivation is carried out, the assumed macrorelationship is shown to be faulty.

Even when researchers postulate a simple, purely individualistic mathematical model and aggregate it by straightforward addition of the individual-level variables, the relationship of macro- to microexplanations can be surprisingly complex. Key individual-level variables, irrelevant to the explanation of individual behavior, may enter at the macrolevel (Schlicht 1985, chap. 5). The relationship of macroeconomics to its microeconomic foundations is the most studied and paradigmatic case (e.g., Shafer and Sonnenschein 1982, on consumer demand), but parallel conundrums in adjacent fields are no less daunting for being less familiar.

The central issue is the "macroconsistency problem." Here we ask whether, given a set of theoretically meaningful microrelationships, a suitable macrorelationship exists at all when the microlevel data are aggregated. The question is not as trivial as it may seem. Consider, for example, Zinnes and Muncaster's stimulating study of the dynamics of hostility in the international system (Muncaster and Zinnes 1984). To avoid the hopeless task of dealing with every nation, they work at the aggregate level. Their model is a differential equation of the form

(A1) $$H' = f(H),$$

where $H = H(t)$ denotes aggregate hostility at time t and $H' = H'(t)$ is its first derivative with respect to time. (H and f must be treated as vector-valued to allow for the second-order derivatives Zinnes and Muncaster actually employ.) This appears to be a perfectly sensible dynamic specification.

Notice, however, that equation (A) does not describe the behavior of any one actor in the international system. No international agency controls the aggregate amount of hostility. Only individual states express hostility. If the equation is to make theoretical sense, then, it must be derivable from the behavior of individual states.[6] The question posed by the macroconsistency problem is this: Under what circumstances does a relationship like (A1) exist?

The most widely used model for the hostility of individual states is Richardson's (1960) equations. In the case of two states, this model expresses the derivative of each state's hostility as a linear function of the hostility directed against it, the level of its current hostility ("fatigue"), plus an intercept ("fear"):

$$(A2) \qquad h_1' = a_1 - b_1 h_1 + c_1 h_2,$$

$$(A3) \qquad h_2' = a_2 + b_2 h_1 - c_2 h_2,$$

where for $i = 1, 2$, $h_i = h_i(t)$ is the ith state's hostility level at time t; $h_i' = h_i'(t)$ is its time derivative; and a_i, b_i, and c_i are fixed positive coefficients. Ordinarily, "hostility" is measured by the level of armaments in this model, but the equations are perfectly general.

Now defining aggregate hostility in the obvious way as $H = h_1 + h_2$, so that $H' = h_1' + h_2'$, we have by simple summation of equations (A2) and (A3):

$$(A4) \qquad H' = a_1 + a_2 + (b_2 - b_1)h_1 + (c_1 - c_2)h_2.$$

Now the problem is apparent. In general, the last two terms cannot be written as a function of H. That is, they cannot be factored with a term $h_1 + h_2$. Thus equation (A4) cannot be written as $H' = f(H)$. Except in the purely accidental case when $b_2 - b_1 = c_1 - c_2$, no aggregate relationship like (A2) exists for the Richardson equations.

Thus if aggregate hostility means what it seems to mean, Zinnes and Muncaster's macroequations are inconsistent with the standard micromodel of state hostility. If one wishes to save Zinnes and Muncaster's equations, or any such equations for the aggregate behavior of the international system, then theoretical meaningfulness requires that replacements for Richardson's equations be found which are equally meaningful substantively and which imply the macroequations. The macroconsistency problem consists precisely of this sort of demand for logical consistency.

In general, one cannot choose an arbitrary set of microrelations and then expect that similar relationships will hold at the aggregate level. One can fix the micro- and macrotheories and attempt to define the aggregate variables so that the microtheories aggregate properly (Klein 1946). Alternatively, one can fix the microtheories and macrovariables and look for macrotheories consistent with them (May 1946). Since social scientists rarely control the aggregation procedures used to generate their data, Klein's approach is the least use-

---

6. Note that the "macrolevel" here is the international system, while the "microlevel" is the individual nation-state. Calling for an emphasis on the theoretically meaningful microlevel, therefore, is by no means to argue for the reduction of all social theories to that of atomistic individual human beings. In arguing for a certain approach to macrodata, we need take no position on the philosophical issues of methodological individualism.

ful, and we will concentrate on methods in the spirit of May. In particular, we follow Green (1964) in preferring, when the microlevel is the theoretically meaningful domain, that macrolevel models be explicitly derived from micro-level assumptions. Without that constraint, macrolevel research too easily slips into studies of the interrelationships of meaningless statistical aggregates. Only when both macrotheoretical propositions and statistical assumptions are rigorously inferred from the microlevel can we have faith in macrolevel studies.

APPENDIX B

A Method to Determine Statistically the Sociological and Demographic Structure of Voting in Secret Elections   By F. Bernstein

Little is known about the sociological and demographic structure of the results of secret elections, even though this question is of great importance from the most varied points of view. Our ignorance follows naturally from the fact that such elections *are* secret.

However, it is easily shown that the difficulty in answering this question—an exclusively statistical question by the way—is only apparent. Consider an election comprising a large number of districts, for which the results are known. One sees easily that whatever connections exist between certain categories of the population and their voting must become visible, and do indeed become visible, in that the demographic characteristics of the various districts are observable, and lead to differences in the electoral results. Thus the political contrasts between city and countryside, between the workers' quarter and the suburb, etc., are quite clear, and allow us to recognize certain connections between social structure and parties.

In what follows we will develop a method to put this observation—which cannot of itself provide us with quantitative solutions—on an objective basis. We will then apply the method to a simulated example of a real problem, ascertaining how an election result would be changed if the voting age were changed from 20 to 25. I am primarily interested here in demonstrating the general method, not concentrating on any particular application.

Let us select for examination across the electorate some social category, such as age or occupation. The category should be one that is easily retrieved from the electoral rolls either through simple counting or from knowledge of the place of residence of the voters

Without loss of generality, let us posit that three party lists have been submitted. We wish to ascertain the percentage distribution of the social category

Translated by W. Phillips Shively from F. Bernstein, "Über eine Methode, die Soziologische und Bevölkerungs-statistische Gliederung von Abstimmungen bei Geheimem Wahlverfahren Statistisch zu Ermitteln," *Allgemeines Statistisches Archiv* 22 (1932): 253–57. We include this selection both for its continuing scientific value, and as a tribute to a fine scholar who disappeared in the 1930s and presumably died in the Nazi camps.

across the party lists. We shall designate the number of voters for the three party lists as A, B, and C. These sum to L, the total number of voters in the election. The total number of voters belonging to the social category under consideration will be designated as l. The quantity l is known, or can be calculated. On the other hand, we will designate as a, b, and c the unknown numbers of the selected social category who voted for each of the three party lists.

As our unknowns, we take the three ratios

$$x = \frac{a}{A},$$

$$y = \frac{b}{B},$$

$$z = \frac{c}{C}.$$

From the definitions, it follows that

(B1) $$Ax + By + Cz - l = 0.0.$$

In order to solve for the unknowns, we can use our knowledge of the voting results in the various districts. Let A_i, B_i, and C_i be the election results for the ith district, with L_i their sum and l_i the (known) number of voters of the selected social category in the ith district.

Now, if our unknown ratios x, y, and z were invariant across all districts, then the equations

(B2) $$A_ix + B_iy + C_iz - l_i = 0$$

would be true for each district. In actuality, however, these equations will not be valid, and the left side will deviate sometimes above zero, sometimes below. There is no particular reason to expect that deviations would occur more strongly in one direction than the other, since the values of x, y, and z are means of the values for the individual districts. It also follows from the nature of means that, at least most of the time, small deviations will be more numerous than large deviations. Therefore, since the number of districts, N, is generally much larger than the number of party lists, the conditions for the application of the method of least squares are satisfied. The individual solutions for the various districts are significant in proportion to the relative number of voters in the district; therefore, the number of voters in a district should be used as a weight. If we designate the weights as g_i and the left-hand side of equation (B2) as v_i, then we must minimize the following sum of squared deviations:

(B3) $$\sum_{i=1}^{N} v_i^2 g_i = [vvg].$$

From this is derived the following system of equations:

(B4)
$$[AAg]x + [ABg]y + [ACg]z + kA = [Alg],$$
$$[ABg]x + [BBg]y + [BCg]z + kB = [Blg],$$
$$[ACg]x + [BCg]y + [CCg]z + kC = [Clg],$$
$$Ax + By + Cz = l \quad .$$

Total Number of Voters	Voters over 25	Election Result		
		Party A	Party B	Party C
250	150	120	90	40
400	200	300	60	40
1,000	600	500	400	100
300	150	160	70	70
200	110	100	60	40
150	100	80	50	20
450	250	300	100	50
700	400	500	100	100
400	250	220	80	100
300	200	160	40	100
800	500	350	180	270
900	600	300	350	250
250	150	150	50	50
150	100	100	30	20
400	250	250	100	50
550	400	200	120	230
600	350	400	100	100
750	450	450	120	180
600	350	350	120	130
350	250	200	80	70
9,500	5,810	5,190	2,300	2,010

This system is most easily solved with the help of the well-known method of Gauss, which also allows us to estimate the unique solution for the mean error. Before I proceed with the example, I would like to point out the conditions for applying the method.

First, the method becomes illusory if the categories do not vary enough across the districts. In this case the various equations become identical and no longer provide identification of the unknowns. This source of error is one we need not fear greatly.

Second, there is a problem if it happens that the electorate is partitioned into geographic parts across which the relationships between the selected social category and the party lists vary systematically. Here we are not dealing with statistical error, but with an important problem in its own right. However, the method is so designed that it automatically lets us know if this is a problem, in the following way:

As we check for the goodness of fit, then as is well known, our determination of the fit depends on the value of the sum of squared errors which is being minimized, while the expression

(B5)
$$m^2 = \frac{[vvg]}{(N + 1) - 3}$$

presents these errors multiplied by a known value. The problem under consideration will be revealed by the fact that the sum of squared errors becomes too large, and therefore the fit will not be sufficiently precise.[7] In other words, the dispersion of the errors v will prove to be too large. This is most easily checked by sketching the frequency distribution of v, a form of dispersion test as proposed by the geodetic surveyors (Helmert [reference not provided in original]).

I will now present an example of 20 electoral districts and three party lists. For each district it is known how many voters are of a certain age—say, 25 or older. We seek to determine what the outcome of the election would have been, if the voting age had been raised to 25.

From the calculations, we see that the 5,810 voters who were 25 or older would have divided themselves as follows:

$$\text{Party A:} \quad 2{,}514 \pm 103,$$
$$\text{Party B:} \quad 1{,}584 \pm 87,$$
$$\text{Party C:} \quad 1{,}712 \pm 93.$$

Thus, party A would have had only a plurality, not a majority, even if the average error that is presented here is taken into account in the most unfavorable way.

---

7. This is in fact not correct. The specification problem Bernstein correctly identified will not necessarily cause a weak fit at the aggregate level.—Trans.

TWO

ECOLOGICAL REGRESSION
AND ITS EXTENSIONS

This chapter sets out in detail the most widely used statistical model for aggregate data analysis, the ecological regression technique discovered by Bernstein (1932), and customarily attributed to Goodman. For concreteness, we focus on its most common application, the estimation of voter transition rates. However, the same methods apply when aggregate data are used to estimate the entries in any contingency table.

As noted in the first chapter, Goodman's technique is meant to circumvent Robinson's (1950) ecological problem and to allow us to use aggregate data to learn about individuals. In chapter 1, however, we discussed only the aggregate-level version of the voter transition model and only the two-party case without abstention. Here we show how the model may be derived from individual-level assumptions, how it may be extended to deal with multiple parties and abstention, and how control variables may be used to improve the fit.

We intend the chapter to provide both an introduction to ecological regression and a critical review. Thus we also discuss the weaknesses of the technique and summarize certain closely related methods from the recent literature, assessing their promise as improvements of ecological regression, or replacements for it.

Most of the methods discussed are in common use; in effect, we mean the chapter to be a summary of contemporary standards of good ecological regression analysis. We begin with an introductory, informal discussion and move toward an intermediate level of statistical formality. Readers new to the subject and those interested primarily in applications are invited to read selectively.

Important prior discussions, in addition to Goodman (1953,

1959), include Stokes (1969), Kousser (1973), Langbein and Lichtman (1976), Hannan (1991), Madansky (1959), Hawkes (1969), Lee *et al.* (1970), and Kalbfleisch and Lawless (1984), with the first six treating substantive issues and data analysis, and the latter four developing the statistical theory. These references emphasize the estimation of transition rates; Haitovsky (1973) discusses the more general problem of regression analysis with grouped data, and Stoker develops methods related to the special problem of estimating average marginal effects (Stoker 1984, 1985, 1986; Powell and Stoker 1985).

VOTER TRANSITIONS WITH INDIVIDUAL-LEVEL DATA

We now take up again the subject of voter transition rates, beginning with the simple two-party, no-abstention case. To derive the Goodman model, we assume initially that individual-level data are available. Thus suppose that a simple random sample of the population of voters is taken. All respondents are asked which party they chose in the current election (either the Democrats or the Republicans). They are also asked how they voted at the previous election, and they reply truthfully and accurately. For the moment, we shall assume that everyone votes.

Voter stability now may be assessed in the obvious way by examining the 2×2 cross-tabulation of current vote on prior vote. Figure 1 displays this simple table. Its entries are the "transition rates"; the conditional probabilities that a voter who chose a particular party last time will either remain loyal or defect from it at the current election. Notice that columns add to 1.0: for example, a voter who chose the Democrats last time must choose either the Democrats or the Republicans this time, and so the probabilities of doing either one or the other must sum to one. The table is just (the transpose of) a conventional transition matrix for a Markov chain.

		TIME 1 VOTE	
		Democrat	Republican
TIME 2 VOTE	Democrat	p	q
	Republican	1-p	1-q

Figure 1. Transition rates between votes at two successive elections

The same statistical relationship may be expressed as a linear regression. For voter i ($i = 1, \ldots, N$), let d_{2i}, the dependent variable, represent the vote at the second election. Then $d_{2i} = 1$ if i voted Democratic, 0 if Republican. Similarly, d_{1i} is i's vote at the initial election. For those who voted Democratic at time 1, let the probability of voting Democratic at time 2 be p ("loyalty"), and for those who voted Republican at time 1, let the probability of voting Democratic at time 2 be q ("defection"). Notice that p and q are precisely the same quantities as the p and q of figure 1. Finally, let u_i be a disturbance term equal to the difference between the actual vote (which must be either 0 or 1) and the probabilities p and q. Of course, the disturbance term u_i must average zero across the population; that is just another way of saying that p and q are the relevant probabilities.

The regression format equivalent to the 2×2 cross-tabulation is then

(1) $\qquad d_{2i} = pd_{1i} + q(1 - d_{1i}) + u_i \quad (i = 1, \ldots, N).$

This is a regression equation with two independent variables and no intercept. To see that this equation reproduces the cross-tabulation, consider first those who voted Democratic at time 1 ($d_{1i} = 1$). Substituting for d_{1i} above shows that, for this group, the term involving q drops out, so that the right-hand side reduces to p plus the disturbance. Since the disturbance averages zero across the population, the average vote at time 2 among this group is just p. That is, those who initially voted Democratic do so again with probability p, just as in figure 1. Similarly, for those who voted Republican at time 1 ($d_{1i} = 0$), the right-hand sided reduces to q plus the disturbance, meaning that time-1 Republican voters have probability q of defecting to the Democrats, as in figure 1. Thus the regression equation (1) and the 2×2 table of figure 1 are equivalent forms of the same relationship.

Equation (1) is not quite in standard regression format. However, it may be rewritten in an obvious way as

(2) $\qquad d_{2i} = q + (p - q)d_{1i} + u_i,$

which is just a simple bivariate regression with intercept q and slope $p - q$. Estimates of slope and intercept are therefore easily produced: in a sample of voters such as might be taken from a public opinion survey, one simply regresses the current vote on the prior vote. The intercept is the estimated defection rate, q, and the slope is the estimate of $p - q$. (The loyalty rate p may be estimated by adding the slope and the intercept.) From either equation (1) or equation (2), the conventional least squares regression estimates will reproduce exactly the same estimates as the 2×2 cross-tabulation.[1] Thus as one would expect, no difficulties arise in the estimation of transition rates when individual-level data exist.

ECOLOGICAL REGRESSION: THE SIMPLE GOODMAN MODEL

The "ecological inference problem" arises when the researcher has access to data not from individuals but only from aggregates of voters. For example, election returns like those discussed in the previous section may be tabulated by precinct, county, constituency, or province. Learning the individual transition rates p and q from these aggregate returns presents a very different inference problem. Most obviously, whereas the individual-level survey data were discrete (zeroes and ones), the aggregate data are usefully displayed only in continuous form. They consist of percentages or fractions—the vote proportions obtained by the parties in each geographic unit. Thus the appropriate display for the data from two elections is a regression plot, not a cross-tabulation. A regression line can be fitted to the points in the plot, and such regressions were computed frequently in political science and sociology during the first half of this century (*e..g.*, Gosnell 1937, 1942). These quantitative pioneers understood that the resulting coefficients told them something about the individual voters, but Bernstein's (1932) derivation of the individual-level loyalty and defection rates was not known to them.

Working in a different substantive context, Miller (1952) was the first to use a microlevel model to explicitly derive a macrolevel regression equation for Markov chain transition rates. Goodman (1953, 1959) applied Miller's ideas to aggregate electoral data, arguing that the method circumvented Robinson's (1950) "ecological fallacy." Goodman's procedure is to begin with the regression equation (2) and then average it within each geographic district (which we will suppose is a constituency). The result is a new regression equation of the same form but with a unit of observation equal to the constituency. Under the crucial assumption that the transition rates are constant across constituencies, the aggregate-level regression may be estimated

1. Perhaps surprisingly, these statistical estimates have the usual desirable properties in spite of the dichotomous dependent variable; see chap. 4.

with constituency data and the coefficients interpreted at the individual level.[2]

To spell out the derivation, suppose that the sample consists of n_j individuals from each of m constituencies ($j = 1, \ldots, m$), so that the full sample is $N = \Sigma n_j$. Let d_{1ji} be the vote of the ith person in the jth constituency at time 1, and define d_{2ji} similarly. Define the constituency means as $D_{1j} = (1/n_j)\Sigma_{i=1}^{n_j} d_{1ji}$, and similarly for D_{2j}. Denoting the individual-level disturbances by u_{ji}, define the aggregate disturbance as $U_j = (1/n_j)\Sigma_{i=1}^{n_j} u_{ji}$.

Now averaging both sides of equation (2) is straightforward. Since the loyalty and defection rates, p and q, are assumed constant, one may find the means of both sides simply by averaging the independent and dependent variables, along with the disturbance. In effect, one simply replaces these three quantities by their constituency means, which yields the two-party version of the "simple Goodman model":

(3) $\qquad D_{2j} = q + (p - q)D_{1j} + U_j \quad (j = 1, \ldots, m).$

Equation (3) is an "ecological regression." To estimate the slope and intercept, one simply calculates the bivariate regression in which the dependent variable is the constituency Democratic vote at time 2 and the independent variable is the constituency Democratic vote at time 1. Just as with individual-level data, the resulting intercept is $\hat{q}$, the estimated Republican-to-Democrat defection rate. The slope is the estimate of $p - q$. Hence the sum of the estimated slope and intercept is $\hat{p}$, the estimated Democrat-to-Democrat loyalty rate.[3]

Standard errors for the estimated probabilities $\hat{p}$ and $\hat{q}$ are easily obtained. Of course, the standard error for $\hat{q}$ is just the standard error for the intercept. The standard error for $\hat{p}$, or its square, the variance, is derived by noting that

(4) $\quad \mathrm{var}(\hat{p}) = \mathrm{var}(\text{slope} + \text{intercept})$

$\qquad = \mathrm{var}(\text{slope}) + \mathrm{var}(\text{intercept}) + 2\mathrm{cov}(\text{slope, intercept}).$

---

2. Alternatively, it is often assumed that the variation in transition rates may be absorbed into an uncorrelated disturbance term. For discussion of this "sophisticated Goodman model," see below and chap. 4.

3. Researchers who wish to avoid adding slopes and intercepts may estimate eq. (1) instead of eq. (2). The technique is to enter both Democratic and Republican vote fractions on the right-hand side as independent variables while suppressing the regression intercept. The coefficients then estimate p and q directly.

The last three quantities on the right are available from the variance-covariance matrix printed with the regression statistics in standard statistical software, and so var($\hat{p}$) is easily computed. The square root gives the standard error. Statistical tests then may be carried out in the usual way.[4] Of course, these sampling error calculations depend on the use of the correct variance-covariance matrix, which in ecological regression is not always the same as the values produced by the OLS calculations; see below.

As noted earlier, nothing requires that current votes be regressed on past votes. Current votes might be expressed as a function of social class, or religion, or any other dichotomous variable. One might also use entirely different dependent variables: for example, social class might be regressed on religion to learn how Catholics and non-Catholics distributed themselves between worker and nonworker categories. The logic is precisely the same, and the methods of this chapter apply with only the obvious changes in notation. For notational and intuitive simplicity, however, we maintain the single running example of estimating voter transition rates.

When votes or other social variables have more than two possible values, the Goodman model must be extended. It is to that topic that we now turn.

THE SIMPLE GOODMAN MODEL IN MULTIPARTY SYSTEMS

In practice, most ecological regressions have been bivariate; that is, they were based on the assumption that the voters faced just two alternatives. However, most of the world's electoral systems are multiparty, so that the bivariate version of ecological regression is inapplicable. Ignoring the vote for third and fourth parties, or collapsing them into their larger ideological neighbors, will sometimes be satisfactory, but the danger always exists that the vote for tertiary alternatives will vary across constituencies in parallel with major-party votes, so that one set of effects will be confounded with the other.

---

4. If the disturbances are spatially correlated, as will often be the case, then the regression coefficients are unbiased but their estimated standard errors are erroneous, even if all the other assumptions hold. Typically, the standard errors are too small. At present, due to the large number of parameters involved, the problem can be addressed only by making strong, often rather implausible assumptions about the pattern of the spatial autocorrelations (Cliff and Ord 1973; Ripley 1981; Anselin 1988). In practice, both theoretical and empirical researchers have tended to ignore the problem but it deserves additional investigation. See King (1980) for a clear-sighted exposition.

Even in two-party systems, the assumption of two alternatives is restrictive. The citizenry always have a third choice, which is to stay
home or abstain.[5] Indeed, abstention is widespread in many democracies. It should be understood, however, that abstention per se is not
problematic for Goodman. The point is perhaps clearest in the pure
case in which the same people always abstain. Then no matter how
large a proportion of the eligible electorate the abstainers are, they
never appear in the voting population. Ignoring them and defining the
population as the actual voters thus poses no special difficulties for ecological regression. When this situation is approximated in practice, ignoring abstention will be statistically satisfactory.

Abstention creates biases only if the abstainers are systematically
different people from one election to the next. That is, two-party transition probabilities estimated from bivariate ecological regression will
mislead when constituency turnout is correlated with vote fractions.
Substantial changes in turnout are a warning signal. For example, if
American cities turn out very weakly at time 2 compared to time 1, the
Democratic percentage of the vote will drop, even if in the pool of those
who voted both times, everyone who backed the Democrats at time 1
backed them again at time 2. If an ecological regression is computed
using just the two-party vote, Democrats will falsely appear to have
suffered from voter defections to the Republicans. The error occurs be-

5. "Abstention" is a purely residual category encompassing any failure to vote by a
member of the relevant population. Thus it includes those who become ill, move away,
or die, as well as those who are too young at time 1 (but come of age at time 2). The
"relevant" population is usually taken to be the total eligible population (e.g., those who
were adult citizens at either time 1 or time 2), or in the American case, perhaps those
who were eligible and registered.

A minor subtlety is that neither at time 1 nor at time 2 do population statistics or
voter rolls give the correct count of the relevant population for Goodman regression.
When abstention counts as a vote choice, those who die, move in or out, or come of age
between elections should be counted as part of the eligible pool of voters, but they will
appear in only one of the two population counts. Thus both population counts are too
low, and there are more "abstainers" than there appear to be.

When abstention is ignored, a similar point applies to the vote totals. Some citizens
appear at the polls at one time period and not at the other. Since the relevant population
is the voters who appeared at both time periods, the vote counts at each time period are
too high.

These fine points are always ignored in practice. The implicit assumption is that ad-
justing for the nonvoters would not change the vote fractions. That is, those who miss an
election due to death, youth, or residential mobility are assumed to resemble the rest of
the population. Localities undergoing rapid growth may not meet these conditions if the
time period under study extends over a decade or more (Converse 1969). Except in these
unusual circumstances, however, the resulting biases seem likely to be very small.

cause turnout varies across districts as a function of residential location, which is correlated with the vote. Thus party loyalty effects are compounded with turnout effects, and ecological regression using the two-party vote is biased.

Happily, the logic of bivariate ecological regression extends readily to include additional parties and abstention. One simply treats abstention as a "party" and then estimates additional regressions. For example, suppose that three "parties" compete, the Democrats, the Republicans, and the abstainers. Now consider the Democrats. At time 2, they can receive votes from the electorate in any of three ways: by maintaining the loyalty of their own voters, by drawing defections from Republican voters, or by mobilizing those who did not vote at the first election. Denote their fractional success in each group as p_{11}, p_{21}, and p_{31}, respectively. (Thus, e.g., p_{21} refers to those who vote initially for party 2 [Republicans] but end up with party 1 [Democrats]; similar probabilities are defined for transitions toward the Republicans and toward abstention.) The task is to estimate the transition rates among the parties. In effect, we are filling in a 3×3 table (fig. 2).

In constituency j, denote the fraction of the vote for Republicans at time 1 by R_{1j}. Notice that this fraction, as well as the fraction of the vote obtained by every other party, is expressed as a proportion of the total eligible electorate, not as a proportion of the two-party vote. Thus a 60–40 Democratic victory with 50% turnout would translate to Democratic, Republican, and abstention fractions of .3, .2, and .5, respectively. It is the latter numbers which must be used when abstention is included in voter transition tables.

An aggregate-level regression for the movement of voters into the Democratic fold at time 2 might follow the form of either equation (1) or equation (2), depending on whether the intercept is suppressed. For simplicity here we keep the form with the intercept, and write

| | | TIME 1 VOTE | | |
		Democrat	Republican	Abstain
TIME 2 VOTE	Democrat	p_{11}	p_{21}	p_{31}
	Republican	p_{12}	p_{22}	p_{32}
	Abstain	$1-p_{11}-p_{12}$	$1-p_{21}-p_{22}$	$1-p_{31}-p_{32}$

Figure 2. Transition rates between votes or abstentions at two successive elections

(5) $\quad D_{2j} = p_{31} + (p_{11} - p_{31})D_{1j} +$

$$(p_{21} - p_{31})R_{1j} + U_{1j} \quad (j = 1, \ldots, m).$$

Here the Democratic vote at time 2 is regressed on the Democratic vote and the Republican vote at time 1. The intercept is p_{31}, and the slopes are the terms in the parentheses. The individual probabilities are recovered in the obvious way: for example, p_{21}, which is the fraction of Republicans who defect to the Democrats at time 2, is found by adding the intercept to the Republican coefficient. A similar procedure with the Democratic coefficient gives the loyalty rate. And the intercept alone gives the fraction of abstainers who were mobilized for the Democrats at time 2. Standard errors for probabilities are obtained in the same way as in the bivariate regression case.

A parallel equation is needed to characterize vote transitions toward the Republicans:

(6) $\quad R_{2j} = p_{32} + (p_{12} - p_{32})D_{1j} +$

$$(p_{22} - p_{32})R_{1j} + U_{2j} \quad (j = 1, \ldots, m).$$

The individual probabilities are derived in the same way as in the Democratic case. Combined with the probabilities from the previous regression, these estimates determine all the entries in the table of figure 2. We have generated rows 1 and 2, and since columns sum to 1.0, the third row is implied.

The third row of figure 2 might also be estimated by another regression, with abstention at time 2 as the dependent variable and Democratic and Republican votes at time 1 as independent variables. In the same manner as the first two regressions, the coefficients of this equation would decompose abstention into its three sources in prior Democratic votes, prior Republican votes, and prior abstention. However, there is no new information in these estimates. It is not hard to show that one gets numerically identical results for the third row of figure 2 whether this third regression is estimated or whether the row entries are inferred from the previous two regressions. Put another way, any two of the three regressions may be chosen for estimation without affecting the findings.

The extension to additional parties is obvious. In general, suppose that a party system has k parties, one of which might be abstainers. The task is to fill in the probabilities in the $k \times k$ table of transition probabilities between the elections at times 1 and 2.

The procedure is, first, to set aside the vote fractions for one of the parties; the choice is arbitrary. Then taking the remaining parties one at a time, one regresses their fraction of the vote at time 2 on all the party fractions at time 1 except the one set aside. Thus in the jth such regression, the jth party vote at time 2 is regressed on $k - 1$ party fractions at time 1, including its own. Only the set-aside party fraction is omitted as an independent variable. Some party must be excluded for the intercept term to make sense or, equivalently, for perfect collinearity to be avoided.

This procedure yields $k - 1$ regressions, each with $k - 1$ independent variables plus an intercept. In each, the intercept term is the fraction of the set-aside party who defect to party j at time 2. Adding the intercept to each regression coefficient gives the proportion of the corresponding party vote which defects to party j at time 2. As before, the standard errors for the probabilities are easily computed, and the regression for the set-aside party is implied by the others and need not be run.

If abstention is included as a "party," one first converts the vote proportions to fractions of the total eligible electorate (not fractions of the total vote). Then everything proceeds as before. Typically, abstainers constitute the set-aside group.

If some of the parties are small, estimation of their transition rates is often demanding in practice. The central difficulty is that small parties have petite effects on vote totals, and thus minor specification errors loom large in their estimates. This difficulty is sometimes confounded by voting rules which create peculiar incentives in certain constituencies. For example, voters' aversion to wasting their votes under plurality rule may lead them to abandon their first choice in favor of a candidate with a better chance to win. Such behavior systematically alters transition probabilities in certain constituencies, inducing a correlation between vote totals and transition rates, and thus invalidates the Goodman assumptions.

To cope with small-party anomalies in Goodman regression, combining the lesser parties with ideologically adjacent parties whose transition rates are similar may be helpful. In addition, voter turnout may be systematically lower in districts with no real contest, so that better estimates are obtained by controlling for this source of turnout variability or by ignoring abstention entirely (Crewe and Payne 1976).

THE EXTENDED SIMPLE GOODMAN MODEL:
DETERMINISTIC HETEROGENEOUS TRANSITION RATES

From the beginning, the simple Goodman model has encountered severe difficulties in practice. We discuss these problems in detail in other chapters. Here we simply set out some of the extensions of the model which have been proposed as partial remedies. For ease of exposition, we begin with the two-party case with abstention ignored.

Computational experience and political common sense both testify that transition rates are not constant across electoral districts. Voters who pull the Democratic lever at time 1 because they are coal miners will behave differently at the next period from voters who pull it because they are movie stars (see the simulation in the preceding chapter). This elementary fact of political life suggests that the transition rates p and q should vary across districts as a function of the demographic or political composition of the district (Boudon 1963; Przeworski 1974; Hanushek et al. 1974; and many others). Bias is introduced unless the variation in rates is captured with control variables.

For simplicity, consider the simplest version of this approach, proposed by Goodman himself (1959, pp. 624–625), in which p and q depend linearly and deterministically on one exogenous constituency-level variable, such as income or religion, whose value in the jth constituency is denoted X_j.[6] Subscripting the two transition rates to indicate that they now vary across districts, we have

(7) $$p_j = \alpha_1 + \beta_1 X_j,$$

(8) $$q_j = \alpha_2 + \beta_2 X_j,$$

where $\alpha_1, \alpha_2, \beta_1,$ and β_2 are unknown constants. These assumptions mean that the transition rates vary across districts but are constant within them. The idea is that heavily working-class districts make everyone in them more loyal to the Democrats, not just the workers.[7]

---

6. To avoid the determinism, disturbance terms may be added if, after substitution into the regression, they may be absorbed into the disturbance. See the "extended sophisticated Goodman model" below.

7. This assumption is probably more plausible than the alternative, that only workers' transition rates are influenced by having other workers around. The latter case is more difficult to estimate, since different transition rates now apply to workers and non-workers. E.g., to carry out the estimation, one must know the proportion of the electorate at time 1 who were simultaneously workers and Democratic voters. Typically, such fractions are not available from aggregate data, and to our knowledge, no one has tried estimating them for this purpose. The obvious approach—use one ecological regression

Substituting into the conventional Goodman equation (3) yields the simplest case of the "extended simple Goodman model":

$$(9) \quad D_{2j} = \alpha_2 + \beta_2 X_j +$$
$$(\alpha_1 + \beta_1 X_j - \alpha_2 - \beta_2 X_j) D_{1j} + U_j \quad (j = 1, \ldots, m).$$

Rearranging, we obtain

$$(10) \quad D_{2j} = \alpha_2 + \beta_2 X_j + (\alpha_1 - \alpha_2) D_{1j}$$
$$+ (\beta_1 - \beta_2)(X_j D_{1j}) + U_j.$$

This is a regression equation with three independent variables, X_j, D_{1j}, and an interaction between them, along with an intercept. In other words, one regresses the Democratic vote at time 2 on the exogenous variable, the Democratic vote at time 1, and on their product.[8] The estimate of the parameter α_2 is the intercept from this regression, and the estimate of β_2 equals the slope coefficient on X_j. The parameter α_1 is obtained by adding the intercept to the slope on D_{1j}, while the estimate of β_1 is found by adding the estimated β_2 to the slope on the interaction term. Standard errors for α_1 and β_1 are obtained in the same way as for the simple Goodman model, that is, by using the variance-covariance matrix from the regression statistics and recalling that the variance of a sum is the sum of the variances plus twice the covariance (cf. eq. [4] above).

To estimate p and q, the average loyalty and defection rates, researchers conventionally average p_j and q_j over constituencies using estimates of p_j and q_j obtained by substituting the estimates of $\alpha_1, \beta_1, \alpha_2$, and β_2 into equations (7) and (8). That is, they compute the mean over constituencies of X_j and then substitute it into $p_j = \alpha_1 + \beta_1 X_j$, and similarly for q. This is equivalent to setting $p = \Sigma p_j / m$ and $q = \Sigma q_j / m$.

The conventional wisdom is mistaken here. By averaging the loyalty and defection rates over constituencies, the usual estimate gives equal weight to districts with many Democratic voters and to those with few.

---

equation to estimate the fraction of workers who were Democratic voters at time 1 and another ecological regression which allows for different voter transition rates for workers and nonworkers—is not identified from the regression coefficients. The second equation contains three estimable coefficients and four unknowns.

8. Notice that the crude approach of simply adding the control variable linearly to the equation without including the interaction term imposes the assumption that $\beta_1 = \beta_2$. This assumption is often rejected in applications; i.e., the interaction term enters the equation with a substantively and statistically significant coefficient.

But p is an average over Democratic *voters*, just as q is an average over Republican *voters*. When means are computed over constituencies, the resulting averages are not comparable to estimates of p and q obtained from surveys (for additional detail, see chaps. 4 and 5).

When control variables are used in ecological regression, the appropriate estimate of p is a *weighted* average over constituencies of the estimated $\hat{p}_j$ from equation (7), with the weights being the number of Democratic voters in each constituency at time 1.[9] If at time 1 there were n_{dj} Democratic voters in constituency j and n_d Democratic voters altogether in the electorate, then define p as

(11) $$p = \sum n_{dj} p_j / n_d.$$

An unbiased estimate $\hat{p}$ may then be obtained by substituting $\hat{p}_j$ for p_j in this equation.

Similarly, q is a weighted average of the q_j from equation (8), with weights proportional to the number of Republican voters in each constituency. If n_{rj} is the number of Republican voters in the jth constituency and n_r is the total number of Republican voters, then

(12) $$q = \sum n_{rj} q_j / n_r.$$

An unbiased estimate is obtained in the same way as for $\hat{p}$. Both $\hat{p}$ and $\hat{q}$ are directly comparable to the estimates obtained from surveys.

To see that the appropriate values of p and q cannot be obtained simply by substituting the mean value of the independent variable into equations (7) and (8), consider the simplest case, in which all m constituencies have the same number of voters, namely, n. In that case, $n_{dj}/n_d = [n_{dj}/(mn)]/[n_d/(mn)] = D_{1j}/(mD_1)$, where $D_1 = \sum_{j=1}^{m} D_{1j}/m = n_d/(mn)$ is the national time-1 Democratic vote. Thus in the case of p, for example, we have from equation (11)

$$p = \frac{\sum D_{1j} p_j / m}{D_1}$$

(13)
$$= (1/D_1) \sum D_{1j} (\alpha_1 + \beta_1 X_j)/m$$

$$= (1/D_1)(\alpha_1 D_1 + \beta_1 \sum D_{1j} X_j / m)$$

$$= \alpha_1 + (\beta_1 / D_1) \sum D_{1j} X_j / m.$$

9. In both equations, if all constituencies have approximately the same number of voters, percentages may be substituted for the raw voter counts.

Notice that the last expression is not the same as $\alpha_1 + \beta_1 \sum X_j/m$, which is the value obtained by substituting the mean of X_j over constituencies into $p_j = \alpha_1 + \beta_1 X_j$. Only if D_{1j} and X_j are uncorrelated in the sample will the two expressions coincide.[10]

All these procedures extend easily to the case of multiple control variables and multiple parties. With two parties plus abstention, for example, one simply replaces the single control variable in equations (7) and (8) with a linear sum of several control variables, substitutes the result into equations (5) and (6), and solves for the implied regression equation. In addition to the intercept, the resulting independent variables will include each of the control variables, the vote shares for the two parties, plus interactions between each party's vote and each control variable. As before, the abstention rate (or the set-aside party fraction, if abstention is ignored) will not appear in the equations, neither as independent nor as dependent variable, and neither on its own nor in interactions. Averages for p and q are obtained from equations (11) and (12) by averaging the estimates of p_j and q_j over constituencies with weights equal to the number of Democratic and Republican voters, respectively.

To find the variance of the estimate of p, let X_p be the $m \times k$ matrix of exogenous variables used to forecast p_j, where m is the number of districts and k is the number of variables used in the forecast (including the intercept). Denote by n_d^* the m-dimensional (column) vector whose typical element is n_{dj}. Let Ω_p be the appropriate variance-covariance matrix of the coefficients in the equation generating p_j. For example, in the simplest case, p_j is given by equation (7) above, so that Ω_p is the variance-covariance matrix of the estimated coefficient vector $(\hat{\alpha}_1, \hat{\beta}_1)$, and the elements of Ω_p are derived from the variance-covariance matrix for the ecological regression (10). (We remind the reader that the ordinary regression variance-covariance matrix is not necessarily appropriate; see below.)

Under these conditions, we have:

$$(14) \qquad \text{var}(\hat{p}) = n_d^{*\prime} X_p \Omega_p X_p^\prime n_d^* / n_d^2.$$

The variance formula for $\hat{q}$ follows that for $\hat{p}$, with n_r^*, X_q, and Ω_q replacing their counterparts.

Ecological variables are usually highly correlated relative to their

---

10. In that case, by definition of uncorrelatedness, $\sum D_{1j} X_j/m - D_1 \sum X_j/m = 0$, and substituting $D_1 \sum X_j/m$ for $\sum D_{1j} X_j/m$ in eq. (13) shows the equivalence of the two calculations.

individual-level counterparts, so that, particularly in the case of multiple parties, adding interaction terms as in equation (10) may produce substantial collinearity. Although the regression coefficients are unbiased, their standard errors may be large. In dramatic cases, certain exogenous variables may need to be dropped as controls. However, it is worth remembering that the individual regression coefficients are generally of lesser importance and that p and q are the parameters of interest. Those two fractions are often determined with excellent precision in spite of the noise in their component parts. Then the collinearity may be ignored. (For more aggressive approaches to coping with collinearity, such as ridge regression, see Miller 1972.)

In the study of voter transitions, prior votes are customarily the most useful and powerful predictors of transition probabilities (Upton 1978). Thus a special case of control variables in Goodman regression occurs when a party's vote at the prior election is used to modify the transition rates: $X_j = D_{1j}$. Treating the prior vote as predetermined and substituting as before gives a quadratic in D_{1j}, so that there are only three coefficients, including the intercept, instead of four. Solving backward to $\alpha_1, \alpha_2, \beta_1$, and β_2 is now impossible without additional identifying information. This case has several special features, and we discuss it in chapter 5.[11]

---

11. The identification problem is particularly severe here, since we cannot distinguish easily between a model in which the Democratic vote at time 1 makes everyone more likely to remain loyal at time 2 and a model in which the initial Democratic vote affects only those who voted Democratic. As noted above in n. 7, the latter sorts of model typically cannot be estimated because they require aggregate information that is unavailable: if the percentage working class influences only Democratic voters, we need to know the fraction of the constituency who are both working class and Democratic voters at time 1 to carry out the regression, and this fraction is usually unknown. However, when the prior vote is the control variable, the problem takes on a different character because the control variable and the time-1 vote are the same. I.e., we need to know the proportion of time-1 Democratic voters who were also time-1 Democratic voters, and that fraction is just the proportion of time-1 Democratic voters. Estimation is easy: the ecological regression is quadratic in D_{1j}.

Thus when the percentage of time-1 Democratic votes influences only Democrats, the same variables and the same functional form are called for as when the Democratic percentage influences all voters. The difficulty is that, using only the regression coefficients, one cannot statistically distinguish between these two substantively distinct theories without additional information, and that causes an additional identification problem (beyond the fact that both models require us to estimate four parameters with three pieces of statistical information). See the related discussion in Sprague (1976).

It should be noted, however, that in general the likelihoods of the two models will not be identical due to the greater heterogeneity in transition rates when members of a group influence only themselves. In particular, the two models' disturbance variances will typi-

Finally, it should be noted that nothing requires the researcher to specify that equations (7) and (8) are linear. Especially in multiparty systems where minor-party vote shares are small, it may be more plausible or convenient to work with nonlinear specifications to avoid implied probabilities that are less than zero or greater than one. Sometimes this is accomplished bluntly, as when constraints are imposed to bound probabilities (e.g., Irwin and Meeter 1969; McCarthy and Ryan 1977). A more attractive approach is to replace the linearity assumptions by the more plausible logit/probit forms (or by robust alternatives), which will also conveniently constrain the probabilities.

In the two-party case, we might write

$$(15) \qquad\qquad p_j = f(X_j)$$

and

$$(16) \qquad\qquad q_j = g(X_j),$$

where $f(\cdot)$ and $g(\cdot)$ are arbitrary deterministic functions of X_j and X_j is a vector of aggregate-level exogenous or predetermined variables from constituency j. Substituting these into the Goodman equation (3) gives

$$(17) \qquad D_{2j} = g(X_j) + [f(X_j) - g(X_j)]D_{1j} + U_j,$$

which might be estimated by nonlinear least squares or maximum likelihood methods. For example, if $f(z_1) = \Phi(z_1)$, with $z_1 = X_j\beta_1$, and $g(z_2) = \Phi(z_2)$, with $z_2 = X_j\beta_2$, where $\Phi(\cdot)$ is the (cumulative) standard normal distribution function and β_1 and β_2 are coefficient vectors, then we have the probit case. Alternatively, setting $f(z_1) = e^{z_1}/(1 + e^{z_1})$ and similarly for $g(z_2)$ gives the logit case (MacRae 1977). (Neither of these, of course, is conventional probit/logit analysis.) Estimates of p and q are computed as in equations (11) and (12), with appropriate sampling variances. For example, if S_p is the variance-covariance matrix of forecasts of p_j under the model, then in parallel with equation (14), $\text{var}(p) = n_d^{*'} S_p n_d^{*}/n_d^2$. The extension to multiple parties is obvious.

Nonlinear equations for p_j and q_j mean that the resulting regression specification will be nonlinear as well, requiring additional time and care in the derivation and estimation. For example, modeling the transition rates as a function of the party vote shares at the initial time pe-

---

cally be different. Hence when one has confidence in a particular specification for the disturbance variances in ecological regression, the two models of group influence might be distinguished empirically.

riod is often the best-fitting specification. As discussed in chapter 5, however, this specification causes underidentification when transition rates are linear functions of vote shares, and near-underidentification when they are probit/logit functions of vote shares with arguments like z_1 and z_2 above. In the two-party case given in equation (16), for example, if z_1 and z_2 are each linear functions of the vote at the first time period, D_{1j}, and if $f(\cdot)$ and $g(\cdot)$ are logit forms, then the equation is identified only because of the slightly nonlinear shape of the logit function—a shape customarily assumed only because all relevant evidence is lacking and familiarity is a comfort. In this as in the multiparty case, estimation will be delicate and inference doubtful (see chap. 5).

Substantive blunders will also be more deeply hidden in nonlinear specifications. Bounding probabilities between zero and one means that a likelihood function straining to produce transition rate estimates of 150% or -20% will be forcibly prevented from doing so, and thus important clues to incorrect specification will be lost. As Stokes (1969, p. 76) puts it, active constraints on ecological coefficients are attempts to make a silk purse from a sow's ear (see also Meckstroth 1974; Upton 1978). Nonetheless, especially with minor parties, the gain in accuracy from nonlinearity may be worthwhile, particularly for new or minor parties, whose transition rates may range from near-zero in some constituencies to robust fractions in others. The curvilinearity of the probit/logit forms will typically be of less value for major parties, since their transition rates typically have standard deviations of only several percentage points across constituencies. The probit/logit forms will often be statistically indistinguishable from linearity over that range. Since transition rates linear in the independent variable translate to quadratic ecological regression, this means that quadratic regression and probit/logit forms will be essentially identical in typical aggregate electoral data. (See the applications of quadratic regression in chap. 5.)

MAXIMUM LIKELIHOOD AND GENERALIZED LEAST SQUARES ESTIMATES FOR THE SIMPLE GOODMAN MODEL

To this point we have proceeded somewhat informally, with no attention to the assumed probability model underlying the observations. In consequence, sampling distributions of the estimators have been ignored. We now take up these issues.

Consider again the simplest Goodman model (3), with two parties, no abstention, and transition rates fixed across constituencies. A vote for the Democrats is scored one, a vote for the Republicans zero. Each voter who chose the Democrats at time 1 chooses them again with probability p. Thus, conditional on a Democratic vote at time 1, each citizen's vote is a Bernoulli random variable with the usual variance $p(1 - p)$.[12] Similarly and independently, initial Republican voters select the Democrats at time 2 with probability q and hence variance $q(1 - q)$. Summed over the relevant voters, each of these distributions becomes binomial with variances $n_{dj}p(1 - p)$ and $n_{rj}q(1 - q)$, respectively, where again, n_{dj} and n_{rj} are the total Democratic and Republican votes in constituency j at time 1.

Thus under the simple Goodman model (3), the total number of Democratic votes in a given constituency at time 2 is a convolution of two binomial distributions; that is, it consists of a sum of two independent random variables, the loyal votes and the defections, each with binomial distributions.[13] This probability distribution is discrete: only a finite set of integral values have nonzero probability mass. (See chap. 8.)

In principle, one might use maximum likelihood estimation (MLE) to estimate the model directly. However, with sample sizes of even a few thousand voters for each party, estimation will be computationally intensive, since the likelihood in each district must be summed over the thousands of possible combinations of loyalty and defection which would generate the time-2 vote.[14] Moreover, as has been repeatedly noted in the literature, this numerical effort is pointless. With a few thousand voters, a convolution of binomials will generate a density extremely well approximated by normality.[15] In that case, the log-

12. From this perspective, we are interested not in the actual voters before us, but rather in the universe from which they were drawn. Since the voters choose probabilistically, we are making explicit allowance for the possibility that, although the actual electorate might have had a loyalty rate of 97%, that rate occurred only by sampling error, and the true rate in the larger universe was 90%. This conceptual oddity stems from ignoring the fact that, in most ecological inference problems, we have a complete sample of a finite population. Thus the likelihood model is hypergeometric, not binomial. We have a complete count of every vote, and we wish to know the transition rates that occurred *in this particular election*. However, for reasons of simplicity the binomial perspective is standard in much of the literature, and we follow it here. We return to the subject below and in chap. 4.

13. Brown and Payne (1986) refer to this distribution as "aggregated binomial," but there seems little reason to overturn the ancient usage.

14. The range of possible combinations is that given by the method of bounds; see chap. 8. The computations multiply rapidly as additional parties are added.

15. An exception would occur when, in a constituency, the expected number of defections from prior vote became a small integer for either party. Survey data show that voters are too mobile between parties under even the most static political conditions for this theoretical point to have practical importance.

likelihood function (shorn of additive constants) takes the familiar normal-regression form:

$$(18) \quad L(p, q) = -\frac{1}{2} \sum_{j=1}^{m} \{\log \sigma_j^2 +$$

$$[D_{2j} - q - (p - q)D_{1j}]^2/\sigma_j^2\},$$

where σ_j^2 is the variance of the convolution of binomial distributions. To obtain this variance, we sum the two binomial variances, $n_{dj}p(1 - p)$ and $n_{rj}q(1 - q)$ and convert to vote fractions by dividing by the square of the total vote, n_j^2. Here σ_j^2, which is also the variance of the jth disturbance in the simple Goodman model (3), is

$$(19) \quad \sigma_j^2 = [D_{1j}p(1 - p) + (1 - D_{1j})q(1 - q)]/n_j,$$

where we have used the fact that $D_{1j} = n_{dj}/n_j$ and $R_{1j} = 1 - D_{1j} = n_{rj}/n_j$. Substitution into the likelihood equation then permits a numerical search for the maximizing values of p and q. As usual, the estimate of the asymptotic variance-covariance matrix is the negative of the inverse of the matrix of second partial derivatives of the log-likelihood with respect to the parameters, evaluated at the maximum likelihood estimates.

An alternate and more convenient approach derives from taking the expectation of the convolution of binomial distributions conditional on the vote totals at time 1. Expressed in fractional form, the result is the Goodman regression model (3). The disturbances are uncorrelated with the right-hand-side variable. Thus, as usual with a strictly exogenous right-hand-side variable, OLS is unbiased. With a predetermined regressor such as prior vote, under the usual conditions OLS is (weakly) consistent for p and q. This is the justification for the conventional use of OLS in ecological regression.

As equation (19) shows, however, the disturbances in the ecological regression are heteroscedastic: their variance depends both on the Democratic percentage of the vote and on the number of voters per district. As is well known, if the variance of regression disturbances differs across observations, the coefficient estimates are unbiased but inefficient relative to MLE, and their estimated standard errors are incorrect.

In the presence of heteroscedasticity, the generalized least squares (GLS) estimator has the same asymptotic sampling variance as the MLE. Under GLS, regression analysis is carried out with each observation weighted by the inverse of the true disturbance variance; under the usual assumptions, the result is unbiased, consistent, efficient, asymptotically normally distributed estimates and correct standard errors. If, as in the present case, the weights are not known exactly but must be estimated ("feasible GLS"), then under plausible conditions, the estimates are consistent, and normality, efficiency, and correct standard errors hold asymptotically.[16] Since only the latter estimator is computable for Goodman regression, subsequent references to GLS refer to the feasible version.

In the case of ecological regression, then, after doing one round of unweighted ecological regression to estimate p and q, the estimates should be inserted into equation (19) and the regression rerun with each observation's weight equal to the inverse of the estimated expression in equation (19). This is equivalent to the GLS estimate with a diagonal variance-covariance matrix for the disturbances.[17] Asymptotically (i.e., as the number of constituencies goes to infinity), mild conditions ensure consistent, normally distributed, and efficient estimates, along with correct standard errors for the coefficients.[18]

In the extended Goodman model, the procedure is precisely the same, except that p and q are replaced by p_i and q_i in the variance formula (19). The latter two quantities are estimated, of course, by inserting coefficient estimates from the initial OLS regression into the appropriate formulas such as equations (7) and (8) or (15) and (16).

16. The econometric theory on this point is more subtle than is usually imagined, and many econometrics texts err. See the discussion in Schmidt (1976, chap. 2.5); for a proof when the regressors are bounded, as they often will be in ecological regressions, see Achen (1986a, chap. 3).

17. In the familiar matrix notation, the (feasible) GLS coefficient estimate is $\hat{\beta} = (X'\hat{\Sigma}^{-1}X)^{-1}X'\hat{\Sigma}^{-1}y$, where y is the vector of observations on the dependent variable, X the matrix of observations on the independent variables, and $\hat{\Sigma}$ the variance-covariance matrix of the disturbances. The estimated variance-covariance matrix of the coefficients is $(X'\hat{\Sigma}^{-1}X)^{-1}$. When Σ is diagonal, the estimated diagonal elements of its inverse are the regression weights. I.e., the weights are $1/\sigma_i^2$, where σ_i^2 is defined by equation (19). In this case, it is easily shown that the GLS estimate may be computed by multiplying every variable in the regression equation by the square root of the weight, adding a new variable which is the square root of the weight itself, and then running a new regression with the intercept suppressed. The resulting standard errors of the coefficients will also be the correctly estimated GLS standard errors. The procedure is available in many statistical software packages. However, users should beware: one popular but often statistically inept package alters the value of the number of observations when weights are used, thereby corrupting the estimated standard errors.

18. Since the variances in eq. (19) go to zero as $n_i \to \infty$, weak consistency holds even with the number of constituencies fixed, so long as each of their populations goes to infinity. Kalbfleisch and Lawless (1984) discuss the asymptotics of this model.

The logic of the multiparty case, both the simple and the extended version, is quite similar: To form the expression for the disturbance variances in each regression, one simply enters a term inside the brackets in equation (19) for each party, including the party whose vote fraction was not used as an independent variable. This term entered in equation (19) is just the proportion of the vote for that party at time 1 multiplied by the binomial variance of its transition rate. GLS or MLE then proceeds as before. The resulting estimates are asymptotically efficient as single-equation estimators. Fully efficient estimates with more than two parties require the use of "seemingly unrelated regression" methods. (See Lee et al. 1970, chap. 6.)

The version of GLS implied by equation (19) is rarely used in practice, not even by those authors who appeal to heteroscedasticity as the justification for weighting the observations. For, in practice, focusing on this source of heteroscedasticity is foolish. The variances involved are far too small to be consequential. A typical-sized electoral unit for ecological regression might be an American congressional district of recent decades with approximately 100,000 voters. To estimate its sampling variance, note that neither $p(1 - p)$ nor $q(1 - q)$ can exceed .25. Inserting these values into equation (19) shows that under the Goodman assumptions, the variance of the disturbances in congressional districts is at most .0000025, which makes the square root, the standard error, no more than .0016. Thus if the assumptions of the Goodman model (3) were correct, ecological regressions on American congressional districts would have disturbance standard errors of less than one-sixth of a percentage point.

When theoretical standard errors become this small, they are overwhelmed by other sources of error which are conventionally ignored, including minor errors in vote totals, coding errors in data production, and even arithmetic rounding. For example, one-sixth of a percentage point is only about half the standard error introduced by recording constituency votes just to the nearest percentage point (e.g., 55% rather than 55.2%), and no one familiar with historical election data is a devout believer in the third significant digit in election percentages. Of course, rounding error does not decline with larger numbers of voters. Neither do coding errors. Thus, *even if the Goodman assumptions about constant transition rates hold perfectly,* equation (19) is customarily a poor guide to the actual disturbance variance.

More important, in applications the variance expressed by equation (19) is dwarfed by other sources of heteroscedasticity. The simple

Goodman model is correct only if there is literally no variation in transition rates across districts, or at least no residual variation after control variables are introduced. That is, if each of the mean constituency transition rates, p_j and q_j, were to be regressed on demographic control variables, each regression R^2 would have to be exactly 1.0. This is impossible in practice, of course.

Because the simple Goodman model is imperfect, the transition rates vary across districts, as Goodman (1959) himself noted. Techniques for minimizing cross-district variance in rates include (1) restricting the estimator to regions or provinces rather than the entire country, (2) choosing samples with large districts (or grouping constituencies within the region into larger districts) that are microcosms of the region, and (3) ransacking demographic variables to find those that reduce remaining variation. At the cost of losing statistical information or degrees of freedom, each of these steps makes the observations similar to one another and, hence, minimizes residual variation in transition rates across constituencies. In a model which allows them to assess cross-district heterogeneity, Brown and Payne (1986) take all three steps, but as they remark, many of the resulting cross-constituency heterogeneity estimates remain substantial.

In conventional applications, even after a full set of control variables are introduced as in equation (17), and even in geographic units much smaller than American congressional districts, the resulting standard errors of the disturbances are virtually never less than a full percentage point and are usually considerably more. Thus the disturbance variance induced by varying transition rates is larger than the simple Goodman model's sampling error variance by at least one order of magnitude, and more commonly two or three. For example, the British constituencies discussed in chapters 5 and 7 have approximately 50,000 voters apiece, so that the maximum disturbance variance due to sampling error is easily calculated. Moreover, the constituencies show relatively little parameter variation compared to typical aggregate electoral data. Even so, the actual disturbance variance is at least 50 times larger than equation (19) predicts. Thus pretending that the simple Goodman assumptions are correct and weighting with seriously inaccurate weights from equation (19) is pointless and may well do more harm than good. Heteroscedasticity is generated primarily by variance in transition rates, not by pure sampling error.

THE SOPHISTICATED GOODMAN MODEL:
STOCHASTIC TRANSITION RATES

Due to stochastically varying transition rates, the residuals from ecological regression are virtually always overdispersed relative to the assumptions of the simple or extended simple Goodman model. To model that variation, suppose that for each i, j, we regard p_{ji}, the loyalty rate for the ith voter in the jth district, as constant within districts: $p_{ji} = p_j$. Further suppose that in every district, the probability p_j is a random draw from a mixing distribution common to all districts, with mean p and variance σ_p^2. (The fixed variance across districts is an important assumption; see the section on regression weighting below.) In addition, the draw p_j is taken to be independent of D_{1j}.[19] Thus p_j is constant within districts but varies across them in accordance with a common distribution.

If the density of p_j exists and is denoted by $f_p(p_j)$ and if d_{2dji} is the vote of the ith person in the jth constituency at time 2 who voted Democratic at time 1, then in the country as a whole, the probability of voting Democratic is, for all i, j,

$$\text{Prob}(d_{2dji} = 1) = E(p_{ji})$$

(20)
$$= \int_0^1 p_j f_p(p_j)dp_j$$

$$= p.$$

Similar assumptions are made about q_j. Aggregate vote totals are therefore convolutions of compound binomial distributions. We shall refer to this specification as the "sophisticated Goodman model," since it was proposed informally in Goodman's 1959 article.[20]

Since the convolutions will have very nearly normal distributions in districts of several thousand voters, MLE proceeds with a log-likelihood function that may be written as in equation (18).[21] The sole change is to alter the definition of σ_j^2 from equation (19) to (32) below.

---

19. Thus the transition rates are mean independent of D_{1j}, which is the minimal condition needed for unbiased OLS coefficient estimates (see chap. 1). If the variation in transition rates is not independent of the time-1 vote totals but is instead correlated with them, the regression is biased and no weighting scheme will correct it. We believe that this case is rather common in practice. See chap. 3.

20. Indeed, it is the principal contribution of the article, the "simple Goodman model" having been proposed earlier by Bernstein (1932).

21. Pathological distributions of p_j must be barred to ensure good approximation by the normality assumption. See n. 15.

Alternatively, converting to fractional form and taking expectations conditional on the time-1 fractions yields a random-coefficient regression specification, which may be estimated by GLS. To derive the GLS estimator for this model, some preliminary results are needed.

First, we have for the sampling variance of a single voter

$$\text{var}(d_{2dji}) = E(d_{2dji} - p)^2$$

(21)
$$= E(d_{2dji} - p_j + p_j - p)^2$$

$$= E(d_{2dji} - p_j)^2 + E(p_j - p)^2$$

$$= E[p_j(1 - p_j)] + \sigma_p^2,$$

where $p_j(1 - p_j)$ is the usual binomial variance conditional on p_j and where we have used the fact in the third line that the cross-product term, $E(d_{2dji} - p_j)(p_j - p)$, is zero. Now evaluate the expectation

$$E[p_j(1 - p_j)] = E(p_j) - E(p_j^2)$$

(22)
$$= p - (\sigma_p^2 + p^2)$$

$$= p(1 - p) - \sigma_p^2.$$

Inserting expression (22) into equation (21) gives

(23)
$$\text{var}(d_{2dji}) = [p(1 - p) - \sigma_p^2] + \sigma_p^2$$

(24)
$$= p(1 - p).$$

Thus heterogeneity makes no difference at the individual level; the individual's vote is Bernoulli with parameter p. Note that the term in brackets in equation (23) is the average sampling error variance within the district, conditional on the draw of p_j, and the remaining term is the variance due to the draw itself.

Now consider the variance of $n_{ddj} = \sum_1^{n_{dj}} d_{2dji}$, the random variable whose realization is the total number of votes for the Democrats at time 2 from those in constituency j who voted Democratic at time 1. Now heterogeneity matters, and the variance exceeds the sum of the individual variances. We have, using equation (24),

$$\text{var}(n_{ddj}) = \sum_i \text{var}(n_{2dji}) + \sum_i \sum_{i' \neq i} \text{cov}(d_{2dji}, d_{2dji'})$$

(25)
$$= n_{dj}p(1 - p) + \sum \sum (d_{2dji} - p_j + p_j - p)$$

$$\cdot (d_{2dji'} - p_j + p_j - p)$$

$$= n_{dj}p(1 - p) + n_{dj}(n_{dj} - 1)\sigma_p^2,$$

where we have used the fact in the last line that, conditional on the draw of p_j, the decisions of the voters in the jth constituency have mean p_j and are independent of each other. Similarly, suppose that q_j is random with mean q, independent of D_{1j}. Then by the same logic and in an obvious notation, we have for the variance of the number of defections to the Democrats in each district j

$$(26) \qquad \mathrm{var}(n_{drj}) = n_{rj}q(1 - q) + n_{rj}(n_{rj} - 1)\sigma_q^2.$$

If the draws p_j and q_j are correlated, as seems likely, and since conditional on those draws there are no sampling error covariances across individuals, we have

$$(27) \qquad \mathrm{cov}(n_{ddj}, n_{drj}) = n_{dj}n_{rj}\sigma_{pq}.$$

We now derive the GLS regression form. Because the transition rates vary by district, we add j subscripts and write the individual-level equation corresponding to equation (2) as follows:

$$(28) \qquad d_{2ji} = q_j + (p_j - q_j)d_{1ji} + v_{ji}.$$

Summing the votes within each district j then gives

$$(29) \qquad D_{2j} = q_j + (p_j - q_j)D_{1j} + V_j.$$

Rewriting equation (29) as a conventional Goodman regression yields

$$(30) \qquad D_{2j} = q + (p - q)D_{1j} + U_j,$$

where now $U_j = q_j - q + (p_j - p - q_j + q)D_{1j} + V_j$. By the assumptions already made, this disturbance term has mean zero and is uncorrelated with the Democratic vote at time 1. As noted above in the discussion of the MLE, the disturbance will have an approximately normal distribution, typically to an excellent approximation, and hence weighted least squares (GLS) is asymptotically equivalent to MLE in the first-order efficiency sense.

To find the appropriate weights, we require the variance of $n_{ddj} + n_{drj}$. The individual variances of these two quantities are given in equations (25) and (26); the covariance term is twice the value in equation (27). Summing these and dividing by n_j^2 to convert to the variance of the corresponding fraction gives

$$\mathrm{var}(U_j) = D_{1j}^2\sigma_p^2 + (1 - D_{1j})^2\sigma_q^2 + 2D_{1j}(1 - D_{1j})\sigma_{pq} -$$
$$(31) \qquad [D_{1j}\sigma_p^2 + (1 - D_{1j})\sigma_q^2]/n_j +$$
$$[D_{1j}p(1 - p) + (1 - D_{1j})q(1 - q)]/n_j,$$

which is the disturbance variance of a version of the Hildreth and Houck (1968) random-coefficients regression model.[22] Note that under practical conditions, the disturbance variances will virtually always be strictly larger than those of the simple Goodman case (19), since the first line of equation (31) does not go to zero as $n_j \to \infty$.[23] Thus the sophisticated Goodman model accommodates the overdispersion of the disturbances found in applications.[24]

Unless the districts are both small (fewer than 15,000 voters) and homogeneous (standard error of the regression less than 2 percentage points), the second and third lines in equation (31) will contribute less than 5% of the total variance. In practice, 1% or less is a typical figure. Hence they may ordinarily be ignored.[25] To a good approximation, then,

$$(32) \quad \text{var}(U_j) = D_{1j}^2 \sigma_p^2 + (1 - D_{1j})^2 \sigma_q^2 + 2D_{1j}(1 - D_{1j})\sigma_{pq}.$$

If simple ecological regressions are to be corrected for heteroscedasticity, equation (31) or (32) gives the most defensible set of weights. In the latter case, the procedure is to run a conventional unweighted ecological regression, then regress the squared residuals on the squared Democratic vote, the squared Republican vote, and twice the product of the Democratic and Republican votes, with the intercept term suppressed, as in equation (32). All these vote proportions among the independent variables should be taken from time 1. The resulting three coefficients will estimate σ_p^2, σ_q^2, and σ_{pq}, respectively, and their values may be substituted into equation (32). The inverse of equation (32) is then the regression weight for a final round of estimation, which produces consistent coefficient estimates with the appropriate standard er-

---

22. Note that the first line of eq. (31) is the variance due to the mixing distribution, while the last line is the sampling variance. In the normal-regression random-coefficient analogue, these two kinds of variance sum to produce the total variance. The present result differs due to the Bernoulli individual vote variables, which have variances concave in p. Heterogeneity thus reduces conditional sampling variances; see eq. (22). At the aggregate level, the consequence is that the total variance is reduced by the second line of eq. (31). For this reason, the sampling variance formula given in Lee et al. (1970, p. 194) is (slightly) erroneous.

23. This implies that, to guarantee consistency of the estimates, it is not enough to let sample sizes within constituencies go to infinity as in the simple Goodman model; here the number of constituencies must go to infinity instead.

24. With very strong negative correlation between $D_{1j}p_j$ and $(1-D_{1j})q_j$, the sophisticated Goodman model's disturbance variance becomes less than that of the simple Goodman model, but this point is of purely theoretical interest.

25. If not, of course, there is no difficulty in including them in the calculations below.

rors. The procedure could be iterated, if desired. With or without itera-
tion, the estimator is asymptotically efficient.[26]

Both MLE and GLS may be extended in the obvious way to cope
with transition rates that vary as a stochastic function of strictly exogenous or predetermined control variables ("the extended sophisticated
Goodman model"). Here transition rates are modeled just as in equations (15) and (16) above, or more simply, as in equations (7) and (8),
but with an additive disturbance term on the right-hand side. For example, one might specify that

$$(33) \qquad p_j = \alpha_1 + \beta_1 X_j + e_j,$$

where e_j is assumed to be distributed independently of X_j and D_{1j} and
the other usual regression assumptions hold. One then proceeds as in
the extended simple Goodman case, except that the disturbance variance is of the form (31) or (32), with p_j and q_j replacing p and q, and
$p_j(1 - p_j)\sigma_p^2$, $q_j(1 - q_j)\sigma_q^2$, and $[p_j(1 - p_j)q_j(1 - q_j)]^{1/2}\sigma_{pq}$ replacing σ_p^2, σ_q^2, and σ_{pq}, respectively. In this version of the model, the latter variances and covariances refer to the variance of the disturbance
terms added to equations (15) and (16), not to the variances of p_j and
q_j themselves. They vary as functions of p_j and q_j in the manner of the
binomial case but with the addition of the multipliers σ_p^2, σ_q^2, and σ_{pq},
which are fixed over districts. Finally, note that control variables such
as X_j do not add terms to the disturbance variance.

Multiple political parties pose no special difficulties. The regression
equation is set up in the same manner as in the simple Goodman case,
so that the OLS estimates are unaffected. The only change occurs in
the variance of the disturbances, which now have the form of equation (32). (Eq. [32] is the two-party case; additional terms must be
added for every additional political party in the obvious way.) Apart
from the change in the disturbance variances, the resulting MLE or
GLS estimates have the same form as their simple Goodman model
counterparts. They are asymptotically efficient in the class of single-
equation estimators. Full-system MLE and GLS estimations of this
model are discussed in the appendix to this chapter.

While theoretically sound, MLE and GLS for the sophisticated

26. Eq. (32) with squared residuals standing in for the left-hand side is not a regression equation meeting Gauss-Markov assumptions, so the resulting small-sample efficiency in estimates of p and q in eq. (30) may be less than with other estimators that
correct for the deficiencies in eq. (32) (Judge et al. 1985, chap. 11.2.4). In addition, itera-
tion may not produce the MLE. Of course, numerical search routines may always be
employed to maximize the likelihood directly.

Goodman model are not always of great practical importance. When σ_p^2 and σ_q^2 are approximately the same size and p_j and q_j are positively correlated, as they will tend to be in practice,[27] equation (32) is very nearly constant across the usual range of variation, so that both MLE and GLS are approximately equivalent to OLS. For example, let p_j and q_j be correlated at .5 with identical variances. Then when the Democratic vote varies over the interval from 30% to 70%, the variance as a proportion of σ_p^2 ranges only from .625 to .685. Even if the covariance is zero, the variance as a proportion of σ_p^2 wanders only from .50 to .58 over the same 30%–70% interval. Variance differences of that magnitude will rarely have much effect on either coefficient estimates or standard error calculations. (See the examples in chap. 5, where heteroscedasticity corrections move the transition rate estimates by at most a percentage point, or about half the standard error.)

An additional difficulty is that the sophisticated Goodman model is itself just an approximation. Other, unknowable sources of error in the assumptions, notably the postulate that the remaining stochastic variability (e_j) in the transition rates is itself homoscedastic, will distort the transition rates, so that equation (32) becomes an imperfect guide to weighting in any case. Moreover, in such conditions and with conventional-size aggregate samples, it is questionable whether the variances and covariances in equation (32) can be estimated with enough accuracy to improve on equal weighting, even if the model underlying equation (32) is exactly right. If the standard errors in estimating the variances and covariances are as large as the deviations from homoscedasticity, then estimating the weights may be more inaccurate than assuming them all equal, making the cure worse than the disease.[28]

In summary, unweighted ecological regression may often be a satisfactory option, especially in two-party systems. If so, there is no operational difference between the simple and sophisticated versions of the

27. There is also theoretical reason to expect positive correlation under certain conditions. We prove in the appendices to chap. 5, that if selection of voters into districts is a function just of the dependent variable, then positive correlation between p_j and q_j is implied.

28. Similar remarks apply, of course, to maximum likelihood methods and to OLS with heteroscedasticity-consistent estimates of standard errors that require no knowledge of the heteroscedasticity's functional form, such as White (1980) and MacKinnon and White (1985). However, in small samples these estimators seem likely to be worse than equal weighting when heteroscedasticity is slight. It would be useful to have careful studies of the relative merits of these estimators in samples with the size and characteristics of ecological data.

Goodman model: both estimate the same equation by OLS, and which-
ever model is true, the standard errors will be approximately correct.

Precisely when more elaborate methods are worthwhile is difficult to
say in the absence of sufficient research on the topic. However, if one
transition rate has rather larger variance than the other or if the vote
fractions vary widely and include numerous constituencies with vote
fractions of 20% or less, and if in addition the sample is relatively large
so that one can learn the variances and covariances with some confidence, then, to that extent, MLE and GLS methods become more desirable. OLS with heteroscedasticity-consistent estimation of sampling
variances (White 1980) is another option, especially when special features of the data make the nature of the heteroscedasticity uncertain.

What is quite certain is that, when OLS is abandoned, the sophisticated Goodman model should be used in preference to its simpler
cousin. Then if GLS is used, the regression weights in two-party systems should be the inverse of the variance given in equation (31) or
(32). Similar remarks apply to the corresponding procedures for multiparty systems given in the appendix to this chapter.

SHOULD ECOLOGICAL REGRESSIONS BE WEIGHTED BY POPULATION?

In practice, heteroscedasticity is rarely invoked when ecological regressions are weighted. More commonly, the weight on each observation is
set equal to the number of voters (or eligible voters) in the district in
hopes of appropriately averaging the heterogeneity in p_j and q_j (e.g.,
Jones 1972). As noted earlier, the national average p and q are indeed
averages over individuals, not over constituencies, and so the notion of
weighting district observations by their population has intuitive appeal.
However, the statistical logic is virtually never spelled out precisely, and
quite different arguments for weighting, such as heteroscedasticity, are
sometimes invoked simultaneously. The validity of population weighting has received little attention, and many expositions of ecological regression ignore the topic entirely.

The question of whether ecological regression observations should
be weighted by population is more subtle than it may appear. The conceptual difficulty occurs because, to carry out ecological regression
with minimal realism, one must allow for variability in transition rates
across districts. The simplest interpretation of the variability invokes a
"superpopulation model" (Hedayat and Sinha 1991, chap. 10). From
this theoretical perspective, the particular pattern of transition rates

that occurred in the actual population constitutes a single draw from a superpopulation of all such patterns that might have occurred. Specifically, the transition rates in each district are usually specified as being drawn from a certain probabilities distribution for that district. Often, all the constituency transitions are assumed to be taken from the same distribution, as in the sophisticated Goodman model. The researcher then attempts to estimate the mean transition rates in the superpopulation, in just the same way that one seeks the best estimate of the population mean in a sample from an infinite population.

An immediate difficulty now arises. Ecological samples are samples of finite populations. Thus we care very little about the hypothesized means of the superpopulation. What we seek are the mean transition rates that actually occurred *in this sample*. This is just the reverse of the textbook infinite population case, where we typically care little about the sample mean per se. It is useful only as an estimator of the population value. But ecological transitions are quite different.

A little more precisely, suppose that, in the voter transition model, the "loyalty rate" in the jth district is a random variable $\tilde{p}_j$ with mean $\bar{p}_j$. In the current sample, its realization is p_j, the transition rate that actually occurred. We wish to know the average transition rates that occurred in the sample, averaging it over those individuals to whom it applies, namely, those for whom $d_{1ji} = 1$. Thus the parameter to be estimated is $p^* = \Sigma\, d_{1ji} p_j / \Sigma\, d_{1ji}$, where the sums run over the entire population. However, under the superpopulation model, we estimate instead the population mean, namely, $p = \Sigma\, d_{1ji} \bar{p}_j / \Sigma\, d_{1ji}$. Parallel definitions apply to the "defection rates," q and q^*.

Most of the time, the problem of population mean versus sample mean is of minor concern. Typically the estimate of p turns out also to be a good estimate of p^* (and similarly for q and q^*). In particular, if the constituencies in the sample are all the same size or nearly so, then the best estimate of the population mean transitions and the sample transitions will be identical. For example, suppose that loyalty rates are independently drawn in each constituency from the same distribution. Suppose further that the rates are 70% in a third of the sample, 80% in another third, and 90% in the final third and that all three groups contain the same number of people. Then it surely makes sense to expect a desirable estimator, given enough data, to estimate the average loyalty rate as 80%—both the average in the population of rates from which these were drawn and the average in this particular sample.

When constituency sizes differ from each other, however, the similarity between the two mean estimates diminishes. Suppose that a 90% loyalty rate applies to New York City, Albany, and Buffalo, while a 70% rate applies to three hamlets in upstate New York. In this case, if we really believed that each constituency transition rate were drawn randomly from a common distribution, we would still want a good estimator to estimate the population mean of the loyalty rates as 80%. However, the rate that actually occurs in the population would be nearly 90%, since the larger transition rates happened to fall in constituencies with more people. Under the sophisticated Goodman assumptions, a conventional unweighted ecological regression would produce a large-sample estimate of 80%, which is the right answer but the wrong question. Heteroscedasticity weights, though optimal for estimating the population mean rates, do little better in this problem and have no systematic advantage in problems of this type. On the other hand, regression with population weights, though terribly inefficient at estimating the population transition rates, would produce a more reasonable estimate of the actual rate in the sample, close to 90%. Intuitively, this is the argument for population weighting. As a practical matter, when district populations are highly variable, population weighting should ordinarily be used.

The theoretical status of population-weighted ecological regression is uncertain, however. The estimation problem is this: Under the sophisticated Goodman assumptions (or alternative assumptions), what are the best (minimum mean square error) estimates of the finite-sample means, p^* and q^*? Is population weighting of ordinary regression best? To our knowledge, there are no theoretical results available. Learning the answer is an important agenda item for aggregate data analysis, as much for the theoretical light it would shed on newer estimators as for the Goodman weighting problem itself. Answers appear more likely to emerge from the survey sampling literature than from the infinite population techniques that have dominated the ecological inference literature.

Fortunately, these distinctions are rarely of dramatic practical importance in aggregate samples of conventional size and character. First, many electoral data sets contain districts of roughly equal size, so that the problem evaporates. But even when a few districts are relatively large, the difference between estimates of the population mean and estimates of the sample mean will generally be quite small, especially relative to other sources of error. Most transition rates vary only modestly across districts. If this variation in transition rates is random, then the law of large numbers will fairly quickly produce average transition rates across large districts that are very similar to average transition rates across small districts. Hence the difference between the estimate of the sample mean and the estimate of the population mean collapses.[29]

For most practical purposes, then, one may as well pursue the simpler task of estimating the superpopulation means rather than the more subtle task of estimating their average realizations in the sample. We follow the literature in doing so throughout this book. However, it is well to remember that the result is more reliance on regressions unweighted by population than subsequent research may justify.

We now turn to the other, and quite different, justification for weighting, namely, heteroscedasticity. Given that, for theoretical purposes, one wants to estimate the superpopulation means, is population weighting needed to correct for heteroscedasticity? Since finite-sample considerations seem to support population weighting, and since the simple Goodman model implies weights approximately proportional to population (eq. [17]), the two arguments for population weighting have often been used interchangeably.

As we have already seen, however, the finite-sample argument is only intuitive, and the simple Goodman model is wholly implausible. Instead, if the transition rates p_j and q_j vary across districts in accordance with the sophisticated Goodman model, their variation should be explicitly modeled as in equations (15) and (16) or as in equation (34). Then the resulting ecological regression is heteroscedastic (whose correction, as we saw, may or may not produce better estimates). But population weights are not called for.[30] Using them would reduce the efficiency of the estimates.[31]

Thus under the sophisticated Goodman model, if the task is to esti-

29. Of course, if transition rates are not random but are instead systematically related to population, they should be modeled as such. Typically, the correlation between population and transition rates will be due to the association of large cities with left-party partisanship. The solution, then, is not weighting by population, but rather making transition rates depend on partisanship or past votes, which are the cause of the apparent association of transition rates and population. See chaps. 5 and 7.

30. If transition rates vary across districts as a function of exogenous variables, then, as already seen, the resulting estimates of p_j and q_j should be weighted by the number of Democrats and Republicans in each district to estimate the national averages, p and q, as in eqs. (11) and (12). But this population weighting occurs in the computation of averages after the regression has been run and is, of course, quite different from population-weighted regression.

31. Ecological regressions are occasionally carried out in terms of vote counts rather than fractions. For example, the total number of time-2 Democratic votes, n_{2dj}, might be

mate population mean transition rates, population weighting is unjustified. If Utah's transition rates are no more variable than California's, as the sophisticated Goodman model assumes, then both should be counted alike to estimate their average. Heteroscedasticity weights are not population weights.

Alternatives to the sophisticated Goodman model might be considered, in which transition rate variances are not constant over districts. For example, an election might exhibit transition rates whose variances are inversely proportional to district population. In that case, the appropriate regression weights would be the inverses of the variances in equation (29) or (30), with σ_p^2, σ_q^2, and σ_{pq} replaced by σ_p^2/n_j, σ_q^2/n_j, and σ_{pq}/n_j, respectively. These weights are approximately proportional to population, giving perhaps a rough-and-ready justification of population-weighted regression for reasons of heteroscedasticity. But the plausibility of this approach very much depends on a demonstration that the variance in transition rates is proportional to district population.

We know of no studies of how transition rate variation depends on district population. Variances inversely proportional to population would require the variance in statewide Montana or Vermont transition rates to be five or six times the California variance, which seems historically implausible. At the same time, the more plausible assumption of the sophisticated Goodman model, that the transition rate variance is constant across districts of different sizes, remains untested to our knowledge. More general ecological regression models, which allow transition rate variances to depend on population in a variety of ways, are an obvious avenue to improvements in the sophisticated Goodman model.

HETEROGENEOUS TRANSITION RATES WITHIN DISTRICTS

All the models discussed thus far assume that each person in a district has the same voter transition probabilities. That is, p_j and q_j are the same for everyone in the constituency. In the most important sense, this

---

regressed on the corresponding number at time 1, n_{1dj}, and on n_j itself. The intercept is suppressed.

This regression will produce unbiased estimates under OLS, but it is equivalent to weighting the observations by the square of the district population, which induces substantial heteroscedasticity and inefficiency. To correct this aspect of the heteroscedasticity, one must return to the use of vote fractions.

is true tautologically: in every constituency, some fraction of initial Democratic voters were loyal and some fraction defected, and those two fractions define the probabilities p_j and q_j. The probabilities apply to everyone in the sense that a perfectly respectable sample space may be defined (namely, the obvious one with equal-probability sampling) in which a randomly chosen voter from constituency j behaves in accordance with the conditional probabilities p_j and q_j. Hence the Goodman regression residuals in equation (30) are due to variation in p_j and q_j across constituencies, and heteroscedasticity takes the form of equation (31) above.

Alternatively, King (1990) proposes that ecological regression residuals are due to heterogeneity in transition rates *within districts*, and he sets out a strikingly different approach. He endorses Brown and Payne's (1986) closely related proposal as a possible replacement for what he calls the "patchwork" of conventional ecological regression, and he commends their model for its "comprehensive probabilistic framework, enabling one to bring in as much of the substance of the research problem as possible" (King 1990, pp. 13, 14). However, as many prior researchers have learned, the Goodman structure is not easily evaded, and neither Brown and Payne nor King is an exception. Although both are serious proposals for an alternative to Goodman, we show that, ultimately, both reduce to the very structure they seek to replace. We begin by setting out the Brown and Payne model, and then turn to King.

Brown and Payne extend the simple Goodman convolution-of-binomials model by allowing for cross-district heterogeneity in transition rates. Their approach is a special case of the sophisticated Goodman model (30). That is, everyone in a particular constituency has the same transition rates p_j and q_j, but those rates vary stochastically over districts in accordance with a pair of mixing distributions. However, Brown and Payne impose two additional restrictions. First, instead of specifying just the first two moments of each mixing distribution, they require a particular functional form for them, namely, the beta distribution. And second, they assume away the covariance between p_j and q_j across districts, that is, $\sigma_{pq} = 0$.

The density of the beta distribution, $f_B(p_{ji})$, over the interval [0, 1] is

$$(34) \quad f_B(p_{ji}) = \frac{(N_p - 1)!}{(r_p - 1)!(N_p - r_p - 1)!} p_{ji}^{r_p - 1} (1 - p_{ji})^{N_p - r_p - 1},$$

where $N_p \geq 2$ and $r_p \geq 1$. When $N_p = 2$ and $r_p = 1$, the beta distribution becomes the uniform distribution. Otherwise, the beta is unimodal and nonzero inside the open interval (0, 1). The Brown and Payne estimator thus depends on the faith that the distribution of transition rates is unimodal across districts.

The parameters of the first beta distribution are chosen so that the mean constituency loyalty rate is $E(p_{ji}) = p = r_p/N_p$. The variance of the beta (i.e., the variation over districts around this average transition rate) is $p(1 - p)/(N_p + 1)$, so that cross-constituency variation is indexed by the parameter N_p, with larger values of N_p indicating less dispersion. In the limit, as $N_p \to \infty$, the distribution collapses to a point, every district has the same transition rates, and the simple Goodman model is obtained.[32]

A similar prior beta distribution is postulated for q_j, with parameters r_q and N_q but otherwise entirely parallel features. Brown and Payne also discuss an extension to multiple parties, replacing the beta-binomial distributions with their standard generalization, the Dirichlet-multinomial, but no new conceptual issues arise, and for expositional purposes, we shall confine ourselves to the simpler case. Similarly, they discuss the use of exogenous variables in the logit form of equation (17), but again this extension is standard and we ignore it here.

The combination of Bernoulli distributions for individuals plus a prior beta distribution centered at p_j for the constituency as a whole produces a total vote for the Democrats at time 2 from prior Democratic voters which is a compound binomial distribution with a mean of $p_j n_{dj}$. To find its variance, note that, as in the next to last section, the variance for an individual decomposes into the average of the individual variances plus the variance of the prior, where here the prior is known to have a beta distribution. As in equation (20) above, the conditional variances for individuals are uncorrelated with each other, while the draw of p_j is fixed over individuals with the constituency. Hence, as in equation (25), the total variance is n_{dj} times the mean individual variance plus n_{dj}^2 times the prior variance:

$$(35) \quad \text{var}(n_{ddj}) = n_{dj} \int_0^1 p_{ji}(1 - p_{ji})f_B(p_{ji})dp_{ji}$$
$$+ n_{dj}^2 p_j(1 - p_j)/(N_p + 1),$$

32. The paper by King (1990, p. 13), which follows Brown and Payne in using α to represent the dispersion parameter, N_p, contains a small typo at this point: it has $\alpha \to 1$ for the convergence to homogeneity.

where again n_{ddj} is the number of Democratic votes at time 2 from those who voted Democratic initially in constituency j and n_{dj} is the number of Democratic voters in the district at time 1.

In evaluating the integral, the usual tricks with beta or binomial integrals work nicely. In particular, if the integral in equation (35) is multiplied by $(N_p + 1)N_p/[r_p(N_p - r_p)]$, it becomes the integral of the density of a beta distribution with parameters $N_p + 2$ and $r_p + 1$, so that its value is unity. Hence the integral in equation (35) is

$$\int_0^1 p_{ji}(1 - p_{ji})f_B(p_{ji})dp_{ji} = r_p(N_p - r_p)/[N_p(N_p + 1)]$$

$$\text{(36)} \qquad\qquad = r_p N_p(N_p - r_p)/[N_p^2(N_p + 1)]$$

$$= p(1 - p)N_p/(N_p + 1).$$

Substitution into equation (35) yields

$$\text{(37)} \qquad \text{var}(n_{ddj}) = n_{dj}p(1 - p)(N_p + n_{dj})/(N_p + 1),$$

which is the value listed by Brown and Payne (1986, p. 453) in a somewhat different notation. Alternatively, the result may be obtained by substituting $p(1 - p)/(N_p + 1)$ for σ_p^2 in the more general expression (25) above.

Similarly, the Democratic fraction from time-1 Republican voters has mean q_j and variance $n_{rj}q(1 - q)(N_q + n_{rj})/(N_q + 1)$. Summing the variances from the two vote sources and converting to vote fractions gives equation (39) below.

Now, as Brown and Payne note, since the means are identical across districts, we may write their model in Goodman form as

$$\text{(38)} \qquad D_{2j} = q + (p - q)D_{1j} + U_j,$$

which is just equation (30) again. The variance of the disturbances is a special case of equation (31), reparameterized in terms of N_p and N_q instead of σ_p^2 and σ_q^2, and with $\sigma_{pq} = 0$:

$$\text{(39)} \quad \text{var}(U_j) = [D_{1j}p(1 - p)n_p^* + (1 - D_{1j})q(1 - q)n_q^*]/n_j,$$

where $n_p^* = (N_p + n_{dj})/(N_p + 1)$ and $n_q^* = (N_q + n_{rj})/(N_q + 1)$. In practice, n_j will nearly always be much larger than N_p or N_q. Hence the variance is, typically to a very good approximation,

$$\text{(40)} \quad \text{var}(U_j) = D_{1j}^2 p(1 - p)/(N_p + 1)$$

$$+ (1 - D_{1j})^2 q(1 - q)/(N_q + 1).$$

Since here $\sigma_p^2 = p(1 - p)/(N_p + 1)$ and $\sigma_q^2 = q(1 - q)/(N_q + 1)$, the isomorphism with equation (32) when $\sigma_{pq} = 0$ is apparent.

As noted above, with district sample sizes as large as they are, the disturbance term is very well approximated by normality assumptions; Brown and Payne themselves abandon the convolution of compound binomials in favor of normality for purposes of estimation. Thus there is little reason to engage in elaborate numerical search for the maximum likelihood estimates as Brown and Payne do. Ordinary linear least squares with heteroscedasticity corrections will perform as well asymptotically.[33] The Brown and Payne model is a special case of the sophisticated Goodman model of 1959, which it spells out in a usefully rigorous way but does not modify conceptually. Indeed, Brown and Payne's applied example, using British data, exhibits precisely the usual Goodman problems—loyalty rates straining to exceed 100%, defection rates constrained to zero to prevent their being negative, and poor estimates for third parties.

We now turn to King (1990). He proposes that the Brown and Payne model be interpreted differently. Instead of using the mixing distribution to describe differences in average transition rates *across* constituencies, he applies it to differences among individuals *within* constituencies. Thus Brown and Payne have heterogeneous constituencies with homogeneous voters within each of them; King has homogeneous constituencies with heterogenous voters within them.[34]

King's intuition is that constituencies in which everyone has the

33. Brown and Payne use demographic control variables in logistic form, so that nonlinear least squares with heteroscedasticity corrections will be required to match their estimator, but again, software for carrying out the procedure is commonly available.

34. King (1990, p. 14) says that his model is a special case of the Brown and Payne (1986) framework, and the mathematics is indeed similar. Conceptually, however, the two models are quite different and the implied statistical models distinct, as the succeeding paragraphs in the text demonstrate. Note in particular that, for Brown and Payne, parameter variation across districts is random and would change in repeated samples, while for King, parameter variation within districts (which he describes as "randomly distributed" in parallel with Brown and Payne) is actually treated in his calculations as fixed in repeated samples. And rightly so. It is straightforward to show that if within-district parameter variation were treated as random instead, King's heterogeneity parameters would be unidentified.

The unidentifiability is not due to an unfortunate choice of mixing distribution: In a mixture of Bernoulli distributions, any mixing distribution with mean p is indistinguishable from any other (see eq. [24]). This is a special case of the general result that when binomial distributions with parameters p and n are mixed, the mixing distributions are identified only up to a class of distributions whose first n moments are identical (Maritz 1970, p. 21).

same p_j and q_j will behave differently in repeated samples than those that have heterogeneous transition rates. Hence the variability of the vote fractions would allow us to infer the underlying within-district heterogeneity in transition rates. King (1990, p. 1) states that "one is not only able to infer the transition probabilities, but, perhaps even more significantly, we can also study the variation in these probabilities across people within districts. . . . This approach requires more sophisticated mathematics than usual . . . , [but] once the mathematics are understood, the approach also meets my what-did-you-do-to-those-data criterion, since the stochastic model is quite clear."

We follow King in abstracting from multiple parties, abstention, and demographic control variables to focus on the conceptual issues. In the case of two parties with no abstention, then, King specifies that an individual voter i in constituency j who chose the Democrats at time 1 has a fixed loyalty rate, p_{ji}, distributed across voters according to the beta distribution (34). Given this transition rate, she votes Democratic again with conventional Bernoulli probability p_{ji} and variance $p_{ji}(1 - p_{ji})$, independently of every other voter. In every district, voters are distributed according to the same beta distribution, so that each district is equally heterogeneous.

King does not spell out the details of his model, but as he indicates, it is not difficult to fill them in. As we have seen in the sophisticated Goodman and the Brown and Payne models, the variance of district total votes may be found by summing over the individual variances. Since we no longer have a single transition rate for the constituency but rather separate fixed rates for each individual, the total variance is just n_{dj} times the mean of the individual variances, which in the case of the beta mixing distribution yields

(41)
$$\text{var}(n_{ddj}) = n_{dj}\int_0^1 p_{ji}(1 - p_{ji})f_B(p_{ji})dp_{ji}$$
$$= n_{dj}p(1 - p)N_p/(N_p + 1).$$

Similarly, the variance of the number of defections to the Democrats in constituency j is

(42)
$$\text{var}(n_{drj}) = n_{dj}q(1 - q)N_q/(N_q + 1).$$

Both these variances are just the usual homogeneous binomial variances weighted by a fraction less than one. That is, both values are *less than* the variance when all the time-1 Democratic voters and all the time-1 Republican voters are each perfectly homogeneous with the same mean transition rates. (This is a consequence of Jensen's Inequality and the concavity of the binomial variance: If x is a real random variable defined on a bounded interval, and if $f(\cdot)$ is a continuous concave function over that interval, then $E[f(x)] \leq f[E(x)]$.)

Now taking expectations within constituencies and making use of the homogeneity assumption across districts, the King model implies a heteroscedastic normal linear regression equation:

$$(43) \qquad D_{2j} = q + (p - q)D_{1j} + U_j.$$

After the usual conversion to vote fractions, the total variance of constituency votes in the King model is, from equations (41) and (42),

$$(44) \quad \text{var}(U_j) = [D_{1j}p(1 - p)N_p/(N_p + 1) +$$
$$(1 - D_{1j})q(1 - q)N_q/(N_q + 1)]/n_j.$$

Equations (43) and (44) are, of course, almost a perfect replica of the simple Goodman model (2) and (19). The stochastic variation in parameters across districts of the sophisticated Goodman model is missing. The comprehensive probabilistic framework and nonlinear MLE produce essentially the simplest version of the "patchwork" Goodman model, whose difficulties have already been discussed above.

The sole change is that King's disturbance variances are allowed to be smaller than those of the simple Goodman model. But as we noted above, even after control variables have been introduced, the homogeneous binomial variances in the simple Goodman model are already too small to fit actual historical election disturbances—often by two or three orders of magnitude. King's proposal is to make them smaller still. By its nature, then, a likelihood approach to this kind of within-district heterogeneity cannot replace sophisticated Goodman regression.

If King's approach were combined with Brown and Payne's, so that transition rates varied stochastically both within and across districts, the data would be better served. Even in that case, however, we are doubtful that within-district heterogeneity can be reliably recovered. The heterogeneity parameters N_p and N_q influence only that part of the disturbances due to pure binomial sampling error. In King's model, there is no other source of variability. In that case, equation (44) shows that the heterogeneity parameters have the effect of making fractional changes in the sampling error. Once district-level parameter variation is allowed for, however, the sampling error itself routinely dwindles to less than 1% of the total disturbance variance, as we have seen. Thus the estimation of heterogeneity will be extremely delicate. Even if one has perfect confidence in all the distributional assumptions and perfect confidence in all the significant digits in the data, parameters whose identification depends on influencing less than 1% of second- and higher-order moments are not good candidates for tight estimates from aggregate data. Once the evanescent heterogeneity parameters are dropped, however, this hypothetical Brown-Payne-King model reduces to the sophisticated (or extended sophisticated) Goodman model of 1959.

CONCLUSION

This completes our exposition of ecological regression and its extensions. As we noted at the beginning of the chapter, Goodman's method remains the workhorse of ecological inference. In some applications, it performs dependably and produces sensible results. Certainly, it is the starting point for any statistical study of transition rates using aggregate data. The endless parade of new methodological suggestions demonstrates, however, that dissatisfaction with the Goodman model is widespread. Empirical experience with it has often been disappointing, particularly in the estimation of voter transitions, and none of the extensions has enjoyed consistent success.

We believe that the reason for the failure of ecological regression, including the extensions by Brown and Payne (1986) and others, is that it deals with *derivative* probabilities rather than with *microlevel fundamentals*. Voter transition rates in particular are not causal relationships. At both time 1 and time 2, voters choose one party or another on the basis of party identification and other factors. Such specifications are fundamental, in the sense that, at least ideally, they represent microlevel relationships that hold across the sample. Given those statistical specifications, the loyalty and defection rates may be *derived*. But Goodman's p and q have no independent casual status.[35] They are a consequence of the fundamental relationships, not fundamentals themselves.

The distinction is important because, at the aggregate level in particular, our intuitions about derived relationships are often rather poor. For example, instead of thinking about the elusive relationship of a time-2 vote to a time-1 vote, consider the more obvious relation-

35. "Causal status" is a shorthand expression and somewhat misleading. See chapter 4.

ship of each of them to party identification. In particular, suppose that within each constituency, each Democratic party identifier has the same probability of remaining loyal to her party at time 1. Across constituencies, the loyalty rates are drawn independently from a common beta distribution. Assume that the same is true at time 2: within constituencies, each Democrat supports the party with the same probability; across constituencies, loyalty rates are again drawn independently from a (different) beta distribution. Assume further that, at each time period, the Republican identifiers have their own beta distributions from which they draw their common constituency transition rates. Thus we have a total of four mutually independent beta distributions, each one giving the distribution of the transition rate from party identification to vote, for a particular party and time period. These assumptions about "party identification transition rates" are microlevel fundamentals: party identification causes vote choices, and we have considerable experience with the likely range of probabilities that tie votes to the underlying party identifications. In particular, unimodal distributions like the beta are a plausible hypothesis.

Now consider the derivative, noncausal probabilities—the transition rates across constituencies between the vote at time 1 and the vote at time 2. The distribution of these Goodman transition rates p_j and q_j are mathematically implied by what has already been said. What is their statistical distribution? If the party identification transition rates are beta, do the Goodman voter transition rates have the mathematically convenient, but otherwise unsupported, beta distributions Brown and Payne assume? In fact, as a bit of arithmetic will demonstrate, the answer is no. For plausible parameter values, the implied distributions of both p and q are bimodal mixtures of two betas, with the heights of the two modes varying by the party identification in the district. In short, if party identification affects the vote in this conventional way, the Brown and Payne distributional assumptions will be seriously inaccurate. Other party models actually support them. But in the absence of derivations from fundamentals, we have no way to choose.

Inaccurate distributional assumptions are the Achilles' heel of MLE. The example makes it clear just how remote from our substantive knowledge is the postulated distribution of transition rates that is so crucial to likelihood models like that of Brown and Payne. Even in sophisticated work like their own, the critical assumptions are not derived from substantive fundamentals at the microlevel, and the trustworthiness of their estimates is unavoidably in doubt.

The fault is not unique to Brown and Payne, of course, nor are they particularly blameworthy. Given the weaknesses of voting theories, Brown and Payne share with Goodman and everyone else who writes on the subject a certain inescapable theoretical fragility. In any discipline, the connection of statistical theory to powerful substantive assumptions happens over decades and is the work of many scholars. The present lack of that connection accounts, we believe, for the well-known troubles of ecological regression.

The next chapter discusses in detail the difficulties ecological regression has encountered in practice. It then takes a step toward better microfoundations for voter transition studies by assuming that party identification causes the vote. The Goodman transition rates are derived as consequences. The result is used to explain why ecological regression too often fails.

APPENDIX

MLE and GLS for the Sophisticated Goodman Model in the Multiparty Case

With aggregate data, single-equation methods often give very satisfactory fits whose sampling errors are smaller than their suspected specification errors. Thus additional statistical efficiency is not always of great concern. For completeness, however, and because not all aggregate regressions fit well, this appendix gives an outline of full-system estimation in the sophisticated (random-coefficient) Goodman model, an issue that arises when there are three or more parties. The idea is to take advantage of correlation among the disturbances of competing parties in order to improve statistical efficiency. To be concrete, we will discuss transition rates among parties over time, but the same formulas apply when the right-hand-side variables are demographic.

We suppose that observations of party fractions of the vote are taken from m constituencies or districts at each of two times, with n_j votes cast in constituency j each time. Each constituency's votes are assumed independent of the votes in other constituencies. Let there be K parties, exclude one as usual, and let Y_j be the $(K - 1)$-dimensional row vector of the remaining vote proportions in the jth constituency at time 2. Similarly, let X_j be the K-dimensional row vector of all party proportions in constituency j at time 1, so that X_{jk} is the vote for party k in constituency j. Denote by P the $K \times (K - 1)$ transition matrix, where $p_{kk'}$ is the national average fraction of those who supported party k at time 1 who defect to party k' at time 2. Then for the (unextended) sophisticated Goodman model, using the normal approximation to the likelihood discussed in the text, the log-likelihood function may be written as

$$(A1) \quad L(P, \sigma) = -\frac{1}{2} \sum_{j=1}^{m} [\log|\Sigma_j| + (Y_j - X_j P)\Sigma_j^{-1}(Y_j - X_j P)'],$$

where Σ_j is the $(K - 1) \times (K - 1)$ variance-covariance matrix of the disturbances in the jth constituency and σ is a vector of coefficients defined below. The same arguments used in the two-party case in the text at equation (32) may be used to show that, to a very good approximation, the k'th diagonal element of Σ_j is $\Sigma_{k=1}^{K} X_{jk}^2 \sigma_{kk'}^2 + 2 \Sigma_{k=1}^{K} \Sigma_{k'>k}^{K} X_{jk} X_{jk'} \sigma_{kk'k''}$, where $\sigma_{kk'}^2$ is the cross-district variance of $p_{kk'}$ and $\sigma_{kk'k''}$ is the corresponding covariance between $p_{kk'}$ and $p_{kk''}$. All these variances and covariances are collected in the vector σ, which therefore appears in the argument of the likelihood function. Each of the elements of σ is unknown and assumed constant across districts. Note that the elements of Σ_j will need slight adjustment in the extended version of sophisticated Goodman regression; see the discussion at equation (33).

The number of parameters increases rapidly with additional parties, and aggregate data are rarely rich enough to recover them. Customarily, all the covariances $\sigma_{kk'k''}$ are set to zero, as in the general random-parameter model of Hildreth and Houck (1968). In addition, following Brown and Payne (1986), it is convenient to reduce the number of parameters still further by constraining the variances $\sigma_{kk'}^2$ to those generated by independent Dirichlet mixing distributions with multinomial components, so that variation in transition rates from party k are independent of those from party k', and for each party, its transition rates jointly have a Dirichlet-multinomial distribution. In that case, the k'th diagonal element of Σ_j is $\Sigma_{k=1}^{K} X_{jk}^2 p_{kk'}(1 - p_{kk'})/(N_k + 1)$, while the (k', k'') off-diagonal element is $-\Sigma_{k=1}^{K} X_{jk}^2 p_{kk'} p_{kk''}/(N_k + 1)$. Thus only K additional parameters N_k are required beyond those of the simple Goodman model, and they form the elements of the vector σ in this case. The extended version of the model may be handled by essentially the same formulas; one simply allows $p_{kk'}$ to vary by constituency.

MLE proceeds by setting the partial derivatives of $L(P, \sigma)$ to zero and solving the resulting equations numerically. Under the usual regularity conditions, the result is estimates which are consistent, asymptotically normal, and asymptotically efficient. (See Kalbfleisch and Lawless 1984 for a detailed discussion of the parallel simple Goodman case.)

Under similar conditions, feasible GLS is a convenient and asymptotically efficient alternative for estimating P, which may be iterated if desired. The feasible GLS estimator is

$$(A2) \qquad \hat{P}_{GLS} = \arg \min \sum_{j=1}^{m} (Y_j - X_j P) \hat{\Sigma}_j^{-1} (Y_j - X_j P)',$$

where $\hat{\Sigma}_j$ is a consistent estimate of Σ_j. The estimator may be computed numerically or expressed in closed form (see below).

A simple way to produce the estimate $\hat{\Sigma}_j^{-1}$ generalizes the two-party method discussed after equation (32). The elements of Σ_j depend only on X_j plus unknown constants. To estimate the constants, begin with an initial OLS regression estimate of P

$$(A3) \qquad \hat{P}_{OLS}' = \left(\sum_{j=1}^{m} X_j' X_j \right)^{-1} \sum_{j=1}^{m} X_j' Y_j.$$

This estimator $\hat{P}_{OLS}$ is simply the regression of each party's vote share at time 2 on all party shares at time 1. It is assumed that the specification is good enough to eliminate out-of-bounds transition probability estimates at this stage.

Next, compute the residuals. Then for each party at time 2, the jth squared residual may be regressed on the corresponding diagonal element in Σ_j to estimate the unknown constants in that element. Estimates of every $p_{kk'}$ from equation (A3) are inserted into each Σ_j before the regression is run, so that only the parameters N_k remain to be estimated. These regressions are most easily carried out in terms of new parameters γ_k, defined as $1/(N_k + 1)$; doing so produces linear regressions without intercepts. Inserting the resulting estimates into the corresponding terms in each Σ_j produces $\hat{\Sigma}_j$ for insertion into equation (A2). It may be necessary to constrain the resulting estimates to ensure that $\hat{\Sigma}_j$ is positive-definite and hence invertible.

Finally, for both MLE and GLS, transitions to the omitted Kth party (the "missing column" of P) may be estimated from the fact that the sum of all transition probabilities out of each party must be unity.

Notice that the present setup closely resembles "seemingly unrelated regression" (SUR). When the regressors in each equation are identical, as they are here, it is well known that OLS and GLS are equivalent in the SUR case, which would make the methods of this appendix unnecessary. However, equation (A1) is not quite in SUR form, since Σ_j varies by constituency instead of being constant. We have not investigated either finite-sample or asymptotic efficiency gains from full-system methods in the present problem, though they seem likely to be small since highly correlated regressors across equations are known to reduce efficiency gains in the SUR case.

Of course, the list of right-hand-side variables is not always the same across parties, particularly not in the extended Goodman case, where the list of control variables may differ from party to party. In that instance, the regression setup cannot be written in the convenient form of equation (A1). Instead, a "seemingly unrelated heteroscedastic regressions" version of SUR is appropriate. The closed form of the GLS estimator in equation (A2) may also be derived from the heteroscedastic SUR formulation. Both are obvious generalizations of the usual SUR case, and in the end, just special cases of GLS. However, these estimators are somewhat inconvenient for applied work, and we omit them here. (See the closely related discussion in Kalbfleisch and Lawless 1984. For discussions of SUR, see any econometrics text, e.g., Judge *et al.* 1985, chap. 12.)

THREE

BIAS IN GOODMAN
ECOLOGICAL REGRESSION

Partisanship Models

Just one technique for handling ecological data has been widely adopted in practice: the linear (unextended) version of Goodman ecological regression (1953, 1959). As we saw in the preceding chapter, Goodman's task is to find the national proportion of Democratic voters at time 1 who voted Democratic again at time 2, and the proportion of Republican voters at time 1 who switched to the Democrats at time 2. As before, denote these proportions by p and q, respectively, and let the fraction of Democratic votes in constituency j at the two time periods be D_{1j} and D_{2j}. Suppose that everyone votes, so that the fraction of Democratic votes and the fraction of Republican votes sum to unity. Then as we have seen, at the aggregate level we have

$$(1) \qquad D_{2j} = q + (p - q)D_{1j} + U_j,$$

where U_j is a disturbance term introduced to cope both with pure sampling error and possible variation in the transition rates across constituencies. It is assumed to be uncorrelated with D_{1j}.

Equation (1) has the form of a bivariate regression with intercept q and slope $p - q$. Thus under the Goodman assumptions, the researcher need only regress the Democratic vote at time 2 on the Democratic vote at time 1 to estimate the coefficients. As discussed in the previous chapter, the model extends smoothly to multiple parties, abstention, controls for demographics, and so on.

Linear ecological regression has enjoyed widespread use across political science, history, and sociology. However, it has a well-known weakness. All too often, the estimated loyalty rate exceeds 100%, or the estimated defection rate is negative, or both (e.g., Kousser 1974, pp. xi–xii). The same problems occur when the independent variable is social class rather than prior vote (Miller et al. 1974). Of course, such probabilities are meaningless, and adding control variables often fails to improve them. Even forcing the probability estimates above 0.0 and below 1.0 (e.g., Irwin and Meeter 1969; Crewe and Payne 1975) guarantees only that the estimates will be interpretable, not that they will be accurate. Typically, the corrected versions are only slightly more believable than the logical impossibilities they replaced.

What is particularly odd about the Goodman anomalies is that they coexist with wonderful regression fits. In Stokes's (1969) justly famous article, for example, the correlation exceeds .98, and the coefficients are known with great precision. Yet the estimates are far from the truth (as estimated from a panel survey), and in fact the estimated defection rate is negative. As usual in ecological regression, sampling error is not the culprit: the hypothesis that the defection rate is zero or positive is rejected at well beyond the 1% level. (See chap. 5 for additional discussion of this standard data set.)

This chapter focuses on the anomalies of ecological regression in the study of voter transitions, where they have received the most attention. Ecological regression may be used more widely, as we have already seen, and related anomalies occur in those applications as well. However, we emphasize the voter transition problem and its origins in citizen partisanship. We suspect that analogous underlying dispositions account for the erroneous estimates that occur when the Goodman method is applied to other sorts of aggregate data.

HOW OFTEN DOES ECOLOGICAL REGRESSION FAIL?

While researchers are agreed that out-of-bounds estimates are often encountered in ecological regression, it is no easy matter to document their frequency. Journals do not publish meaningless estimates, and scholars do not include them in their articles. Published ecological regressions therefore consist almost entirely of sensible results.

Fortunately for our purposes, scholars were unaware of how to interpret ecological regression coefficients before Goodman's work, and so meaningless results were not censored. Hence one may use the early literature to form an honest estimate of how often ecological regression breaks down. A particularly useful source is Harold F. Gosnell's *Grass Roots Politics* (1942, pp. 166–76). Gosnell computes bivariate ecological regressions and correlations using county-level voting data within each of Pennsylvania, Wisconsin, and Iowa. Thus the regressions are estimated on relatively homogeneous data sets and with relatively disaggregated units of observation, both conditions that should improve the estimates. As in the Stokes data, the correlation coefficients (r) are excellent: of the 24 reported, three-quarters exceed .80 and almost half exceed .90. Yet of the 21 regressions included, two-thirds have a loyalty rate exceeding 100% or a defection rate below 0% or both. Some of the illegal estimates are not misdemeanors: One estimated loyalty rate is 145%; another is 209%! Worse yet, the errors accumulate as the fit improves: of the 14 regressions with correlations above .85, all but one have an out-of-bounds coefficient.[1]

Even disaggregating with Chicago data to racially homogeneous units smaller than wards brought no improvement. In another classic study, Gosnell (1937, pp. 107, 123) studied 147 geographic units comprising virtually the entire white population of the city. He plotted the 1932 Roosevelt vote against the 1928 Smith vote, and the 1936 Roosevelt vote against the 1932 Roosevelt vote. Both graphs are very close to linearity, and the r-values are .94 and .96.[2] However, both loyalty rate estimates equal 103%.

Logically impossible estimates in ecological regression are not flukes. They are encountered perhaps half the time, and more often as the statistical fit improves. Ecological regression fails, not occasionally, but chronically.

Ecological regression has theoretical difficulties as well. As we noted in the previous chapter, it is a purely descriptive specification with no pretense of causality. In consequence, it lacks theoretical suppleness. For example, consider the case of "uniform swing," in which, on average, all constituencies move δ percentage points toward the Democrats.[3] This striking phenomenon has often been closely approximated

1. In fairness, we have excluded from this summary Gosnell's study of the LaFollette era in Wisconsin, in which the vote for a Republican candidate with Progressive affiliations is regressed on the prior vote for a "regular" Republican, or vice versa. Gosnell's correlations are relatively low in this era, with two of the three actually negative. Both of the two regressions reported from this period also include an out-of-bounds estimate. The difficulty, of course, is that, although these early Progressive-era races are two-candidate, Democratic-Republican fights and thus have the Goodman form, they are essentially three-party contests, with one party being eliminated in the Republican primary. Indeed, within a few years, a full three-party system came into being.

2. As in the Stokes (1969) case, a close look shows evidence of slight curvilinearity. See chap. 5.

3. More precisely, divide all the districts into homogeneous groups according to the proportion of the vote they gave to the Democrats at time 1. Then "uniform swing" is the condition that each of these groups will increase or decrease its mean Democratic percentage from time 1 to time 2 by the same number of percentage points. That is, the vote change is mean independent of the time-1 vote.

in Britain (e.g., Butler and Stokes 1969, pp. 135–36, 303–12), and historically, it has been a reasonably accurate description of American elections as well, at least within broad geographic regions (Gosnell 1942, chap. 2; see also McCarthy and Tukey 1978). Yet the Goodman model implies that uniform swing is impossible (Stokes 1969; Achen 1983b).[4] Extensions and special cases of Goodman, such as the Brown and Payne (1986) and King (1990) models of the previous chapter, also rule out uniform swing. The inelegant theoretical underpinnings of ecological regression can no more fit the beauty of uniform swing than the stepsister's foot can enter the glass slipper.

The purpose of this chapter is to account for all these anomalies of ecological regression. Focusing on bivariate ecological regression, we show that if party identification influences the vote, as has long been known to survey researchers, then the Goodman anomalies are implied: loyalty rate estimates will be too high, defection rate estimates too low, and out-of-bounds estimates will occur frequently. At the same time, the regression will be perfectly linear and R^2 will be near unity. Thus if party identification matters, ecological regression is biased in the manner familiar to empirical researchers. The problems of ecological regression stem from fundamental features of political life. (Some of the following results appeared in less general form in Achen 1983a.)

PARTY IDENTIFICATION AND AGGREGATE VOTING DATA

A commonplace of the voting literature of the last several decades is that party identification has a strong influence on the vote. This view is most strongly associated with *The American Voter* (Campbell et al. 1960), where party identification is measured by the respondent's self-identification and is regarded primarily as a relatively fixed aspect of her social-psychological makeup. But party identification can also be interpreted as a conceptual simplification to help the voter sort out the welter of political information (Schumpeter [1942] 1976, chap. 22), as a summary "retrospective" judgment about past performance of the parties (Jackson 1975; Fiorina 1981), as a rational "prospective" forecast about future performance (Lewis-Beck 1988; Achen 1992), or

---

4. The exception occurs when the swing is zero, in which case setting $p = 1$ and $q = 0$ in the Goodman model will generate this rather special instance of uniform swing. However, apart from cases in which one party gets all the votes at some time period, this is the sole exception.

even as a mere proxy for the actual causal factors, such as social class. Needless to say, these alternatives are neither mutually exclusive nor exhaustive, and for our purposes, we need not choose among them. Whatever party identification may mean and whatever its actual effect, there is general agreement that most voters have a persistent "behavioral" tendency to vote for one party rather than another. For present purposes, that *tendance* will be called "party identification," regardless of what the voter would say in response to a survey or what an outside observer would regard as the cause of the vote. Party identification here is a revealed preference. Whether it is also (or actually) an attitude, a rational choice, or a position in the social structure makes no difference.

The strategy of this chapter is to postulate an electoral system in which only party identification influences the vote, and then to investigate how well unextended ecological regression performs in that system. The model of party voting is as simple as we can make it. The goal is not to match in detail the behavior of actual voters, but rather to produce a conceptually uncluttered model as a test case for ecological regression. If ecological regression fails in this stylized world, its problems will multiply when confronted with causal subtleties.

Consider, then, a two-party system in which voters are either Democrats or Republicans; there are no independents. Each party group is homogeneous: at each election, every member of a party has the same probability of voting for her party's candidate. Within each party, voting is independent across voters and over time. That is, knowing that a Democrat defected from her party identification last time tells us nothing about what she will do this time or what her Democratic and Republican neighbors did either time, beyond what we already know about them from their party identifications.

In constituency j, let the fraction of the vote for the Democrats at the two time periods be written as D_{1j} and D_{2j}. Denote the proportion of Democratic identifiers in the constituency by D_j^*, so that the fraction of Republican identifiers is $1 - D_j^*$. These party fractions are unknown to the researcher; in general, it is not assumed that party registration exists, nor if it does, that the fraction of registered Democrats is the same as the proportion of citizens who *vote* Democratic regularly.

Let p_1^* and p_2^* be the fractions of Democratic identifiers who vote for their parties at times 1 and 2, and let q_1^* and q_2^* be the fractions of Republican identifiers who defect to the Democrats at the two time periods. Notice that these are loyalty and defection rates from *party iden-*

tification, while the Goodman loyalty and defection rates are from the prior *vote.*

Now aggregate within constituencies in the obvious way, so that, by analogy with the Goodman equation (1) above, the *j*th constituency's vote for the Democrats at times 1 and 2 may be written as

$$(2) \qquad D_{1j} = q_1^* + (p_1^* - q_1^*)D_j^* + U_{1j}^*,$$

$$(3) \qquad D_{2j} = q_2^* + (p_2^* - q_2^*)D_j^* + U_{2j}^*,$$

where U_{1j}^* and U_{2j}^* are disturbance terms embodying pure sampling error plus random variation in the coefficients, and the coefficients are constant across constituencies, by assumption. The disturbances have mean zero and are uncorrelated with D_j^*. So long as the party balance remains the same, this framework may be extended to any number of elections simply by adding an equation for each additional contest.

Equations (2) and (3) are the macrolevel specification of the "ecological party identification model" to be analyzed in this chapter. The equations constitute a factor-analytic setup, where the D_{ti} are the items, the D_j^* are factor scores, and the coefficients $p_1^* - q_1^*$ and $p_2^* - q_2^*$ are factor loadings. With factor scores and items transformed to *z*-scores, as in conventional factor analysis, the q_1^* and q_2^* intercept terms would drop out, and these equations would generate a single-factor structure with one loading for each election.

Historically, excellent statistical fits have been obtained by applying factor analysis to aggregate voting data (e.g., Gosnell 1937, app. B; Rogin 1967, app. B; MacRae and Meldrum 1969; related work includes Thomsen 1987). The usual result is a powerful first factor that seems to rank-order the geographic units on a kind of partisanship scale, just as in equations (2) and (3). But the underlying framework that deduced the factor-analytic assumptions from a coherent tale about political life has been missing. It has never been quite clear what the factor scores and loadings meant. In consequence, this use of psychometric techniques on historical records has largely disappeared.

The framework of equations (2) and (3) answers the question of why ecological factor analysis has so often worked well. Apart from the *z*-score transformations, the factor scores are the proportions of Democratic identifiers, and the loadings are the difference between the party loyalty and defection rates. Hence if party identification influences the vote in the manner of equations (2) and (3), factor analysis will not only fit well, but will be perfectly interpretable substantively. The ecological party identification model explains what ecological factor analysis means substantively and why it works.[5]

An ecological party identification specification also copes with uniform swing. As mentioned above, the theoretical anomaly of ecological regression is that it cannot account for this commonly observed feature of electoral systems. By contrast, the model of equations (2) and (3) deals with it easily. Suppose that

$$(4) \qquad\qquad p_2^* = p_1^* + \delta$$

and

$$(5) \qquad\qquad q_2^* = q_1^* + \delta.$$

That is, both the party loyalty rate for Democrats and the party defection rate for Republicans change by the same amount δ from one election to the next. Substituting these two expressions into equation (3), one obtains

$$(6) \qquad D_{2j} = q_1^* + (p_1^* - q_1^*)D_j^* + \delta + U_{1j}^*.$$

Substituting from equation (2) yields

$$(7) \qquad\qquad D_{2j} = D_{1j} + \delta + U_{2j}^* - U_{1j}^*.$$

Hence, in expectation,

$$(8) \qquad\qquad E(D_{2j}) = E(D_{1j}) + \delta,$$

which is just what is meant by uniform swing.

ECOLOGICAL REGRESSION WHEN PARTY IDENTIFICATION MATTERS

Suppose now that equations (2) and (3) describe voter behavior. What happens when Goodman ecological regression is applied? That is, if the actual causal process is that party identification influences the vote with constant party loyalty rates across districts, what is the implication for Goodman voter transition rates? This chapter shows that under the party identification model, Goodman ecological regression may behave in the manner familiar to empirical researchers, with the estimated loy-

---

5. For details of identification and estimation in this and other ecological party identification models, see chap. 7.

alty rate too high and the estimated defection rate too low. In short, the party identification model accounts for the Goodman anomalies.

The underlying intuition may be grasped by thinking about a simple case in which, say, the voters are evenly divided nationally between the parties and each party is 80% loyal to its party identification at each time period. We assume for simplicity that the constituency sizes are so large that sampling error may be ignored. Then to find the Goodman rate p, the loyalty rate for those who vote Democratic initially, note that at time 1 the Democrats receive the vote of 80% of the Democratic identifiers and 20% of the Republican identifiers. Among these time-1 Democratic voters, 80% will remain loyal at time 2 (the Democratic identifiers), while only 20% of the remainder will do so (the Republican identifiers). The true overall loyalty rate is therefore $p = .8(.8) + .2(.2) = .68$, or 68%. By a similar calculation, the true Republican defection rate, q, is 32%.

Consider now the result of a Goodman ecological regression on the data from these two elections. Because the party identification loyalty and defection rates are identical at each election, so are the vote outcomes. That is, the time-1 vote and the time-2 vote are the same in every constituency, and their graph is the 45° line. Hence the Goodman slope is 1.0 and the intercept is 0.0, yielding the highly inaccurate estimates of loyalty rate $\hat{p} = 100\%$ and defection rate $\hat{q} = 0\%$. Thus the loyalty rate is too high and the defection rate too low. In fact, many actual ecological regressions are close to this case: they imply more voter stability than surveys find.

It is not difficult to produce hypothetical but realistic examples in which ecological regression fares even worse. Another simple case with three constituencies and very conventional party loyalty and defection rates is exhibited (in another context) in table 1A of chapter 7. The true $p = 74\%$, and the true $q = 34\%$. The Goodman ecological estimates are $\hat{p} = 122\%$ and $\hat{q} = -38\%$.

Whether the assumed causal variable is party identification, social class, or some other factor, the reader who tries out a few plausible sets of parameter values will see that the Goodman rates bear little systematic relationship to the true loyalty and defection rates. In this stylized model, as in practice, the loyalty rate is typically too high, often greater than 100%, while the defection rate is too low, often less than 0%.

The next sections show that these features are endemic to ecological regression. That is, if party identification matters, ecological regression is biased.

ASSUMPTIONS

First, we formalize the argument slightly by establishing notation and making certain assumptions. We suppose that there are N voters partitioned into disjoint subsets, D and R, the *Democratic identifiers* and *Republican identifiers*. We let D^* denote the national proportion of Democratic identifiers, meaning that the subsets D and R have ND^* and $N(1 - D^*)$ members, respectively.

The voters are also partitioned into m *constituencies* or *districts*, each with n elements. Thus, for convenience, all constituencies are assumed to have the same size voting population, and $N = mn$. We let D_j^* be the proportion of Democratic identifiers in the jth district, so that $(1 - D_j^*)$ is the proportion of Republican identifiers.

Let d_{1ji} be the vote of person i in constituency j at time 1 ($d_{1ji} = 1$ if i votes Democratic, $d_{1ji} = 0$ if i votes Republican), and similarly for d_{2ji}. Define the mean Democratic vote in constituency j at each period t as $D_{tj} = \Sigma_{i=1}^{n} d_{tji}/n$ ($t = 1, 2$).

We now make three assumptions: first, that districts are not all alike in their partisan tendencies; second, that the vote is a function of party identification plus other factors independent over voters and over time; and third, that partisans are more likely to vote for their party than other voters are. We show that these three postulates imply that ecological regression is biased.

The first assumption is that districts are not all identical in their partisan composition:

Assumption 1 (Geographic Variation):

$$\text{var}(D_j^*) > 0.$$

This assumption implies that the national average proportion of Democratic identifiers is neither zero nor one: $0 < D^* < 1$.

Second, we specify the individual-level assumptions about party identification that generate the ecological party identification model of equations (2) and (3). Thus we assume that, in each time period, every individual in a given party has the same probability of remaining loyal (though the probability may vary over time and across parties). Moreover, these votes are independent of how she herself voted at the other time period and of how everyone else voted at both periods.

To express these assumptions about party identification precisely, consider a given voter i in constituency j at time t, and denote by A_{tji} the set of votes of everyone else at times 1 and 2 plus her own vote at the other time period. Thus, if A is the set of all votes at both time periods ($A = \{d_{tji} | t = 1, 2; j = 1, \ldots, m; i = 1, \ldots, n\}$), we have defined $A_{tji} = A - \{d_{tji}\}$. Then for Democratic identifiers at $t = 1, 2$, the probability of voting for the Democrats is:

Assumption 2 (Causal Role of Party Identification):

$$(9) \qquad \text{Prob}(d_{tji} = 1 | A_{tji} \ \& \ i \in D) = \text{Prob}(d_{tji} = 1 | i \in D)$$

$$= p_t^*.$$

Similarly for Republicans, the probability of choosing the Democrats is:

$$(10) \qquad \text{Prob}(d_{tji} = 1 | A_{tji} \ \& \ i \in R) = \text{Prob}(d_{tji} = 1 | i \in R)$$

$$= q_t^*.$$

Equations (2) and (3) are an immediate consequence.

Third, and finally, to avoid dealing with certain logical possibilities of little substantive interest, we also make the assumption that at each time period, Democratic identifiers are more likely than Republicans to support Democrats, and vice versa:

Assumption 3 (Relative Party Loyalty):

$$(11) \qquad\qquad\qquad p_1^* > q_1^*$$

and

$$(12) \qquad\qquad\qquad p_2^* > q_2^*.$$

Assumption 3 does not rule out Democrats voting more heavily for Republicans than for their own party (party loyalty rates below 50%). It merely excludes the case in which the Democrats support the Republican candidate more strongly than the Republicans do. There is no difficulty in analyzing the latter case, but its omission simplifies the exposition.

BIAS IN ECOLOGICAL REGRESSION

We now derive the biases in ecological regression under assumptions 1–3 above. Throughout most of this chapter, we shall work with the case in which the disturbances in the party identification equations (2) and (3) are sufficiently small that they may be ignored. In fact, under assumption 2, the only source of disturbance variance is sampling error, which declines in inverse proportion to the constituency population, n. We shall therefore investigate the Goodman estimates for the case in which, in every constituency simultaneously, $n \to \infty$. In the limit, sampling error is zero, so that both the factor-analytic disturbances and the Goodman regression disturbances are all zero, and $R^2 = 1$. This case is often approximated in practice, and focusing on it highlights the basic forces at work. For example, issues of sampling error and heteroscedasticity disappear: OLS is the appropriate estimator, and all estimates attain their asymptotic values. We discuss a relaxation of the restriction at the end of the chapter.

Before proceeding, we require certain preliminary results. From equations (2) and (3), we find that, as $n \to \infty$, $\text{var}(D_{1j}) = (p_1^* - q_1^*)^2 \cdot \text{var}(D_j^*)$ and $\text{var}(D_{2j}) = (p_2^* - q_2^*)^2 \text{var}(D_j^*)$. Hence by assumptions 1 and 3, not all constituencies generate precisely the same vote totals: $\text{var}(D_{1j})$, $\text{var}(D_{2j}) > 0$. This implies that, at each time period, both Democrats and Republicans get at least one vote nationwide: $0 < \bar{D}_1$, $\bar{D}_2 < 1$. These technical implications are needed to ensure the meaningfulness of the transition rates and the existence of the Goodman estimates.

We now proceed to compare the true values of the Goodman transition rates with the estimates produced by ecological regression. First, define the true values of Goodman's p and q under the above assumptions. Since p is just the probability of voting Democratic at time 2, conditional on having done so at time 1, and since those probabilities vary by party membership, we have from equations (2) and (3) that the true value of p is given by

$$p = \frac{\text{Prob}(d_{2ji} = 1 \ \& \ d_{1ji} = 1)}{\text{Prob}(d_{1ji} = 1)}$$

(13)
$$= \frac{p_1^* p_2^* D^* + q_1^* q_2^* (1 - D^*)}{p_1^* D^* + q_1^* (1 - D^*)}$$

$$= \frac{q_1^* q_2^* + (p_1^* p_2^* - q_1^* q_2^*) D^*}{q_1^* + (p_1^* - q_1^*) D^*}.$$

By a similar argument, the true value of q is

(14) $$q = \frac{(1 - q_1^*) q_2^* + [(1 - p_1^*) p_2^* - (1 - q_1^*) q_2^*] D^*}{1 - q_1^* + (q_1^* - p_1^*) D^*}.$$

One may also solve straightforwardly for the Goodman estimates of p and q from OLS applied to equation (1). To do so, note that, from equations (2) and (3), as $n \to \infty$, $\mathrm{cov}(D_{2j}, D_{1j}) = (p_1^* - q_1^*)(p_2^* - q_2^*)\mathrm{var}(D_j^*)$. Then using the expression for $\mathrm{var}(D_{1j})$ derived above, we have by the usual formula for the regression slope, β,

$$\lim E(\hat{\beta}) = \lim E(\hat{p} - \hat{q})$$

(15)
$$= \lim E\left[\frac{\mathrm{cov}(D_{2j}, D_{1j})}{\mathrm{var}(D_{1j})}\right]$$

$$= \frac{p_2^* - q_2^*}{p_1^* - q_1^*}.$$

By assumption 3, we have $\lim E(\hat{\beta}) > 0$. That is, the ecological regression line slopes upward, as usual.

For the intercept, note that the mean of the time-1 Democratic vote is, by equation (2), $\bar{D}_1 = q_1^* - (p_1^* - q_1^*)D^*$, where again D^* is the mean of the D_j^*. Similarly, $\bar{D}_2 = q_2^* - (p_2^* - q_2^*)D^*$. Then by the standard formula for the intercept, we have after substitution, as $n \to \infty$,

(16)
$$\lim E(\hat{q}) = \bar{D}_2 - \hat{\beta}\bar{D}_1$$

$$= q_2^* - \beta q_1^*.$$

Now adding the slope and intercept estimates and rearranging gives

(17)
$$\lim E(\hat{p}) = p_2^* + \beta(1 - p_1^*).$$

Now we may solve for the biases in ecological regression. Equations (9) and (13) imply, after some straightforward manipulation, that the bias in the loyalty rate estimate is

(18)
$$\lim E(\hat{p}) - p = \beta\omega^2/\bar{D}_1,$$

where ω^2 is the individual-level variance of the vote at time 1,

(19)
$$\omega^2 = D^*p_1^*(1 - p_1^*) + (1 - D^*)q_1^*(1 - q_1^*).$$

Similarly, equations (10) and (14) imply that the bias in the defection rate is

(20)
$$\lim E(\hat{q}) - q = -\beta\omega^2/(1 - \bar{D}_1).$$

Thus under the assumptions of this chapter, ecological regression is biased. The biases in the transition rate estimates are given by equations (18) and (20). Thus if party identification influences the vote, Goodman transition rate estimates are not to be trusted.

EXPLAINING THE GOODMAN ANOMALIES

The results of the previous section are essentially special cases of the aggregation bias results due to Theil (1955; see also Erbring 1990). However, voter transition rates have a number of special characteristics not shared by aggregate data generally, and this feature imposes additional substantive structure. In conjunction with that structure, the bias formulas may be used to characterize the Goodman anomalies more meaningfully.

We derive three implications of the bias formulas. First, we show that, in ecological regression quite generally, expected loyalty rate estimates are too high and expected defection rate estimates too low. This is, of course, the pattern seen in applications. Second, we demonstrate that if the time-2 election is more polarized along party lines than the time-1, then the biases in the defection rates will be so large as to carry both estimates outside the meaningful bounds of 0% and 100%. Third, we prove that if an electoral system is characterized by uniform swing, then every ecological regression will have at least one transition rate estimate outside the meaningful bounds. Together these results go some distance toward explaining why ecological regression behaves so badly in practice.

Our first result is that the expected Goodman estimate of the loyalty rate is too high and the expected estimated defection rate too low.[6] The result holds quite generally; the sole exception occurs in the fanciful case in which party loyalty is perfect in both parties at time 1. We continue to discuss the limiting case with no sampling error, so that the biases occur in spite of perfect fit ($R^2 = 1$).

Proposition 1. Suppose that party loyalty at time 1 is not perfect ($p_1^* < 1$ or $q_1^* > 0$ or both). Then under assumptions 1, 2, and 3, as $n \to \infty$,

---

6. Under the special assumptions of this chapter, the proposition shows that Goodman's $\hat{p}$ is biased upward and Goodman's $\hat{q}$ biased downward. The conclusion remains true if we attempt to estimate the regression eq. (1) in the reverse direction by regressing the time-1 vote on the time-2 vote. Of course, the transition rates being estimated in that case are not the same as when the regression is done conventionally, but both sets of estimates refer to the entries in the same table, the sole difference lying in whether the probabilities are summed horizontally or vertically. Either set may be used to infer the other. Hence, if one set of estimates yields a lower estimated loyalty rate and a higher estimated defection rate, those estimates are necessarily nearer the truth (cf. Shively 1969). We note, however, that our argument supports this result only when eqs. (2) and (3) hold exactly and when constituency sample sizes are large enough that sampling error may be ignored. We have not worked out conditions in which it holds more generally.

(21) $$\lim E(\hat{p}) > p,$$

(22) $$\lim E(\hat{q}) < q.$$

Proof. We have already shown that assumptions 1 and 3 imply that $\beta > 0$ and $\bar{D}_1 > 0$. Hence the bias in equation (18) has the same sign as ω^2, which is nonnegative. But from the definition in equation (19), we have $\omega^2 = 0$ only if both $p_1^*(1 - p_1^*)$ and $q_1^*(1 - q_1^*)$ are zero, and in light of assumption 3, this is possible only when both $p_1^* = 1$ and $q_1^* = 0$. But the latter is the case of perfect party loyalty at time 1, which has been excluded by assumption. Hence $\omega^2 > 0$, and $\hat{p}$ is biased upward. The same argument applied to equation (20) shows that $\hat{q}$ is biased downward. Q.E.D.

The proposition shows that bias is essentially unavoidable in ecological regression. Even when the estimates are in bounds, they are distorted. Thus constraining the estimates to the [0, 1] interval merely treats the symptoms: the problem with ecological regression is not sampling error, but bias (Stokes 1969).

As an aside, we note that the proposition also has implications for the study of "contextual effects." Many empirical researchers have believed that social influences were at work in ecological data, raising the loyalty rate in districts with many Democratic voters and lowering it in districts with few Democratic adherents ("breakage effects"—Berelson et al. 1954, pp. 98–101). Communication networks were said to be responsible. However, the proposition shows that the same effect will be produced even when every voter acts independently. When $\hat{p}$ is too high and $\hat{q}$ is too low, the slope is too high and the intercept is too low, which in turn means that the highly Democratic constituencies appear to have above average loyalty rates and the less Democratic constituencies below average rates. But this happens under our assumptions even when every single voter in every constituency obeys precisely the same probabilities, with no influence whatever from the constituency, as in assumption 2. Thus ecological data will exhibit pseudocontextual effects whether context matters or not. Only individual-level data can establish the existence of contextual effects. (See chap. 9 for additional discussion.)

Corollary 1.1. Under assumptions 1, 2, and 3, as $n \to \infty$, Goodman ecological regression is unbiased only when there is perfect party loyalty at time 1.

The corollary shows that bias is inevitable. However, it may also be read as a guide to those instances in which ecological regression will work relatively well. When the initial election is highly partisan, with nearly all voters loyal to their party identification, the bias in the Goodman method will be relatively small. The more dangerous situation occurs when the reverse is true, so that the second election is more polarized along party lines, as the next proposition and its first corollary demonstrate.

The next proposition accounts for the tendency of ecological regression to produce meaningless probability estimates. In the limit as constituency sizes become large, if the ratio of the defection rates for Democrats exceeds the ratio of Republican loyalty rates, then on average $\hat{p}$ will be out of bounds, while if the ratio of Republican defection rates exceeds the ratio of Democratic loyalty rates, then on average $\hat{q}$ will be out of bounds.

Proposition 2. Under assumptions 1, 2, and 3, as $n \to \infty$, the necessary and sufficient condition for $\lim E(\hat{p}) > 1$ is

$$(23) \qquad \frac{1 - p_1^*}{1 - p_2^*} > \frac{1 - q_1^*}{1 - q_2^*}.$$

Under the same assumptions, the necessary and sufficient condition for $\lim E(\hat{q}) < 0$ is

$$(24) \qquad \frac{q_1^*}{q_2^*} > \frac{p_1^*}{p_2^*}.$$

Proof. The ratio condition (23) for $\hat{p}$ implies that

$$(25) \qquad 1 - (1 - q_1^*)(1 - p_2^*) > 1 - (1 - q_2^*)(1 - p_1^*).$$

Rearranging, we have

$$(26) \qquad (p_2^* - q_2^*)(1 - p_1^*) > (1 - p_2^*)(p_1^* - q_1^*).$$

Dividing by the nonzero quantity $p_1^* - q_1^*$, we obtain

$$(27) \qquad \beta(1 - p_1^*) > 1 - p_2^*.$$

Substituting into equation (17) then implies that

$$(28) \qquad \lim E(\hat{p}) > 1,$$

which proves sufficiency; reversing the steps establishes necessity.

For $\hat{q}$, the ratio condition (24) implies that

$$(29) \qquad p_2^* q_1^* - q_1^* q_2^* > p_1^* q_2^* - q_1^* q_2^*.$$

Factoring each side and dividing by $p_1^* - q_1^*$ gives

$$(30) \qquad \beta q_1^* > q_2^*,$$

which upon substitution into equation (16) gives

$$(31) \qquad \lim E(\hat{q}) < 0,$$

which establishes sufficiency. Again necessity may be demonstrated by reversing the steps. Q.E.D.

How likely to hold are these conditions for out-of-bounds estimates? The proposition's first corollary shows that a sufficient condition for logically impossible estimates of both p and q is that the second election be more polarized by party than the first. That is, each group of party identifiers must be more loyal to its party at time 2 than at time 1.

Definition. The election at time 2 will be said to be *more polarized* than the election at time 1 if both

$$(32) \qquad p_2^* > p_1^*$$

and

$$(33) \qquad q_2^* < q_1^*.$$

Corollary 2.1. Under assumptions 1, 2, and 3, suppose that the election at time 2 is more polarized than that at time 1. Then as $n \to \infty$,

$$(34) \qquad \lim E(\hat{p}) > 1$$

and

$$(35) \qquad \lim E(\hat{q}) < 0.$$

Proof. Equations (32) and (33) immediately imply that the left-hand sides of conditions (23) and (24) exceed unity, while the right-hand sides are less than unity. Hence both conditions of the theorem are satisfied. Q.E.D.

We note that, if the reverse electoral situation obtains, in which the time-1 election is more polarized than the time-2 election, then in the limit neither $\hat{p}$ nor $\hat{q}$ is out of bounds.

The final implication of partisan voting for ecological regression is in many respects the most damaging. We know that many familiar electoral systems are characterized by approximately uniform swing. This last corollary shows that when uniform swing holds, *every* ecological regression will have an out-of-bounds coefficient.

Corollary 2.2. Under assumptions 1, 2, and 3, uniform swing with $\delta > 0$ implies that, as $n \to \infty$,

$$(36) \qquad \lim E(\hat{p}) > 1$$

but $\lim E(\hat{q})$ is in bounds. On the other hand, if $\delta < 0$,

$$(37) \qquad \lim E(\hat{q}) < 0$$

but $\lim E(\hat{p})$ is in bounds.

Proof. Substitute equations (4) and (5) into each side of equations (23) and 24).[7] Q.E.D.

Thus the two corollaries show that all eventualities are possible: both Goodman estimates in bounds, both out of bounds, or one in and one out. However, as we saw in the Gosnell regressions, the most common pattern is just one coefficient out of bounds. As fits improved, nearly all his ecological regressions failed in that manner. The second corollary explains why: Under nonzero uniform swing, every ecological regression will have one coefficient or the other out of bounds, but not both. Thus, to the extent that actual election systems approximate uniform swing and the regression fit approaches $R^2 = 1.0$, Goodman estimates will always produce exactly one logically impossible probability estimate.

In practice, this conclusion needs qualification. Both propositions and their corollaries assume that the ecological regression disturbances are vanishingly small. In applications, electoral data typically produce small but not vanishingly small disturbances. Under our assumptions, the disturbances are due to nonzero sampling error in the partisan voting structure underlying the data (eqs. [2] and [3]). Realistically, specification errors will add to the disturbance as well. These errors imply that the usual Goodman ecological regression contains random measurement error in the independent variable, which depresses the esti-

---

7. The proof may also be done geometrically. In the limit, as we saw above, two elections with zero swing have a 45° regression line through the origin, so that the slope is unity and the intercept zero. A nonzero swing displaces the graph δ units up or down the y-axis without changing the slope. Thus when $\delta < 0$, the intercept is negative, meaning that q is out of bounds. On the other hand, when $\delta > 0$, the intercept is positive, so that, when it is added to the slope to estimate p, that estimate is out of bounds.

mate slope and raises the estimated intercept. Both factors make the biases less dramatic than in the idealized cases considered above. Thus ecological regression will not produce meaningless estimates every single time. However, as the interested reader may demonstrate, with the R^2 as large as it usually is in ecological regression, the actual bias will be only modestly less than in the propositions above, perhaps 5 to 10 percentage points less in many applications. This often leaves a substantial bias, as the Gosnell regressions show.

We now set out the consequences of the party identification model for the extensions of the Goodman model discussed in the previous chapter. There we discussed various models for allowing the Goodman transition rates to vary by constituency, and we argued that the assumptions underlying the models were distant from substantive intuitions and thus doubtful. Here we illustrate the point by deriving the rather surprising form of the constituency-level transition rates under the party identification model.

We begin by solving for the constituency-level rates, p_j and q_j. To do so, simply specialize the argument that preceded the derivation of the national-level rates in equations (13) and (14). The results are

$$(38) \qquad p_j = \frac{q_1^* q_2^* + (p_1^* p_2^* - q_1^* q_2^*)D_j^*}{q_1^* + (p_1^* - q_1^*)D_j^*}$$

and

$$(39) \quad q_j = \frac{(1 - q_1^*)q_2^* + [(1 - p_1^*)p_2^* - (1 - q_1^*)q_2^*]D_j^*}{1 - q_1^* + (q_1^* - p_1^*)D_j^*}.$$

The first denominator is D_{1j}; the second is $1 - D_1$. Moreover, in light of equations (2) and (3), as $n \to \infty$ the numerators may be expressed as linear deterministic functions of D_{1j}. Thus we have established the following proposition, which gives the functional form for the Goodman transition rates under the assumptions of the party identification model.

Proposition 3. Under assumptions 1, 2, and 3, let $n \to \infty$. Then in the limit, Goodman's p and q vary by constituency:

$$(40) \qquad p_j = \frac{\alpha_1 + \beta_1 D_{1j}}{D_{1j}},$$

$$(41) \qquad q_j = \frac{\alpha_2 + \beta_2 D_{1j}}{1 - D_{1j}},$$

where

$$(42) \qquad \alpha_1 = -p_1^* q_1^* (p_2^* - q_2^*)/(p_1^* - q_1^*),$$

$$(43) \qquad \beta_1 = (p_1^* p_2^* - q_1^* q_2^*)/(p_1^* - q_1^*),$$

$$(44) \quad \alpha_2 = [p_1^*(1 - q_1^*)q_2^* - (1 - p_1^*)p_2^* q_1^*]/(p_1^* - q_1^*),$$

and

$$(45) \qquad \beta_2 = [(1 - p_1^*)p_2^* - (1 - q_1^*)q_2^*]/(p_1^* - q_1^*).$$

This final proposition shows that the Goodman assumption of fixed transition rates conflicts with the assumption that party identification influences the vote; if one is true, the other is false. Nor is allowing for random variation in transition rates helpful. The assumption that the transition rates are random but mean independent of D_{1j}, discussed in the previous chapter, is also contradicted by proposition 3. By their nature, Goodman transition rates vary by constituency *as a function of the Democratic vote at time 1.* Of course, this correlation violates regression assumptions and induces bias. Indeed, the usual analysis of regression bias when the disturbances are correlated with the independent variable may be used to derive proposition 1.

As one may see by substituting the conclusions of proposition 3 into equation (1), the implied Goodman equation is linear. That is, when party identification influences the vote in the manner of this chapter, ecological regression will show no sign of nonlinearity, in spite of the fact that the transition rates vary nonlinearly as a function of D_{1j}. Though the coefficients are estimating something quite different from Goodman transition rates, a straight line will fit beautifully, no matter how large the biases in the estimates. Allowing the transition rates to vary as a linear function of demographic variables or prior votes might be tried in this case, but all the control variables will prove to have zero coefficients. Thus neither high R^2 nor linearity of the fit is a sign of a healthy ecological regression, as empirical researchers have learned to their sorrow.[8]

---

8. In practice, ecological regressions are sometimes slightly nonlinear even in two-party systems, and they may be more obviously nonlinear in multiparty systems. We discuss these complications in subsequent chapters. However, evidence of nonlinearity is no escape for the basic Goodman model, which assumes linearity.

CONCLUSION

This chapter has argued that the familiar difficulties of linear ecological regression have a common source. If a simple underlying model is specified in which party identification influences the vote, then as a logical consequence, loyalty estimates are too high, defection estimates are too low, and out-of-bounds estimates will abound. The biases are not accidents of sampling error; the ecological regression coefficients converge arbitrarily closely to these erroneous estimates as the sample size increases. Moreover, the biases will persist even as the regression fit approaches $R^2 = 1$. Simply put, conventional ecological regression is a failure as a statistical estimator.

We repeat that nothing in this chapter requires party identification as the underlying causal factor. While empirical studies customarily find that the first factor in ecological data is partisanship, the division of the voters into Democrats and Republicans might be given some other name without changing the mathematics. Dichotomized versions of social class or religion would serve as well.[9] The same propositions hold.

In general, the biases of ecological regression are not curable by the social scientist's universal panacea and elixir, controlling for demographic variables. The underlying problem is unmeasured causal variables, which demographic variables can proxy for but never replace. In some cases, demographic controls may palliate the biases enough to produce satisfactory answers, though experience with such variables in ecological data has been unsatisfactory (Upton 1978). Truly satisfactory statistical procedures must deal with the vote outcomes and their causes, not with substitutes. Transition rates vary as a function of vote totals or partisanship.

The findings of this chapter indicate that three paths remain open to students of aggregate voting data. The first is to make much weaker assumptions than Goodman did, as in the method of bounds. The second is to use the extended Goodman regression specification to allow for transition rates that vary across districts as a function of the prior vote, as mentioned in chapter 2. And finally, the third option is to de-emphasize the study of voter transition rates in favor of party identification transition rates, as in the ecological party identification model of

9. Both social class and religion should be defined behaviorally, not by survey responses, income levels, or parish registers. Thus they have the same relationship to their measurable manifestations as party identification has to party registration.

this chapter. We explore each of these possibilities empirically in subsequent chapters.[10] First, though, we spell out in the next chapter the meaning of the fundamental "proper specification" condition that such models must meet.

10. With American data, another possibility is using party registration data as proxies for constituency party identification rates. Doing so would convert the ecological party identification model of eqs. (2) and (3) from factor analysis to regression: Voting proportions would be regressed on party registration rates. Of course, party registration may differ greatly from behavioral partisanship, so that the method is likely to work only in relatively homogeneous samples. By clustering similar observations, McCue (1992) applies the technique successfully to subsets of Los Angeles precincts. He also shows that, empirically, Goodman regression produces biases of the sort derived by Theil (1955) and Achen (1983b).

FOUR

PROBLEMS OF SPECIFICATION
IN CROSS-LEVEL MODELS

It is widely believed among social scientists that regression analysis with aggregate data produces unbiased coefficients if the corresponding individual-level regression is "properly specified." This proposition, if true, would make ecological inference no more difficult than any other regression application. In fact, however, the proposition is false. This chapter shows that coefficients in properly specified linear microregressions are generally biased when estimated with aggregate data, and specific conditions are given which avoid bias. These conditions lead away from pure issues of fit: Simply improving the microspecification, in the sense of adding statistically significant and substantively relevant variables to a regression, can actually make the aggregate biases worse. Instead, meeting the conditions requires the use of substantive knowledge to control for the ways in which individuals group themselves geographically. (An earlier version of this chapter appeared as Achen 1986b.)

PROPER SPECIFICATION AND ECOLOGICAL REGRESSIONS

Perhaps the single most influential suggestion for coping with the biases of ecological regression was given by Hanushek et al. (1974). Returning to Robinson's (1950) data on illiteracy, they showed that his "ecological fallacy" evaporated when the level of education was statistically controlled. They then argued with considerable skill that the bias was due to specification error, so that proper aggregate specification would produce the same statistical results at the individual and aggregate levels. And of course, this argument is correct: If an individual-level model is aggregated and, after aggregation, meets Gauss-Markov assumptions, the aggregate estimates will be attractive estimates of the individual-level effects. Hanushek et al. illustrated their argument with a second empirical example, as well as Robinson's original data set. In each case, they demonstrated that inclusion of additional relevant independent variables may reduce or virtually eliminate aggregation bias. Since specification error is a familar and unfrightening bugaboo in the study of individual-level regression, free interpretation of Hanushek et al. led many researchers to believe that ecological inference held no new terrors. King (1990), for example, followed Brown and Payne (1986) in arguing that ecological inference may be tamed by specifying microlevel distributional assumptions, from which the aggregate statistical specification is then derived. The ecological inference problem was thought to be "solved" in the sense that it disappeared if microlevel models were specified adequately, a requirement to which all statistical work is held in any case.

Unfortunately, aggregation bias cannot be escaped so easily. As one of us has argued informally elsewhere (Achen 1983a, pp. 85–86), the proper inference to be drawn from Hanushek et al. is more subtle. While it is almost tautologically true that the absence of macrolevel specification error avoids bias, it need not follow that the absence of *microlevel* specification error guarantees adequate macrospecification (Langbein and Lichtman 1978, pp. 13–21). In general, as will be seen below, it does not. Even causally accurate individual-level linear regression equations meeting Gauss-Markov assumptions are typically biased when estimated with aggregate data.[1] No matter how carefully and accurately specified are the microlevel distributions and aggregating procedures, macromodels will in general confound conventional statistical procedures (Erbring 1990, pp. 264–65; see also Haitovsky 1973). Thus there is not necessarily anything comforting or familiar about the result of Hanushek et al.: It directs our attention to the poorly understood topic of proper macrolevel specification, a subject with no simple relation to the microlevel setups where our theories and intuitions apply.

What is needed are the conditions under which microlevel regressions will aggregate consistently and without bias. In the nonlinear

---

1. The bias should not confused with "contextual effects," whereby individuals living in a geographic district influence each other. Even if such effects are modeled properly or are nonexistent, bias persists. See chap. 9.

regression case, the answer is quite pessimistic, for it is well known that, in general, nonlinear micromodels do not aggregate to the same functional form at the macrolevel. (An excellent summary is Green 1964, chap. 5; see also app. A to chap. 1, above.) Typically, the macro-specification derived from a nonlinear micromodel depends on purely individual-level data and cannot be estimated with macrolevel data alone. Thus it is particularly obvious in the nonlinear case that simply translating a properly specified microlevel model to the aggregate level and replacing its variables with their macrolevel equivalents will generally not produce an accurately specified macromodel.

By contrast, linear micromodels aggregate to linear macromodels. Thus, in the linear case, replacing microlevel variables by their macro-level counterparts does not by itself produce a specification error. However, the properties of the coefficient estimates remain to be determined. In the remainder of this chapter, then, we restrict ourselves to the conditions for unbiased aggregate estimation in the linear case. What additional conditions on properly specified linear microlevel regressions ensure proper macrolevel specification?

Theil (1955) and others have studied aggregation bias of linear models in the time-series context: A single population, each member with unique but unvarying coefficients, is followed through time. This chapter takes up the somewhat different cross-sectional case more common outside economics, in which each individual appears just once. Given a properly specified micromodel, we derive sufficient conditions for unbiased estimation at the aggregate level for the special case of Goodman regression. The new results for that case are then related to previous work in more general cases by Zellner and Erbring. (For related results, see Alker 1969 and Ansolabehere and Rivers 1992a).

Intuitively speaking, this chapter shows that aggregate cross-sectional regression is unbiased only when the microlevel specification is good enough to make geographic location useless as a predictor of the dependent variable. In practice, the standard statistical methods will fail to meet these conditions; special methods suited to aggregate data are needed to avoid bias. The chapter also shows that, in the absence of these conditions, simply improving microlevel specifications (better functional form, distributional assumptions on coefficients, more causally relevant variables, improved standard errors and R^2) may actually increase bias. The real enemy of aggregate-level inference is not causal misspecification but rather "intraconstituency spatial autocorrelation"—the tendency of individuals in the same geographic unit to resemble each other in unmeasured ways. The ecological fallacy is circumvented by eliminating or rendering harmless this kind of spatial autocorrelation.

"PROPER SPECIFICATION" IN ORDINARY REGRESSION ANALYSIS

Informally, a regression equation is "properly specified" if it meets a set of assumptions guaranteeing that its parameter estimates will possess some desirable set of statistical attributes. Thus there can be no single definition of "proper specification." Depending on the nature of the data, the estimation procedure, and the statistical properties desired, "proper specification" takes on different meanings.

For the purposes of this chapter, we adopt a minimalist definition: We shall say that a "properly specified" regression equation is defined as a regression equation whose coefficients may be estimated without bias by OLS. Of course, unbiasedness has strict limits as a statistical criterion, and much stronger properties are customarily required of estimators. However, unbiasedness would certainly be expected of any estimator in a regression with nonstochastic regressors, and asymptotic failures of unbiasedness would imply other failures as well. Thus all the essential points of this chapter can be made with unbiasedness as a minimal definition of properness. Adding or substituting (weak) consistency as a condition, for example, complicates the arithmetic while adding no real insights.[2]

By defining the properness of regression specifications in terms of the unbiasedness of their OLS coefficient estimates, we make concrete the notion of "finding the right causal variables." This attractive, but vague and often misleading, idea animates much empirical work; we mean to give it clear statistical content. In our terms, the list of causal variables in a linear regression is satisfactory if the resulting OLS estimates are unbiased. This definition allows simultaneously for cases in which all major causal variables are included, for cases in which some or most causal variables are unmeasured and relegated to the disturbance term, and also for purely descriptive regressions which make no causal claims whatsoever. In each instance, the properness of the specification depends not on imprecisely defined features external to the model, such

---

2. Minor modifications to the arguments of this chapter are required if the right-hand-side variables in the regression equation must be regarded as stochastic rather than fixed, as, e.g., when they consist of voting returns at the previous time period. In that case, probability limits replace expectations, and we define proper specification to be

as how elaborately it attempts to model some causal process, but rather on its statistical properties. If in expectation, OLS gives the right answer, then the specification is "proper" in our sense.

Given this definition, the central theoretical issue raised by the work of Hanushek et al. (1974) may be stated in statistical terms. Suppose that an individual-level linear regression is properly specified in the sense that its OLS coefficients are unbiased. Suppose further that the observations each belong to geographic units ("constituencies"), so that averages of all the variables may be computed in each constituency. Now replace the individual-level variables in the regression by their corresponding constituency averages, so that the unit of observation becomes the geographic unit. Then what additional conditions, if any, are needed to guarantee proper specification in this aggregate-level regression?

We begin with the specification of the individual-level model. For concreteness, consider first the simple case of a cross-tabulation of vote against social class in a sample of individuals from a given geographic unit (constituency). As in the previous chapter, assume for simplicity that there are just two parties (Democrats and Republicans), that everyone is either working class or middle class (suitably defined), and that everyone votes. Then in each constituency, the relationship between vote and social class is just a 2×2 table whose entries are the probabilities that a working-class or middle-class voter will choose either the Democrats or the Republicans.

The same relationship can be represented in regression format. Let d_{ji}, the dependent variable, be a dummy variable for the vote of person i in the jth district ($d_{ji} = 1$ if i votes Democratic, 0 otherwise); let w_{ji}, the independent variable, measure membership in the working class ($w_{ji} = 1$ if i belongs to the working class, $w_{ji} = 0$ if i is middle class.) To keep the arithmetic to a minimum, suppose that the sample is taken from m constituencies, each with the same number, n, of observations. Thus the full sample size is $N = mn$.

Next, we allow for intraconstituency spatial autocorrelation—the unmeasured similarity of voters in the same district. In the jth constituency, define p_j as the probability of voting Democratic if the person is working class ("loyalty"), and define q_j as the probability of voting Democratic if the person is middle class ("defection"). These proba-

---

(weak) consistency rather than unbiasedness. In all other respects, the findings are essentially identical.

bilities vary by district due to spatial autocorrelation; they are the same as those of the 2×2 cross-tabulation of vote against social class in constituency j. Finally, let v_{ji} be a disturbance term to capture the difference between the actual outcomes (which must be either 0 or 1) and the probabilities (which fall in between). Then the regression format for the individual-level relationship between voting and social class in the jth constituency is

$$(1) \quad d_{ji} = p_j w_{ji} + q_j (1 - w_{ji}) + v_{ji}$$

$$(i = 1, \ldots, n; j = 1, \ldots, m).$$

We shall adopt a generalization of the sophisticated Goodman model of chapter 2, in which p_j and q_j are treated as realizations of random variables. The underlying probability space is defined by a superpopulation model, each draw from the space consisting of an entire finite voting population (see, e.g., Hedayat and Sinha 1991, chap. 10). In particular, we assume that in each constituency, the probabilities p_j and q_j are draws from the bivariate distribution function $F_j(\cdot)$, which may differ by constituency. Thus p_j and q_j may be correlated with w_{ji}.

We wish to estimate p and q, the national average probabilities. That is, p is the mean of p_j among workers and q is the mean of q_j among the middle class: Letting $W_j = \Sigma\, w_{ji}/n$, we note that

$$p = \sum_{j,i} w_{ji} E(p_j)/\sum_{j,i} w_{ji} = \sum_j W_j E(p_j)/\sum_j W_j$$

and

$$q = \sum_{j,i} (1 - w_{ji}) E(q_j)/\sum_{j,i} (1 - w_{ji})$$

$$= \sum_j (1 - W_j) E(q_j)/\sum_j (1 - W_j),$$

where the weights w_{ji} and $1 - w_{ji}$ are used to restrict the averages to the appropriate social class.[3] Of course, all these expectations exist since F_j has support only on the square $[0, 1] \times [0, 1]$, and thus it and its marginals have finite moments of all orders.

---

3. In practice, of course, it is not p and q that are of interest, since they are only the averages of the *expectations* of p_j and q_j. We wish to know instead the averages of the actual transition rates that occur in the sample, namely, $p^* = \Sigma\, w_{ji} p_j/\Sigma\, w_{ji}$ and $q^* = \Sigma(1 - w_{ji}) q_j/\Sigma(1 - w_{ji})$. However, when the Goodman model is properly specified, typically the estimates of p and q turn out also to be good estimates of p^* and q^* (see n. 9, and pp. 57–61 above). Hence we do not belabor the distinction.

Rewriting the previous equation in the usual way gives the standard regression format:

$$(2) \qquad d_{ji} = q + (p - q)w_{ji} + u_{ji},$$

with $u_{ji} = (p_j - p)w_{ji} + (q_j - q)(1 - w_{ji}) + v_{ji}$.[4]

Given, for example, a simple random sample of voters from a national population, OLS applied to equation (2) will produce unbiased estimates. This conclusion follows easily from conventional Gauss-Markov considerations.[5] The underlying intuition is particularly simple in this case: p and q are population means of Bernoulli (dichotomous) random variables; the OLS estimates are the sample means. It is well known that, under virtually any conventional equiprobability randomized sampling scheme, these sample means are unbiased for the population means, p and q.[6]

If, in addition, the observations are independent and if, as $N \to \infty$, $\text{var}(w_{ji})$ converges to a positive constant, then weak consistency and asymptotic normality follow as well, since under independent sampling, the sample proportions from Bernoulli distributions are consistent and asymptotically normal. They are also efficient. Indeed, in that case, the sample proportions are the maximum likelihood estimates. Thus, under quite mild conditions, the OLS coefficient estimates of equation (2) have very attractive properties.[7] Even if one insists that "proper specification" means more than just unbiasedness, equation (2) is certainly properly specified.

4. Of course, it makes no difference whether we use a linear probability model, a probit, or a logit specification for this problem. The model is "saturated"; i.e., it contains one parameter for each possible configuration of the right-hand-side variables. Hence, after translation to the original probability scale, each specification produces precisely the same estimates of p and q (Achen 1986b, chap. 6).

5. Note that the usual Gauss-Markov conditions ensuring unbiasedness, namely, $E(u_{ji}) = 0$ and $E(w_{ji}u_{ji}) = 0$, need not be independently assumed, since they are implied by the other assumptions. In particular, they follow from taking expectations conditional on w_{ji} in eq. (1) and making use of the definitions of p and q.

6. In particular, the fact that p_j and q_j vary by district is irrelevant. We require only that the sample contain both working-class and middle-class voters, so that the variance of w_{ji} is positive. Independent sampling is not required so long as membership in the sample is not influenced by v_{ji}.

7. Of course, the conventional OLS estimated sampling variances are inaccurate due to heteroscedasticity. Some will imagine that the OLS coefficient estimates will therefore be inefficient and should be replaced by GLS or MLE. However, a little arithmetic will show that the heteroscedasticity does not affect the efficiency of the estimates. In fact, OLS and GLS produce precisely the same regression coefficients, and both are identical with MLE.

Because there is occasionally some confusion on the point, it is worth noting that, while equation (2) is properly specified and has desirable OLS coefficient estimates associated with it, it expresses a purely descriptive relationship. In general, social class will have a true causal impact quite different from the simple bivariate relationship in equation (2), and in extreme cases might have none at all. As a *causal* setup, then, equation (2) is typically hopelessly inaccurate. But the specification is proper, in the sense that the OLS coefficient estimates are unbiased. Indeed, these regression coefficients would be perfectly well estimated even if, say, the underlying causal relationships were unknown, highly nonlinear equations unique to each individual in the sample, each one depending on hundreds of variables and coefficients and meeting no conventional assumptions whatever. There is no statistical requirement that regression equations express true causal relations—a fortunate fact for social scientists. "True causal relationships" and "proper specification" are simply different concepts. One may often do useful descriptive work with individual-level data and well-specified models without knowing much about the underlying causal laws.

THE GOODMAN MODEL

We are now ready to investigate the additional conditions needed at the macrolevel to ensure aggregate unbiasedness.

As above, let d_{ji} be the vote of the ith person in the jth constituency, w_{ji} the person's social class, and v_{ji} the disturbance. As usual with aggregate data, we assume that the sample in each constituency exhausts the population: Everyone's vote is counted, since we have ignored the possibility of abstention. Then we define the constituency means as $D_j = (1/n) \sum_{i=1}^{n} d_{ji}$, $W_j = (1/n) \sum_{i=1}^{n} w_{ji}$, $V_j = (1/n) \sum_{i=1}^{n} v_{ji}$, and $U_j = (1/n) \sum_{i=1}^{n} u_{ji}$. Now computing the average of each side of equation (2) within each constituency and assuming that the constituencies do not all have the same fraction of working-class voters ($\text{var}(W_j) > 0$), one obtains an ecological regression, in which the observations are constituencies and the fraction Democratic vote in each constituency is regressed on the fraction working class:

$$(3) \qquad D_j = q + (p - q)W_j + U_j \quad (j = 1, \ldots, m),$$

with $U_j = (q_j - q) + (p_j - p - q_j + q)W_j + V_j$. Notice that, in general, $E(U_j) \neq 0$, since $F_j(\cdot)$ may differ by constituency, and hence it is not necessarily the case that $E(p_j) = p$ nor that $E(q_j) = q$.

As noted in earlier chapters, the Goodman specification has been a disaster in applications, with estimates for p and q routinely falling several standard errors above 100% loyalty or below 0% defection. Ecological regression is biased, often grossly so. Yet at the microlevel, Goodman regression is properly specified, essentially by definition, as was seen above. Indeed, no collection of purely causal variables could ever enjoy the same confidence of meeting the unbiasedness conditions at the microlevel. Yet the macromodel is biased. Thus proper micro-specification is no guarantee of avoiding ecological bias.

What conditions guarantee unbiasedness in the Goodman model? Since the disturbances in the sophisticated Goodman model need not have mean zero, conventional Gauss-Markov analysis is inapplicable. The principle tool needed for assessing unbiasedness is a set of minimal conditions for OLS regression estimates to be unbiased. The following well-known lemma gives necessary and sufficient conditions for unbiased OLS regression in the bivariate regression case. A similar result for multiple regression appears below.

Lemma 1. Let $y_i = \alpha + \beta x_i + u_i$ ($i = 1, \ldots, n$), with y_i and x_i observed and u_i an unobserved random variable, the disturbance. The real numbers α and β are unknown parameters to be estimated. It is assumed that the x_i are fixed and that in the sample, $\text{var}(x_i) > 0$. Then the conventional OLS estimates of α and β are both unbiased if and only if both (a) and (b) hold:

$$\text{(a)} \quad \sum_{i=1}^{n} E(u_i) = 0,$$

$$\text{(b)} \quad \sum_{i=1}^{n} E(x_i u_i) = 0.$$

Proof. The OLS slope estimate is

$$(4) \qquad \hat{\beta} = \frac{\text{cov}(x_i, y_i)}{\text{var}(x_i)}.$$

Letting $\bar{x} = (1/n) \sum x_i$ and similarly for $\bar{y}$, the last equation may be written as

$$(5) \qquad \hat{\beta} = \frac{\sum (x_i - \bar{x})(y_i - \bar{y})}{\sum (x_i - \bar{x})(x_i - \bar{x})}.$$

Recall that $\sum (x_i - \bar{x}) = 0$, so that $\sum (x_i - \bar{x})\bar{y} = \sum (x_i - \bar{x})\bar{x} = 0$. Hence,

$$(6) \qquad \hat{\beta} = \frac{\sum (x_i - \bar{x})y_i}{\sum (x_i - \bar{x})x_i}.$$

Proceeding in the usual manner, substitute $y_i = \alpha + \beta x_i + u_i$ and use again the fact that $\Sigma (x_i - \bar{x}) = 0$. This yields

$$(7) \qquad \hat{\beta} = \beta + \frac{\Sigma (x_i - \bar{x})u_i}{\Sigma (x_i - \bar{x})x_i}.$$

Since the denominator in the last term is fixed, we have that $\hat{\beta}$ is unbiased $(E(\hat{\beta}) = \beta)$ if and only if

$$((8) \qquad \Sigma (x_i - \bar{x})E(u_i) = 0.$$

Next, using the OLS estimate $\hat{\alpha} = \bar{y} - \hat{\beta}\bar{x}$, substituting for $\hat{\beta}$ from equation (7), and proceeding in a similar way, we find after a little arithmetic that $\hat{\alpha}$ is unbiased if and only if

$$(9) \qquad \text{var}(x_i) \Sigma E(u_i) - \bar{x} \Sigma (x_i - \bar{x})E(u_i) = 0.$$

Now as just seen, if and only if $\hat{\alpha}$ and $\hat{\beta}$ are both unbiased, equations (8) and (9) hold. Thus to prove the "only if" part of the lemma, one must show that equations (8) and (9) imply conditions (a) and (b). Multiplying equation (8) by $\bar{x}$, adding it to equation (9), and dividing by the positive constant $\text{var}(x_i)$ gives

$$(10) \qquad \Sigma E(u_i) = 0,$$

which is condition (a). Then, since $\bar{x}$ in equation (8) is fixed, equation (10) implies that equation (8) may be written as $\Sigma E(x_i u_i) = 0$, which is condition (b). This establishes the "only if" part.

To show the more obvious converse, one must demonstrate that conditions (a) and (b) imply equations (8) and (9). To do so, multiply (a) by $\bar{x}$ and subtract from (b), giving equation (8). Then multiplying (a) by $\text{var}(x_i)$ and subtracting the product of $\bar{x}$ and equation (8) gives equation (9). Q.E.D.

The principal feature of the lemma is that each disturbance need no longer have mean zero. In the usual Gauss-Markov assumptions for unbiasedness, every element of the sums in conditions (a) and (b) is required to be zero. Here the expected values of these terms are permitted to take on nonzero values so long as their sum is zero. Of course, the conventional Gauss-Markov assumptions imply conditions (a) and (b).

We now test conditions (a) and (b) of the lemma in the case of the Goodman model. Recalling that W_j is fixed, we find that condition (a) holds:

$$\sum_j E(u_i) = \sum_j E[q_i - q + (p_i - p - q_i + q)W_i]$$

$$= \sum_j W_i E(p_i - p) + \sum_j (1 - W_i)E(q_i - q)$$

(11)
$$= \sum_{j,i} w_{ji} E(p_i) - p \sum_{j,i} w_{ji} + \sum_{j,i} (1 - w_{ji})E(q_i)$$

$$- q \sum_{j,i} (1 - w_{ji})$$

$$= 0,$$

by the definitions above of p and q as national averages.

Condition (b), on the other hand, does not necessarily hold. The condition that $\Sigma_j E(W_j u_j) = 0$ is equivalent to

(12) $\quad \sum_j W_j^2 E(p_j - p) + \sum_j W_j(1 - W_j)E(q_j - q) = 0.$

This is the necessary and sufficient condition for a well-specified individual-level model to be estimated in Goodman regression without bias. It is the additional assumption that must be added to proper microspecification to ensure proper macrospecification in the Goodman model.

Apart from accidents in which the two terms in equation (12) take on arbitrary values that happen to cancel, avoiding bias requires that both terms in equation (12) equal zero. In this spirit, researchers often proceed with Goodman regression under the assumption that "each transition rate must be uncorrelated with the aggregate independent variable" (i.e., that p_j and q_j must have zero covariance with W_j). Inspection of equation (12) shows, however, that even after division by the appropriate constants, the two terms on the left are not the aggregate-level covariances between p_j and W_j and between q_j and W_j, respectively.[8] In fact, it is straightforward to demonstrate that the vanishing of the latter covariances is not enough to guarantee unbiasedness.

The language about uncorrelatedness is appropriate, however, under a modified definition of the relevant covariances. Let $\text{cov}_w(W_j, p_j)$ denote the individual-level covariance between W_j and p_j, with the sample space defined as the working class only ($w_{ji} = 1$). That is,

---

8. In fact, neither term is an ordinary covariance at all. E.g., $\Sigma_j\ W_j^2 E(p_j - p)$ is not the covariance of W_j^2 and p_j, since p is not the mean of p_j over districts. The sample spaces must be chosen as in the following paragraph to avoid this difficulty.

using $E_w(\cdot)$ to denote expectation over working-class voters and recalling that by definition $p = E_w(p_i)$, we define $\text{cov}_w(W_i, p_i) = E_w(W_i - \overline{W})(p_i - p) = E_w W_i(p_i - p)$, where $\overline{W} = \Sigma_{j=1}^m W_j/m$. Similarly, we define $\text{cov}_m(W_i, q_i)$ as the covariance over middle-class voters between W_i and q_i. It turns out that these two covariances, set to zero, guarantee that condition (12) for unbiasedness of Goodman regression holds.

To spell out the argument, assume that

$$(13) \qquad\qquad \text{cov}_w(W_i, p_i) = 0$$

and

$$(14) \qquad\qquad \text{cov}_m(W_i, q_i) = 0.$$

Now consider the first term in the unbiasedness condition (12) under the assumption that $\text{cov}_w(W_i, p_i) = 0$:

$$\sum_j W_i^2 E(p_i - p) = \sum_{j,i} w_{ji} W_i E(p_i - p)/n$$

$$(15) \qquad\qquad = k_w \, \text{cov}_w(W_i, p_i)$$

$$= 0,$$

where $k_w = \Sigma_{j,i} w_{ji}/n = \Sigma_j W_j$. Similarly, under the assumption that $\text{cov}_m(W_i, q_i) = 0$, the second term of the unbiasedness condition is also zero:

$$\sum_j W_i(1 - W_i)E(q_i - q) = \sum_{j,i} (1 - w_{ji}) W_i E(q_i - q)/n$$

$$(16) \qquad\qquad = k_m \, \text{cov}_m(W_i, q_i)$$

$$= 0,$$

where $k_m = \Sigma_{j,i}(1 - w_{ji})/n = \Sigma_j(1 - W_k)$. Thus the conditions (13) and (14) imply that equation (12) holds, so that bivariate ecological regression is unbiased.

Unbiased estimation with Goodman regression therefore is guaranteed if "each transition rate is uncorrelated with the aggregate independent variable," in the sense that, if we compute the covariance at the individual level over just those individuals to whom the transition rate applies, then that covariance must be zero. In practice, this is the weakest plausible assumption justifying Goodman ecological regression.

A variety of stronger assumptions are commonly used to guarantee unbiasedness. For example, bias disappears if "mean independence" is assumed:

(17) $$E(p_j|W_j) = p,$$

(18) $$E(q_j|W_j) = q,$$

which, of course, implies zero covariances.[9] In turn, mean independence is implied by the still stronger assumption that each of p_j and q_j
are statistically independent of W_j. Strongest of all is the assumption
that, for all j, $p_j = p$ and $q_j = q$, which implies independence. The last
condition means that the loyalty and defection rates are the same in
every constituency—the simple Goodman model.[10] None of these assumptions is very plausible, and the poor empirical experience with
Goodman regression demonstrates that such conditions routinely fail
in practice. Chapter 3 showed why that failure is to be expected.[11]

The failure is due, not to any features of the individual-level specification, which remains correct and proper, but to the grouping of
individuals within constituencies. Different constituencies will exhibit different loyalty and defection rates, and it is only by quirk that
these differences will fail to correlate with the aggregate independent
variable.

In short, proper macrolevel specification does not follow from its
microlevel counterpart. Put another way, "proper specification" is no
cure-all in aggregate data analysis. Ensuring proper macrospecifications raises special difficulties not subsumed under the conventional
injunction that micromodels be suitably specified. Intraconstituency
spatial autocorrelation must also be controlled.

9. This assumption also implies that estimates of the expected probabilities p and q
will also be good estimates of the actual probabilities that occurred in the sample, p^* and
q^*, as defined in n. 3. E.g., the difference between p^* and p is $\Sigma_j W_j[(p_j - E(p_j)]/\Sigma_j W_j$,
which under the assumption has expected value zero and will converge to zero rapidly in
the usual medium-sized samples with small var(p_j) and district worker populations not
grossly unequal. Hence the distinction between p^* and p is generally unimportant if
Goodman regression is successful at all.

10. Each of the latter assumptions also implies that averaging the expected transition
rates over constituencies gives the same answer as averaging over the relevant pool of
individuals, since $p = \Sigma W_j E(p_j)/\Sigma W_j = \Sigma E(p_j)/m$, and similarly for q.

11. The other meaningful special case in which no bias exists in the OLS estimation
of the Goodman model occurs when $W_j = 0$ or 1 for all j. Thus constituencies consist
entirely of working-class voters or entirely of middle-class voters. Then condition (12)
may be used to show what intuition makes obvious: OLS will perform nicely in this case.
In effect, OLS estimates p simply by taking the mean Democratic vote over the (entirely)
working-class districts, and similarly it estimates q by taking the mean Democratic vote
over the entirely middle-class constituencies. The result is necessarily the observed national proportions p and q.

A MORE GENERAL FRAMEWORK

While Goodman regression is an important special case, as well as a useful context for grasping certain distinctions, in many ways it is unique. Hence we now take up the general linear multiple regression case. Given a well-specified individual-level linear model, under what conditions does it remain well specified at the aggregate level? A slight generalization of lemma 1 is needed in the discussion of this question, and it will be set out first.

Lemma 2. Let $y = X\beta + u$, with y an n-dimensional vector of observations on the dependent variable, X an $n \times K$ matrix of fixed observations on k independent variables, and u an unobserved vector of random disturbances. The elements of the coefficient vector β are unknown parameters to be estimated. It is assumed that X has full rank k. Then the conventional OLS estimate of β is unbiased if and only if for all k

$$(19) \qquad\qquad X'E(u) = 0.$$

Proof. The OLS slope estimate is

$$(20) \qquad\qquad \hat{\beta} = (X'X)^{-1}X'y.$$

Substituting for y and taking expectations gives as usual

$$(21) \qquad\qquad E(\hat{\beta}) = \beta + (X'X)^{-1}X'E(u).$$

Thus $E(\hat{\beta}) = \beta$ (unbiasedness) if and only if the second term on the right-hand side is zero. Since X is fixed and of full rank, so is $(X'X)^{-1}$; hence the latter's product with a vector can be zero if and only if the vector consists entirely of zeroes. Thus equation (21) implies that $\hat{\beta}$ is unbiased if and only if $X'E(u) = 0$.   Q.E.D.

Note that, expressed in scalar form, condition (19) of this lemma is equivalent to $\sum_{i=1}^{n} X_{ik}E(u_i) = 0$ $(k = 1, \ldots, K)$. Thus in the bivariate regression case, since the independent variables consist of the constant plus one other variable, condition (19) reduces to conditions (a) and (b) of lemma 1 above.

Armed with this result, we may take up the multiple regression version of conditions for unbiasedness at the aggregate level. For simplicity, we shall assume that coefficients vary by constituency but are constant within them. Maintaining the assumption of m equal-sized constituencies composed of n individuals each, suppose that the individual-level model is

$$(22) \qquad y_{ji} = x_{ji}\beta_j + v_{ji} \quad (j = 1, \ldots, m; i = 1, \ldots, n),$$

where y_{ji} is the observed value of the dependent variable for individual i in constituency j, x_{ji} is a corresponding (row) vector of fixed values of K independent variables, β_j is a K-dimensional vector of unknown coefficients drawn from the K-dimensional distribution function $F_j(\cdot)$, and v_{ji} is a scalar disturbance term.

We make the assumptions that the full set of observations are not perfectly collinear and that disturbances have mean zero:

(i) Denote the $mn \times K$ matrix of observations on the independent variables by x, so that $x' = [x'_{11}, \ldots, x'_{mn}]$. Then x has full rank k.

(ii) $E(v_{ji}) = 0$, for all i, j.

Define the vector of observations on the dependent variable as $y' = [y_{11}, \ldots, y_{mn}]$. Typically, researchers set $\beta = \Sigma_j E(\beta_j)/m$, so that the coefficient vector to be estimated is the simple mean of the individual constituency vectors (which in this case is equivalent to averaging over persons). Then we have

$$(23) \qquad\qquad\qquad y_{ji} = x_{ji}\beta + u_{ji},$$

with $u_{ji} = x_{ji}(\beta_j - \beta) + v_{ji}$. Note that additional assumptions must be imposed so that $E(u_{ji}) = 0$ and $E(x_{ji}u_{ji}) = 0$. For example, one may assume that for all j, i:

(iii) $E(\beta_j | x_{ji}) = \beta$.

The OLS regression estimate then takes the usual form:

$$(24) \qquad\qquad\qquad \hat{\beta} = (x'x)^{-1}x'y.$$

The inverse, and hence the estimate, exist by assumption (i). Substituting for y from the definition of its constituent elements in equation (23), it is immediate from elementary econometric theory that β is unbiased. Thus, under the minimal assumptions (i) and (ii), the regression setup (23) is well specified in the sense we have defined.

We now move to the aggregate level. Define the constituency-level mean of the dependent variable as $Y_j = \Sigma_i y_{ji}/n$, and let the corresponding vector be $Y' = [Y_1, \ldots, Y_m]$. Similarly, let the constituency-level means of the independent variables be $X_j = \Sigma_i x_{ji}/n$ and $X' =$

$[X'_1, \ldots, X'_m]$; also set $V_j = \Sigma_i \, v_{ji}/n$, $V' = [V_1, \ldots, V_m]$, and $U_j = \Sigma_i \, u_{ji}/n$, $U' = [U_1, \ldots, U_m]$. Then averaging equation (23) within constituencies gives the aggregate regression equation:

$$(25) \qquad\qquad Y_j = X_j\beta + U_j,$$

or in matrix form:

$$(26) \qquad\qquad Y = X\beta + U,$$

where $U = X(\beta_j - \beta) + V$ and $E(V) = 0$. We assume in addition that the aggregate independent variables are not perfectly collinear:

(iv) X has full rank k.

Then the aggregate OLS estimate may be defined in the usual way:

$$(27) \qquad\qquad \tilde{\beta} = (X'X)^{-1}X'Y.$$

Lemma 2 then states that, in equation (27), $\tilde{\beta}$ is unbiased if and only if for all k

$$(28) \qquad\qquad X'E(U) = 0.$$

Then, in matrix terms, the condition for unbiasedness is, from the definition of U in equation (26),

$$(29) \qquad\qquad X'XE(\beta_j - \beta) = 0.$$

This is just the multiple regression generalization of condition (12): A certain set of weighted cross-products of independent variables and regression coefficients must sum to zero.

The interesting feature of this condition for unbiasedness is that it is covered by the assumption about random-coefficient variation already made at the individual level: Assumption (iii) implies equation (29). Thus, in this context, proper individual-level specification indeed implies unbiased aggregation (Zellner 1969). This is an important change from the Goodman ecological regression case. However, in many respects, the difference is more apparent than real, as the following paragraphs explain.

Why does Goodman regression require additional assumptions to guarantee unbiasedness at the aggregate level when other regression models do not? Purely descriptive models like Goodman's have special features which permit individual-level unbiased estimation in the presence of random coefficients. The fact that the model is saturated is of particular importance (see n. 4). When such specifications are estimated with aggregate data, additional conditions are then needed to guarantee unbiasedness.

More general regression models do not share the special features of saturated models, and additional assumptions about uncorrelated parameter variation (such as assumption [iii]) are needed from the beginning. When such assumptions fail to hold, as they often do in practice, bias results at the individual level as well as the aggregate level. Thus, in theory, random parameters correlated with regressors cause the same problems for general linear regression models at both the individual and the aggregate levels.

In social science practice, however, the biases from parameters correlated with regressors in individual-level data tend to be small. The correlations exist, but they are not strong, and so the problem is usually overlooked or ignored. Other approximations in the specification, inevitable in applied work, are generally of far greater consequence. Thus, even when assumption (iii) fails, the consequences at the individual level are often slight. Saturated models like Goodman's do not need assumption (iii), and in practice, more general linear specifications, which do require it, often violate it only mildly.

In aggregate data, however, correlations are stronger. The cause is the averaging process that aggregation imposes on data. After averaging, much individual variation is smoothed out, and central limit theorems have their usual effects. Thus a slight and erratic tendency for *individual* voters in Democratic districts to have higher loyalty rates becomes, after simple aggregation, a strong and highly dependable tendency for Democratic *districts* to have higher loyalty rates. The result is that biases too small to be of great concern in individual-level data become powerful sources of bias in aggregate data. An imperfect but serviceable specification at the microlevel becomes useless at the macrolevel. Both Goodman regressions and more general regression specifications become biased.

In practice, then, the general multiple regression case is not very different from descriptive Goodman regression. Both impose special demands on aggregate work that are customarily safely ignored at the individual level. In both cases, successful individual-level specifications will fail at the macrolevel unless additional conditions are satisfied.

In practice, matters have seemed less bleak. Most researchers have operated on the assumption that, while their specifications were surely imperfect, improving them (in the sense of higher R^2, smaller confidence intervals, and better t-ratios) would never be harmful. They have added control variables to tighten the statistical fit of their regressions, believing that the estimates from the best models were likely to be nearer the truth. Or they have added assumptions at the microlevel concerning the distribution of parameters within constituencies, and then mathematically aggregated to the macrolevel. The next section shows that, while these procedures may sometimes be helpful, improved fit offers no guarantees of better inferences with aggregate data. Absent the conditions guaranteeing unbiased macroestimates, improving the fit may actually make coefficient estimates worse.

AN ALTERNATIVE APPROACH

Another approach to aggregation bias in multiple regression, somewhat more general, is to write equation (25) as

$$(30) \qquad\qquad Y_j = X_j\beta + \delta_j + \epsilon_j,$$

where $\delta_j = E(U_j)$ and $\epsilon_j = U_j - \delta_j$. Thus δ_j is the mean of the disturbance in the jth constituency; it captures the intraconstituency spatial autocorrelation. (An earlier version of this framework appeared in Achen 1986; see also Erbring 1990).

Equation (30) is a random-intercept specification, in which the intercept is unique to the observation. Necessarily, then, for all j, $E(v_j) = 0$ and condition (28) for unbiased macroestimation is satisfied. The difficulty, of course, is that equation (30) contains more coefficients than the number of macroobservations available: there are $K + m$ coefficients and m observations. The equation is not estimable as it stands.

The usual approach, as in equation (27), is to delete the variables δ_j and estimate only β. This procedure amounts to committing the specification error of omitted variables. Assuming that these omitted variables are consequential, it is well known from elementary econometrics that the omitted variables do not bias the OLS estimates only if the included variables are uncorrelated with the effects due to the omitted variables. Thus omitting the δ_j from equation (30) will leave the OLS estimates of β unaffected only if the δ_j are uncorrelated with X_j, i.e., if $X_j'\delta = 0$, where δ is a column vector with typical element δ_j. But this condition for unbiasedness under omitted variables is just the condition (28) for unbiased aggregation: This way of thinking about aggregation bias gives the same conclusion as that of lemma 2.

In practice, researchers often find that macrospecifications are quite sensitive. Particularly troublesome is the common experience of finding additional regression variables which dramatically improve the fit but inappropriately reverse the sign of key coefficients. Equation (30) may be used to explain why the experience of improved fits and meaningless coefficients is to be expected in aggregate regressions. Suppose that equation (30) is the truth, and write it in matrix form:

$$(31) \qquad Y = X\beta + \delta + \epsilon$$

$$(32) \qquad = X_1\beta_1 + X_2\beta_2 + \delta + \epsilon,$$

where X_1 and X_2 are the first K_1 and the last $K - K_1$ columns of X, respectively, and β_1 and β_2 are the corresponding elements of β. Again δ captures the intraconstituency spatial autocorrelation. We suppose that one or more of the elements of β_1 are of primary substantive interest.

The researcher first estimates a regression using just X_1 as independent variables:

$$(33) \qquad \tilde{\beta}_1 = (X_1'X_1)^{-1}X_1'Y.$$

Substituting for Y from equation (32) and taking expectations gives the bias

$$(34) \qquad E(\tilde{\beta}_1) - \beta_1 = B\beta_2 + (X_1'X_1)^{-1}X_1'\delta,$$

where $B = (X_1'X_1)^{-1}X_1'X_2$.

Now suppose that an "improved specification" becomes available, using both X_1 and X_2, in which not all the elements of β_2 are zero. However, δ remains omitted. Define the corresponding OLS estimate as

$$(35) \qquad \hat{\beta} = (X'X)^{-1}X'Y.$$

Then, since additional variables with nonzero coefficients have been added to the regression, in expectation the fit will be better. The adjusted R^2 and standard error of estimate will improve. And, except in those small-sample cases in which the regression is overwhelmed by collinearity and/or vanishing degrees of freedom, confidence intervals will tighten and t-ratios increase.

In this situation, the researcher will be very much inclined to believe that the new estimates of β_1 are superior. Unfortunately, no such conclusion follows. Regression equations with one omitted group of variables are not necessarily superior to those with two omitted groups, particularly if the two groups produce biases in opposite directions which tend to cancel.

Indeed, substituting for Y, partitioning the matrices conformably, applying standard results on the inverse of a partitioned matrix, and taking expectations, one finds that the bias in $\hat{\beta}_1$ is

$$(36) \qquad E(\hat{\beta}_1) - \beta_1 = (X_1'X_1)^{-1}X_1'\delta - BC,$$

where B is defined as in equation (34), $C = S^{-1}X_2'[I - X_1(X_1'X_1)^{-1} \cdot X_1']\delta$, and $S = X_2'X_2 - B'X_1'X_1B$. Note that C is the matrix of regression coefficients when the elements of δ are regressed on X_2 after both have been "purged" by X_1.

There is no reason for the bias in equation (36) necessarily to be smaller than that in equation (34). Both share the bias term $(X_1'X_1)^{-1} \cdot X_1'\delta$. The first expression has another bias term, $B\beta_2$, which is a function of the covariance between X_1 and X_2 and the regression coefficients β_2. This term is replaced in the second case by $-BC$, again a function of the covariance between X_1 and X_2 and also of the partial covariance between X_2 and δ. Roughly speaking, therefore, controlling for X_2 gets rid of a bias term due to its omission, but adds a term due to its covariation with the intraconstituency spatial autocorrelation, δ. Since these covariances can be of any sign, there is no guarantee that the extra control variables are helpful. For example, if X_1 and X_2 are uncorrelated, then $B = 0$, and controlling for X_2 improves the fit but makes no difference in the estimate of β_1. The improved fit is useless.

Controlling for the extra variables will be most helpful, not necessarily when they improve the statistics of fit, but rather when they are close proxies for the intraconstituency spatial autocorrelation, i.e., for the elements of δ. If this kind of spatial correlation can be entirely controlled for, bias disappears. That is, when X_1 and X_2 are jointly perfect predictors of δ, then $BC = (X_1'X_1)^{-1}X_1'\delta$ and the bias in equation (36) is zero. In this case, controlling for the extra variables eliminates bias entirely, no matter how little the extra variables improve the fit. The success of Hanushek et al. in reducing aggregation bias is due precisely to their skill in controlling for this kind of spatial autocorrelation.

The goal in adding control variables, therefore, should be to control for intraconstituency spatial autocorrelation. That is, the control variables should eliminate any differences among constituencies in their mean disturbances which are correlated with the aggregate regressors. Doing so is not easy. The culprit, the vector of expected disturbances δ, cannot be estimated, and the estimated OLS residuals will always disguise the problem. (They are, of course, uncorrelated with the aggregate regressors by the nature of the OLS computations.) Improved R^2 or an elaborate, proper, and causal specification aggregated up from the microlevel is no evidence that bias has been eliminated; a weak R^2 and a simple descriptive specification is no evidence that it has failed.

In some instances, it may be possible to treat δ as fixed over time and use a time series of cross sections to estimate it. This technique is too little used in practical work, and it deserves wider trials than it has enjoyed thus far. But its usefulness is strictly limited to instances in which the assumption of δ fixed over time is credible. This formulation would make little sense in the Goodman regression case we discussed above for instance, in which $\delta_i = W_i E(p_i - p) + (1 - W_i)E(q_i - q)$, a quantity dependent on the transition probabilities and hence sure to vary election by election.

Instead, what is needed for most applications is strong substantive knowledge of how individuals group themselves into constituencies and how best one might control for the resulting differences in mean disturbances. Aggregate data themselves are little help; the bias comes from relationships *within* constituencies that can be known only from other sources. Thus the success of Hanushek et al. (1974) in eliminating the biases in Robinson's (1950) data was due to their understanding that, conditional on educational levels, illiteracy and foreign birth would have the same relationship across the sample, making the district disturbances useless as predictors. Knowledge of that kind is essential. Only when one can be assured that uncontrolled differences across constituencies are negligible or unrelated in the sense of equation (28) can one have confidence in aggregate regression. Microlevel specification is not enough; one must meet this additional macrolevel condition as well.

CONCLUSION

The conclusion of this chapter is that proper specification of micro-regressions is a necessary but not sufficient step toward achieving unbiased estimation of the corresponding macroregression models. Additional conditions on the macrospecification must also be imposed. In the absence of those conditions, well-specified individual-level models estimated at the macrolevel may generate severe biases. And improving the microspecification may make the biases worse. The successful model must cope with threats to validity at both the micro- and the macrolevel.

The other chapters of this book are attempts to propose individual-level models that will meet both microconditions for proper specification and the additional macrolevel condition of minimizing bias due to intraconstituency spatial autocorrelation. Chapter 5 explains how a researcher may estimate a quadratic regression model which would allow (in the example of this chapter) p_j and q_j to vary with W_j, thus eliminating a source of bias. Similarly, chapter 7 shows how models with unobservable variables, such as party identification, can sometimes remove sources of aggregation bias. The message of this chapter is that in each case, such models are useful just to the extent that they eliminate a source of intraconstituency spatial autocorrelation.

FIVE

RELAXING THE GOODMAN ASSUMPTIONS

Improved Estimation Using a Subset of the Assumptions

One obvious way to address problems of Goodman ecological regression such as those raised in the preceding chapters is to incorporate into a Goodman model covariation between transition rates and a set of predetermined variables, that is, between p_j and X_j and between q_j and X_j. One may develop an elaboration on Goodman that no longer requires an assumption that p_j and q_j are independent of X_j, but rather includes as part of the model $p_j = f(X_j)$ and $q_j = g(X_j)$ relationships. In practice, these relationships have usually been approximated as linear, and we too will do so in this and the following chapter.

As will be seen below, specifying linear relationships between the transition rates and the predetermined variable(s) produces a quadratic model at the aggregate level. This is a version of the extended sophisticated Goodman model discussed in chapter 2. Many investigators (Boudon 1963; Przeworski 1974; Crewe and Payne 1976; Iversen 1981; Thomsen 1987; among others) have investigated this model, which was initially noted by Goodman (1959), but they have generally been deterred by the fact that such models are underidentified with regard to inferences at the individual level (Goodman 1959, p. 624).

One might argue that other nonlinear models, with more complex specifications of the relationships between p_j and q_j and the X_j, would be more appropriate than the quadratic. In particular, one might choose a probit or logit form. In the probit case, for example, we set $p_j = \Phi(X_j\beta_1)$ and $q_j = \Phi(X_j\beta_2)$ where Φ is the cumulative normal distribution function and β_1 and β_2 are coefficient vectors to be estimated (See chap. 2). Probit or logit forms might often be a sensible choice, especially when variation in p_j or q_j is substantial and thus the linearity assumption could produce nonsensical, out-of-bounds estimates of the transition rates.

In most electoral situations, however, the predetermined variables modify the transition rates only slightly. Middle-class voters support the Tories more strongly in some places than in others, for example, but nowhere do they give majority support to Labour. Similarly, in the example in this chapter, the standard deviation over districts of the forecasted value of p_j is a matter of 3 percentage points. The linear approximation to the probit or logit form will be extremely close in such cases, well beyond the power of the data to distinguish between them. Only when the transition rates cover a substantial range near the upper and lower bounds are these nonlinear functions for p_j and q_j genuinely useful. In most instances, they produce estimates that are similar to those from the linear specification, as will be seen below. In addition, as will be seen in chapter 6, it is possible when using the quadratic specification to check for most forms of significant nonlinearity in the (p_j, X_j) and (q_j, X_j) relationships.

We believe that the quadratic model, with identification or near-identification forced in varying ways according to one's contextual knowledge and theory, can provide a flexible and useful technique in many situations. Indeed, one special case of it dominates simple Goodman ecological regression if we assume that any existing (p_j, X_j) or (q_j, X_j) relationships are adequately approximated as linear.

In the present chapter, we develop the special case of a model which is just-identified, like Goodman's, but with the distinct advantage that it uses a less-demanding subset of the Goodman assumptions. The technique presented in this chapter may be used for all purposes for which standard ecological regression is now used. And if one accepts the linear approximation for any $p_j = f(X_j)$ or $q_j = g(X_j)$ relationships, it can be shown that the expected bias due to aggregation is less than the expected bias for the simple Goodman estimates.

In chapter 6 we relax the Goodman assumptions further, to address the general quadratic model; this yields a broad family of techniques by which ranges of estimates may be produced on the basis of direct substantive assumptions. That is, we treat the quadratic model's under-identification with regard to individual-level inferences as a virtue, providing flexibility for the investigator to build up the model with direct substantive assumptions; these are added to the model's rather flexible polynomial assumptions, approximations of the unknown functional forms relating p_j and q_j to the independent variable.[1] This allows the investigator to get beyond rigid assumptions almost entirely, and thus holds out the possibility of great reductions in aggregation error. However, it is more cumbersome, and it demands more contextual knowledge than the improved version of standard ecological regression presented in this chapter. Our guess is that the technique as described in the present chapter will be of most immediate practical value, but we hope that readers will also be challenged by the presentation in chapter 6 to develop even better, tailor-made models.

A QUADRATIC MODEL FOR CROSS-LEVEL INFERENCE

Just as so many others have done, let us approximate the $p_j = f(X_j)$ and $q_j = g(X_j)$ relationships linearly, as in equations (1) and (2) (as will be seen in chap. 6, it is possible to test, for most situations, whether the assumption of linearity is a sufficiently close approximation). We now let X_j be a single variable and set

$$(1) \qquad p_j = b_1 + b_2 X_j + e_{p_j}$$

and

$$(2) \qquad q_j = b_3 + b_4 X_j + e_{q_j},$$

for each district j, where e_{p_j} and e_{q_j} are stochastic error terms assumed independent of all the X_j.

For concreteness, we shall treat the case in which the individual-level variables corresponding to X_j and Y_j are dichotomous variables. Taking the basic Goodman model of $Y_j = q_j + (p_j - q_j)X_j + V_j$ and substituting p_j and q_j from equations (1) and (2), we obtain

$$(3) \quad Y_j = b_3 + (b_1 - b_3 + b_4)X_j + (b_2 - b_4)X_j^2$$
$$+ [e_{q_j} + (e_{p_j} - e_{q_j})X_j + V_j].$$

---

1. Technically, the disturbances in the sophisticated Goodman model (of which this is an example) carry information about the transition rates, so identification might be achieved even though knowledge of the regression coefficients alone was insufficient. As discussed in chap. 2, however, the conventional formulas for the disturbances are of doubtful validity. Moreover, even if we credulously adopt the formulas, in practice the disturbance variances are not strongly related statistically to the transition rates, so that the actual relevance of the disturbances to identification is weak. Thus we refer to these "nearly unidentified" models simply as "unidentified."

The error term is uncorrelated with X_j and X_j^2 since, if two variables are independently distributed, any functions of them are uncorrelated.[2]

Temporarily ignoring the heteroscedasticity in equation (3), we estimate b_3, $b_1 - b_3 + b_4$, and $b_2 - b_4$ from an OLS regression of Y_j on X_j and X_j^2. If the parameters of the regression equation are labeled β_0, β_1, and β_2, we derive the underidentified set of equations

(4)
$$b_3 = \beta_0,$$

(5)
$$b_1 - b_3 + b_4 = \beta_1,$$

(6)
$$b_2 - b_4 = \beta_2.$$

The problem is that only b_3 is identified here. This has discouraged most empirical investigators from carrying the quest much further along these lines, and they have usually reverted to the simple Goodman model. Looking at the simple Goodman assumptions in light of this underidentified set of equations, however, we see that Goodman achieves identification by assuming $b_2 = b_4 = 0$; that is, $E(p)$ and $E(q)$ are constant across X_j, so the slopes in equations (1) and (2) will be zero. The Goodman assumptions obviate the need for a quadratic term since $b_2 - b_4 = 0$, and the set of equations (4)–(6) reduces to

$$b_3 = \beta_0,$$

$$b_1 - b_3 = \beta_1,$$

which is precisely the Goodman model of $\hat{q} = \beta_0$ and $\hat{p} - \hat{q} = \beta_1$.

However, it is clear from equations (4)–(6) that we can do better than that. It is not necessary to assume $b_2 = b_4 = 0$ to achieve identification. Rather, identification can be achieved by assuming either $b_2 = 0$ or $b_4 = 0$. Either of these is a less-demanding subset of the Goodman assumptions, and as is demonstrated in appendices A and B, by moving to one of them we can achieve estimation which, under the assumptions of equations (1) and (2), will have less bias than the Goodman estimates.

Specifically, we prove in the two appendices that, given the assumptions of equations (1) and (2), if $\beta_2 \geq 0$, then estimation obtained setting $b_4 = 0$ has a lower expected bias than Goodman estimation. Alter-

---

2. Since the error term in eq. (3) includes a function of X_j, there will be heteroscedasticity in the disturbances. But since the error is uncorrelated with X_j and X_j^2, estimation will be unbiased. For discussion of heteroscedastic corrections in this model, see chap. 2 and p. 128 of the present chapter, below.

nately, if $\beta_2 \le 0$, estimation obtained setting $b_2 = 0$ has a lower expected bias than Goodman estimation.

Appendix A gives the stronger of two proofs of this, which is the proof that for most situations justifies using the quadratic model rather than the simple Goodman model. We prove in appendix A that if one can assume that b_2 in equation (1) and b_4 in equation (2) are both greater than or equal to zero—that is, that neither p_j nor q_j varies negatively with X_j—then given the assumptions of equations (1) and (2), bias from quadratic estimation is less than or equal to bias from simple Goodman estimation.

For most common applications of ecological inference, it is possible to assume $b_2 \ge 0$ and $b_4 \ge 0$. In studies of electoral transition, for instance, we commonly assume that the loyalty rate of Democrats is higher in heavily Democratic districts (i.e., $b_2 \ge 0$), but we also assume that Republican defection rates are higher in heavily Democratic districts (i.e., $b_4 \ge 0$). Similarly, in relating vote to class, religion, or ethnic group, we often expect that where a group is more highly concentrated its members' support for "their" party will increase (i.e., $b_2 \ge 0$); a good example is working-class support for socialist parties in heavily working-class towns. At the same time, we assume that others' support for that party also increases under the same condition (i.e., $b_4 \ge 0$); for example, we expect that middle-class voters are unusually likely to vote socialist if they live in heavily working-class towns.[3] If one can assume $b_2 \ge 0$ and $b_4 \ge 0$, then, the strong result holds that quadratic bias is *always* less than or equal to simple Goodman bias.

In appendix B we prove a more general result, appropriate if one is uncertain about assuming $b_2 \ge 0$ and $b_4 \ge 0$. Remarkably, this proof requires only a weak Bayesian indifference prior in which b_4 is as likely to be negative as to be positive. We prove there, simply given the assumptions of equations (1) and (2) plus the indifference prior, that the expectation of aggregation bias in the quadratic estimators is less than or equal to the expectation of aggregation bias in the Goodman estimators, averaged over the prior.

To sum up: from a sampling theory viewpoint, if one assumes $b_2 \ge 0$ and $b_4 \ge 0$, then in expectation quadratic estimation yields aggrega-

---

3. The argument here is based on assumptions of "contextual" effects (see chap. 9), but we believe further that the effects of usual forms of aggregation, unmediated by "contextual" processes of social interaction, will also produce $b_2 \ge 0$ and $b_4 \ge 0$ if in the full population $p > q$. Proof of this is probability complex, though, and the result is not necessary for the argument provided here.

tion bias that is less than or equal to that of Goodman estimation (app. A). From a Bayesian viewpoint, assuming neither $b_2 \geq 0$ nor $b_4 \geq 0$ but the weak prior that b_4 is equally likely to be positive or negative, bias is less under quadratic estimation than under Goodman estimation when averaged over the prior (App. B).

The result presented above is emphatically *not* the usual finding that if a quadratic is the true regression specification, then it is better to use a quadratic form than a linear form. Instead, we are comparing the linear form (in this case, the simple Goodman model) not with the truth but rather with a quadratic, under a possibly (indeed, typically) false identifying restriction. It should not be obvious what will happen in that case: presumably each specification might sometimes be better. The proof of appendix A shows that inference from the quadratic form is always better, under plausible assumptions, than inference from the Goodman linear form.

ESTIMATING THE POPULATION p AND q

So, either strongly (if we assume b_2 and b_4 nonnegative) or weakly (without this assumption), we can obtain superior estimation by setting $b_2 = 0$ or $b_4 = 0$. What do these estimates look like? The reader will recall from chapter 2 (pp. 40−42) that our estimate $\hat{p}$ of the population p is *not* the same as the expectation of p_j when $X_j = \bar{X}$. That is, it does not equal $b_1 + b_2\bar{X}$, as one might have expected from equation (1). Using the notation of p. 41, let n_{xj} be the number of people in the jth district who are in the first category of the dichotomous variable x, and n_x the sum of n_{xj} over all districts. As before, our estimate of the population p is $\hat{p}$:

$$
\begin{aligned}
\hat{p} &= \frac{\sum n_{xj}\hat{p}_j}{n_x} \\[2ex]
&= \frac{\sum n_{xj}[\hat{b}_1 + \hat{b}_2(n_{xj}/n_j)]}{n_x} \\[2ex]
&= \frac{\hat{b}_1 \sum n_{xj}}{n_x} + \frac{\hat{b}_2 \sum(n_{xj}^2/n_j)}{n_x} \\[2ex]
&= \hat{b}_1 + \hat{b}_2\frac{\sum(n_{xj}^2/n_j)}{n_x},
\end{aligned}
$$

(7)

since $n_x = \Sigma n_{xj}$.

If the n_j are constant across districts (as is approximated in congressional or parliamentary elections), this reduces to

(8)
$$\hat{p} = \hat{b}_1 + \hat{b}_2 \frac{\overline{(X^2)}}{\overline{X}}.$$

Similarly,

(9)
$$\hat{q} = \hat{b}_3 + \hat{b}_4 \frac{\sum(n_{xj} n_{\tilde{x}j}/n_j)}{n_{\tilde{x}}},$$

where $n_{\tilde{x}}$ is the number of individuals in the population having the characteristic $\tilde{x}$, not-x. Or, if n_j is constant across districts,

(10)
$$\hat{q} = \hat{b}_3 + \hat{b}_4 \frac{\overline{[X(1 - X)]}}{1 - \overline{X}}.$$

If $\hat{\beta}_2 > 0$, so that we assume $b_4 = 0$, then as can be seen from equations (1), (2), and (4)–(6),

$$\hat{q} = \hat{b}_3 = \hat{\beta}_0$$

and

$$\hat{p} = \hat{b}_1 + \hat{b}_2 \frac{\sum(n_{xj}^2/n_j)}{n_x} = (\hat{\beta}_0 + \hat{\beta}_1) + \hat{\beta}_2 \frac{\sum(n_{xj}^2/n_j)}{n_x}.$$

Or, if $\beta_2 < 0$, *so that we assume* $b_2 = 0$, then

$$\hat{q} = \hat{b}_3 + \hat{b}_4 \frac{\sum(n_{xj} n_{\tilde{x}j}/n_j)}{n_{\tilde{x}}} = \hat{\beta}_0 - \hat{\beta}_2 \frac{\sum(n_{xj} n_{\tilde{x}j}/n_j)}{n_{\tilde{x}}}$$

and

$$\hat{p} = \hat{b}_1 = \hat{\beta}_0 + \hat{\beta}_1 + \hat{\beta}_2.$$

These estimates are summarized in table 1.[4]

If district sizes are equal, it will prove easier to estimate first the $\hat{p}$ or $\hat{q}$ that does not involve the summations of n_{xj}, $n_{\tilde{x}j}$, and so forth. Thus,

---

4. When $\beta_2 = 0$, we can pick either b_2 or b_4 to equal zero, and the other is therefore also zero since $\beta_2 = b_2 - b_4$. Therefore, both are zero, consistent with the Goodman assumptions, although since we have tested for it in this case by estimating β_2, we have only had to assume *one* of them to be zero, unlike the Goodman procedure.

Note also that we do not observe the true β_2, but rather the estimate $\hat{\beta}_2$, and draw our estimate of the sign of β_2 from that estimate; thus it is possible that one's estimate could have the wrong sign, though the likelihood of this is indicated by the standard error of the estimate.

TABLE 1 Procedures for Estimating $\hat{p}$ and $\hat{q}$

Sign of $\hat{\beta}_2$	Assume	$\hat{p}$	$\hat{q}$
+	$b_4 = 0$	$\hat{\beta}_0 + \hat{\beta}_1 + \hat{\beta}_2 \dfrac{\Sigma \left(n_{xj}^2 / n_j \right)}{n_x}$	$\hat{\beta}_0$
0	b_2 or $b_4 = 0$	$\hat{\beta}_0 + \hat{\beta}_1$	$\hat{\beta}_0$
−	$b_2 = 0$	$\hat{\beta}_0 + \hat{\beta}_1 + \hat{\beta}_2$	$\hat{\beta}_0 - \hat{\beta}_2 \dfrac{\Sigma \left(n_{xj} n_{\bar{x}j} / n_j \right)}{n_{\bar{x}}}$

Note: The formulas are set up in the general form of equations (7) and (9), rather than (8) or (10), so that they apply whether or not the districts are of uniform size.

if we are setting $b_4 = 0$, we first estimate $\hat{q} = \hat{\beta}_0$ from the quadratic equation. Then $\hat{p}$ is easily estimated from known population parameters, since

$$(11) \qquad \bar{Y} = p\bar{X} + q(1 - \bar{X}).$$

That is,

$$(12) \qquad \hat{p} = \frac{\bar{Y} - \hat{q}(1 - \bar{X})}{\bar{X}},$$

since our $\hat{p}$ and $\hat{q}$ must be consistent with the truism of equation (11).[5] (If we are setting $b_2 = 0$, we first estimate $\hat{p} = \hat{\beta}_0 + \hat{\beta}_1 + \hat{\beta}_2$ and then estimate $\hat{q}$ from $\hat{p}$ plus the population parameters.) If district sizes are unequal we must work directly with the formulas of table 1, since it is then not true that $\hat{p}$ and $\hat{q}$ must be consistent with equation (11).

5. To prove that eq. (11) is true of $\hat{p}$ and $\hat{q}$ if district sizes (ns) are equal, note that from the quadratic regression equation it is tautologically true that

$$\bar{Y} = \hat{\beta}_0 + \hat{\beta}_1 \bar{X} + \hat{\beta}_2 \overline{(X^2)}.$$

Add and subtract $\hat{\beta}_0 \bar{X}$:

$$\bar{Y} = \hat{\beta}_0 \bar{X} + \hat{\beta}_1 \bar{X} + \hat{\beta}_2 \overline{(X^2)} + \beta_0 (1 - \bar{X}).$$

Multiply through by n:

$$n_y = \hat{\beta}_0 n_x + \hat{\beta}_1 n_x + \hat{\beta}_2 \frac{\overline{(X^2)}}{\bar{X}} \cdot n_x + \beta_0 n_{\bar{x}}.$$

Substitute from table 1, with $\beta_2 > 0$:

$$n_y = \hat{p} n_x + \hat{q} n_{\bar{x}}.$$

Divide through by n:

$$\bar{Y} = \hat{p} \bar{X} + \hat{q}(1 - \bar{X}).$$

The quadratic model has a particularly attractive characteristic when we work with multicategory individual-level variables. For a dichotomous x, such as we have discussed so far, the quadratic solution is underidentified, and we must struggle to produce identification in the system. For multicategory variables, however, at least with regard to main effects (p, etc., taken as functions of the category on which they are based), *the quadratic solution is just-identified* (see below, pp. 129–31).

AN EXAMPLE: THE BRITISH ELECTIONS OF 1964 AND 1966

Donald Stokes (1969) presented an excellent example of the weakness of ecological regression. Taking only those constituencies in which there was a straight Conservative-Labour contest in both the 1964 and 1966 general elections, he produced an ecological scattergram with an exceptionally tight and apparently linear relationship between the Conservative vote in 1964 and 1966 (fig. 1). If ever ecological regression is to work well, it should be in a case like this. He was able to compare the results of ecological regression with parallel results from the Butler-Stokes panel survey. Stokes presented the comparison graphically and did not state his ecological estimates, but we have recalculated on essentially the same data set the standard least squares ecological regression equation which lay behind his comparison (see table 2).[6]

While the ecological results are not terribly distant from the survey estimates, they clearly are unsatisfactory. The estimate for transition from Labour falls below the logical bound of zero to produce a negative proportion—a problem which has continually plagued ecological regression. (This is not a matter of sampling error; $-.03$ is four standard errors from zero in this estimate.) Overall, to quote Stokes, "the divergence . . . strongly suggests the presence of a bias which has altered the conditional proportions according to the partisanship of the constituency, depressing the ecological regression line

---

6. The data set used here differs slightly from Stokes's set; Stokes apparently included some districts in which Liberals or various nationalists contested a single election, while the set used in this paper is designed to fit Stokes's description: "constituencies which were fought only by Labour and Conservatives at two successive elections" (1969, p. 77). The ecological regression result in table 2 is closely consistent with Stokes's graphical presentation, however, so this does not seem to be a significant disparity. All analysis presented here is performed on the reconstructed data set.

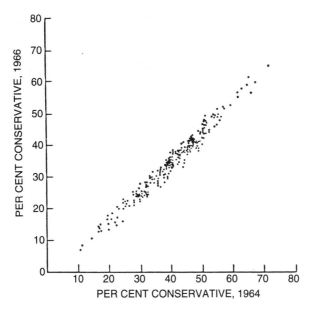

Figure 1. Conservative share of vote in British districts with straight fights in both 1964 and 1966. *Source:* Stokes 1969, p. 78.

TABLE 2 Comparison of Standard Ecological Estimates with Panel Data, from among Voters Living in Constituencies with Straight Fights in Both 1964 and 1966

	Panel	Standard Ecological Regression
Estimated proportion of 1964 Conservative voters Conservative in 1966 (p)	.87 (.02)	.95 (.008)
Estimated proportion of 1964 Labour voters Conservative in 1966 (q)	.03 (.01)	−.03 (.006)

Note: For the regression equation, $R^2 = .972$, $n = 145$, and the standard error of residuals = .0175. Numbers in parentheses are standard errors.

where the Conservatives were weak and raising it where they were strong" (1969, p. 81).

This example provides a strong test case for the technique we have described above. It is a well-known example of the problems of ecological regression, and figure 1 does not obviously display the sorts of nonlinearity which our specification assumes will generally be present if p_i and q_i vary with X_i. Let us see how the proposed technique will work in this case.

Regression of the 1966 Conservative vote on 1964 and on 1964 squared produces the following results, where C66 is the proportion of the 1966 vote Conservative, and C64 is the proportion of the 1964 vote Conservative:

$$
\text{(13)} \qquad \begin{matrix} \text{C66} = .010 + .783 \ \text{C64} + .239 \ \text{C64}^2. \\ \quad (.015) \quad (.076) \qquad (.093) \end{matrix}
$$

Standard errors are given in parentheses; $R^2 = .974$, $n = 145$, the standard error of the residuals is .0172, the mean of C64 is .412, and the mean of C66 is .376.

Though nonlinearity was not obvious in figure 1, there is significant nonlinearity in equation (13); this equation produces the slightly nonlinear track of figure 2.[7] Substituting into equations (4), (5), and (6), we obtain for this case

$$b_3 = .010,$$

$$b_1 - b_3 + b_4 = .783,$$

$$b_2 - b_4 = .239.$$

Since $\hat{\beta}_2$ is positive and we easily reject at the conventional .05 level the hypothesis that its true value is zero or less, we set $b_4 = 0$ and obtain

$$b_4 = 0,$$

$$b_3 = .010,$$

$$b_1 = .783 + b_3 - b_4 = .793,$$

$$b_2 = .239 + b_4 = .239.$$

Since the mean of C66 is .376 and the mean of C64 is .412 (and district sizes are approximately equal, so that the mean of C66 approximates the proportion of the population Conservative in 1966, and

---

7. This curve would fit either a probit or a quadratic form approximately equally well, of course. Estimates using the probit model of Thomsen (1987) on the same data are discussed in chap. 7. Thomsen's probit model requires strong assumptions about the underlying process, though we believe that these may not yet have been fully worked out, and may eventually prove less demanding than what he presents. (See below, pp. 183–88.)

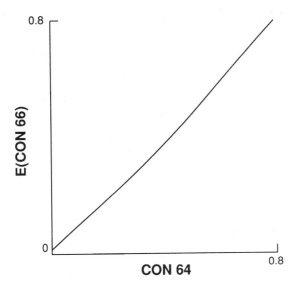

Figure 2. The quadratic slope

ditto for C64), we estimate from table 1:

$$\hat{q} = \hat{\beta}_0 = .010,$$
$$(.015)$$

standard error given in parentheses. We estimate $\hat{p}$ from equation (12):

$$.376 = .412\hat{p} + .588\hat{q},$$
$$\hat{p} = .898,$$
$$(.018)$$

standard error given in parentheses. Referring to table 3, we see that these estimates are close to the panel results of .87 and .03, and distinctly better than the estimates of .95 and $-.03$ obtained from standard ecological regression.[8]

One moral to be drawn from this example is that eyeballing for linearity in a scattergram is not enough in cross-level analysis. Even gentle nonlinearity in the aggregate data, of the sort evident in fig-

---

8. The quadratic regression estimates do not differ significantly from the panel results.

TABLE 3 Comparison of Ecological Regression Estimates with Panel
Data, from among Voters Living in Constituencies with
Straight Fights in Both 1964 and 1966

	Panel	Quadratic Ecological Regression	Standard Ecological Regression
Estimated p	.87	.90	.95
Estimated q	.03	.01	−.03

ures 1 and 2, can lead to serious misspecification in the translation to
individual-level estimates.

HETEROSCEDASTICITY

As we noted at the beginning of this chapter, the quadratic cross-level
inferential model based on linear $f(X_j)$ and $g(X_j)$ implies a particular
form for heteroscedasticity in the data. In chapter 2 we provided appropriate weighting for heteroscedasticity in cross-level inference, but we
argued there that except for some special cases heteroscedastic corrections would make little difference in estimates. In the current example,
comparisons of OLS estimates (uncorrected for heteroscedasticity) and
weighted least squares estimates (corrected) are as follows:

I. Bivariate (standard Goodman regression):
 A. OLS:
$$C66 = -.025 + .974 \; C64, \quad \hat{q} = -.03,$$
$$\quad\;\; (.006) \quad (.014) \qquad \hat{p} = .95,$$
 B. Weighted:
$$C66 = -.023 + .970 \; C64, \quad \hat{q} = -.02,$$
$$\quad\;\; (.005) \quad (.012) \qquad \hat{p} = .95,$$

II. Quadratic:
 A. OLS:
$$C66 = .010 + .783 \; C64 + .239 \; C64^2, \quad \hat{q} = .01,$$
$$\quad\; (.015) \quad (.076) \qquad\quad (.093) \qquad \hat{p} = .90,$$
 B. Weighted:
$$C66 = .003 + .818 \; C64 + .197 \; C64^2 \quad \hat{q} = .00,$$
$$\quad\; (.009) \quad (.051) \qquad\quad (.065) \qquad \hat{p} = .91.$$

Thus, in the Stokes example the difference between weighted and
unweighted estimates is slight, as expected. Note also that the estimates
adjusted for heteroscedasticity are not systematically closer to the survey estimates.

EXTENSION TO MULTIVARIATE REGRESSION

Most applications of ecological regression are not bivariate, but multivariate. For instance, we might investigate interelection transition rates in a system of three parties, x_1, x_2, and x_3, with a 3×3 table of transition rates for the three parties at two elections (see chap. 2, pp. 34–38; note also that for ease of exposition we are dropping the district subscript in this section). The easiest way to estimate the transitions via ecological regression is to perform a separate regression for each row. By regressing X_1 at time 2 on X_1, X_2, and X_3 at time 1, we estimate the rate of transition to party x_1 of voters for party x_1, party x_2, and party x_3—three of the nine transition probabilities. (To avoid collinearity, customarily X_3 is omitted from the equation, but the effect is the same.) We then repeat similar analyses for the other two rows, taking X_2 at time 2 and X_3 at time 2, respectively, as dependent variables.

The same sort of quadratic model as used above extends readily to the multivariate case. As in the bivariate case (where our setting of $b_2 = 0$ or $b_4 = 0$ meant that we worked with a partial system), again we achieve identification by using less than a fully general system, since indirect effects and interactions will be omitted. However, the assumptions required by this are still fewer than the Goodman assumptions. And unlike the case of dichotomous variables, analysis of multicategory variables yields a *fully identified* system with regard to main effects.

Take a 3×3 table for the case in which we wish to estimate p_{11}, the transition rate from x_1 at the first election to x_1 at the second election; p_{21}, the transition rate from x_2 to x_1; and p_{31}, the transition rate from x_3 to x_1; as well as p_{12}, p_{22}, and p_{32}, the transition rates to x_2; and p_{13}, p_{23}, and p_{33}, the transition rates to x_3. For our example, let us look only at the first row: p_{11}, p_{21}, and p_{31}.

Let us specify that p_{11}, p_{21}, and p_{31} each varies linearly with the concentration of its party by district, where X_{kl} is the vote for x_k at the *l*th election:

(14) $$E(p_{11}) = b_1 + b_2 X_{11},$$

(15) $$E(p_{21}) = b_3 + b_4 X_{21},$$

(16) $$E(p_{31}) = b_5 + b_6 X_{31}.$$

Now,

(17) $$E(X_{12}) = p_{11} X_{11} + p_{21} X_{21} + p_{31} X_{31}$$

$$= p_{11} X_{11} + p_{21} X_{21} + p_{31}(1 - X_{11} - X_{21}).$$

Substituting from equations (16), (15), and (14) into equation (17), we obtain

$$E(X_{12}) = (b_1 + b_2 X_{11})X_{11} + (b_3 + b_4 X_{21})X_{21} +$$

$$[b_5 + b_6(1 - X_{11} - X_{21})](1 - X_{11} - X_{21})$$

$$= b_1 X_{11} + b_2 X_{11}^2 + b_3 X_{21} + b_4 X_{21}^2 + b_5 - b_5 X_{11} -$$

$$b_5 X_{21} + b_6 - b_6 X_{11} - b_6 X_{21} - b_6 X_{11} +$$

$$b_6 X_{11}^2 + b_6 X_{11} X_{21} - b_6 X_{21} + b_6 X_{11} X_{21} + b_6 X_{21}^2.$$

Combining terms, we have

$$E(X_{12}) = (b_5 + b_6) + (b_1 - b_5 - 2b_6)X_{11} +$$

(18) $$(b_2 + b_6)X_{11}^2 + (b_3 - b_5 - 2b_6)X_{21} +$$

$$(b_4 + b_6)X_{21}^2 + 2b_6 X_{11} X_{21}.$$

By conducting the regression indicated in equation (18), we obtain the following system of six equations in six unknowns:

(19) $$\hat{b}_5 + \hat{b}_6 = \hat{\beta}_0,$$

(20) $$\hat{b}_1 - \hat{b}_5 - 2\hat{b}_6 = \hat{\beta}_1,$$

(21) $$\hat{b}_2 + \hat{b}_6 = \hat{\beta}_2,$$

(22) $$\hat{b}_3 - \hat{b}_5 - 2\hat{b}_6 = \hat{\beta}_3,$$

(23) $$\hat{b}_4 + \hat{b}_6 = \hat{\beta}_4,$$

(24) $$2\hat{b}_6 = \hat{\beta}_5.$$

From equation (24), we see that $\hat{b}_6 = .5\hat{\beta}_5$; and subtracting $\hat{b}_6$ from $\hat{\beta}_0$ in equation (19), we obtain $\hat{b}_5$. Having identified $\hat{b}_5$ and $\hat{b}_6$, we can solve easily for $\hat{b}_1$, $\hat{b}_2$, $\hat{b}_3$, and $\hat{b}_4$ as well, and the system is identified.

To obtain $\hat{p}_{11}$, $\hat{p}_{21}$, and $\hat{p}_{31}$, we note that p_{11} equals the sum across districts of the product $p_{11j}n_{X_{11j}}$, divided by $n_{X_{11}}$, the number of time-1 x_1 voters in the population; the derivation of equation (7) produces

$$\hat{p}_{11} = \hat{b}_1 + \hat{b}_2 \frac{\sum(n_{X_{11j}}^2/n_j)}{n_{X_{11}}}.$$

From our estimates of b_1 and b_2 and the known values of the $n_{X_{11j}}$, we can thus calculate the estimate of p_{11}. Similarly, we can solve for our estimates of p_{21}, p_{31}, and so forth. Standard errors for these estimates are discussed in chapter 2.

Equations (14), (15), and (16) are not fully general; an unrestricted linear specification of equation (14), for instance, would allow for the effect of X_{21} and (omitted) X_{31} on p_{11}, as in equation (25):

$$(25) \qquad E(p_{11}) = b_1 + b_2 X_{11} + b_3 X_{21}.$$

We have assumed above that the effect of X_{21} on p_{11} was zero and have made similar assumptions in equations (15) and (16). If these assumptions are wrong, aggregation bias will result. As compared with standard ecological regression, however, we have at least incorporated the main effect into our model. In equation (25), for instance, we must assume that b_3 equals zero, but the Goodman assumptions require that b_2 *and* b_3 equal zero. As in the bivariate case, we expect that the estimation procedure outlined here should typically produce results with less bias than one finds with standard regression; however, this is proved in appendices A and B only for the bivariate case.

Note that in a particular research problem, an investigator might well decide to constrain b_2, leaving b_3 or even an additional parameter b_4 free to vary. For instance, it might be that the loyalty of British Liberal Democratic voters is more a function of whether Labour and the Conservatives are closely matched in the district (so that strategic voting matters) than of the number of Liberal Democratic voters in the district. In that case we might specify, similarly to equation (25),

$$E(p_{11}) = b_1 + b_2 \text{Lib}_1 + b_3 \text{Cons}_1 + b_4 |\text{Cons}_1 - \text{Lab}_1|,$$

where Lib_1 is the proportion Liberal Democratic at the first election, Cons_1 is the proportion Conservative at the first election, and $|\text{Cons}_1 - \text{Lab}_1|$ is the absolute value of the difference between the proportions Conservative and Labour at the first election. We would then constrain b_2 and b_3 to zero, allowing p_{11j} to vary as a function of $|\text{Cons}_1 - \text{Lab}_1|_j$. Whatever specification is to be used, of course, only the intercept plus one slope may be left unconstrained if we are to achieve identification.

The multicategory technique presented in this section extends readily beyond the 3 × 3 case.

CONCLUSION

The reader will note that the estimation approach we suggest in this and the following chapter does not achieve the ideal we set in chapter 1:

specification of the aggregation process as well as the individual-level process. Aggregation processes are multifaceted, complex, and subtle; modeling them properly must be extremely difficult, and we do not pretend to do so in these chapters.[9] Actually, for the example used in this chapter, even the individual-level model is probably imperfectly specified. Recall that in chapter 3 we showed that for voter transition problems (such as the Stokes example) a common-factor model makes more theoretic sense than a regression model; in chapter 7 we develop an ecological factor-analytic approach appropriate for such problems, and we will use the Stokes example again at that point.

What we do offer in these two chapters is a flexible, local approximation to processes that probably no one will normally model fully— an approximation that can allow good estimation even in the absence of a full specification of the process. The approximation is local in the sense that it picks up what is happening across the actual cases but would not necessarily be valid if extended to hypothetical cases of zero or one on the independent variable. While the approximation does not model aggregation directly, it takes into account many of the *effects* of aggregation by allowing p_j and q_j to covary with the aggregate independent variable. It provides a flexible functional approximation that allows us to pick up various local features of the underlying individual and cross-level processes, sufficient to get estimation that we believe is superior to linear approximations that share the Goodman assumptions that p_j and q_j are uncorrelated with the independent variable.

We have shown that the model presented here yields estimates that under the assumptions of this chapter yield lower expected biases, should the constraints prove false, than do Goodman linear estimates. Even very gentle aggregate nonlinearities (as in the Stokes example) can induce substantial aggregation error if a linear specification is used; therefore, the quadratic or some other nonlinear specification should always be tested, even when the aggregate relationship "looks" linear. The quadratic model is not the final answer—there *is* no "final answer"—but it is an improved specification as compared with Goodman's. Both theoretical considerations and data-analytic experience have made it clear that simple linear bivariate ecological regression is inadequate and should not be used. As a practical matter, we see no

---

9. This is true even of a relatively simple example such as Stokes's, but it becomes crashingly clear in a more complex example, such as that drawn from W. S. Robinson in the next chapter.

reason why anyone should prefer standard ecological regression to the version of the extended sophisticated Goodman model presented in this chapter, whether or not they also wish to go on to the less determinate quadratic approach of the next chapter, or to other alternatives.

APPENDIX A

Proof that If $b_2 \geq 0$ and $b_4 \geq 0$, Aggregation Error Using the Quadratic Ecological Regression Model Is Less Than or Equal to Aggregation Error Using Linear Ecological Regression, Given the Assumptions of Equations (1) and (2)

We will divide the proof into parts 1–3 in which we prove that, if $\beta_2 > 0$ and b_4 is set to zero, then |Goodman aggregation error| $\geq$ |quadratic aggregation error| and part 4 in which we prove that, if $\beta_2 < 0$ and b_2 is set to zero, then |Goodman aggregation error| $\geq$ |quadratic aggregation error|.

PART 1: AGGREGATION ERROR IN GOODMAN ECOLOGICAL REGRESSION

Goodman linear regression uses the model

$$E(Y_j) = \beta_0 + \beta_1 X_j,$$

and p is estimated as $\beta_0 + \beta_1$.

In the quadratic specification,

(A1) $$E(p_j) = b_1 + b_2 X_j$$

and

(A2) $$E(q_j) = b_3 + b_4 X_j.$$

Thus the quadratic model with parameters β_0, β_1, and β_2 yields the following:

(A3) $$\beta_0 = b_3,$$

(A4) $$\beta_1 = b_1 - b_3 + b_4,$$

(A5) $$\beta_2 = b_2 - b_4.$$

If the Goodman assumptions that $b_2 = b_4 = 0$ are true, then $\beta_2 = 0$, the linear aggregate model is properly specified, and $E(p) = \beta_0 + \beta_1$ as posited in the Goodman inference. If the Goodman assumptions do not hold however, unless $b_2 = b_4, \beta_2 \neq 0$ and we must calculate error in the linear model due to omission of the quadratic term in the model.

Assume that the correctly specified model is

$$E(Y_j) = \beta_0 + \beta_1 X_j + \beta_2 X_j^2,$$

but we estimate

$$E(Y_j) = \beta_0^* + \beta_1^* X_j.$$

Then

$$E(\beta_1^*) = \beta_1 + d_{21}\beta_2,$$

where

$$d_{21} = \frac{\sum(X_j - \bar{X})(X_j^2 - \overline{(X^2)})}{\sum(X_j - \bar{X})^2},$$

i.e., in this case the linear slope of X_j^2 on X_j. (This is a standard result; see, e.g., Kmenta 1971, p. 392.) And,

$$E(\beta_0^*) = \beta_0 + [\overline{(X^2)} - d_{21}\bar{X}]\beta_2.$$

Thus, the Goodman estimate of $\hat{p} = \beta_0^* + \beta_1^*$ has expectation

$$E(\hat{p}) = \beta_0 + [\overline{(X^2)} - d_{21}\bar{X}]\beta_2 + \beta_1 + d_{21}\beta_2.$$

Rearranging terms, we obtain

$$E(\hat{p}) = \beta_0 + \beta_1 + [\overline{(X^2)} + (1 - \bar{X})d_{21}]\beta_2.$$

The actual expectation of p for the population is

$$E(p) = b_1 + b_2\frac{\sum(n_{xj}^2/n_j)}{n_x},$$

from equation (7) in the main text. Therefore, the bias (expected error) in estimating p by linear ecological regression is

$$E(\hat{p}) - E(p) = \beta_0 + \beta_1 + [\overline{(X^2)} + (1 - \bar{X})d_{21}]\beta_2$$
$$- b_1 - b_2\frac{\sum(n_{xj}^2/n_j)}{n_x}.$$

Substituting from equations (A3)–(A5), we obtain

$$E(\hat{p}) - E(p) = b_3 + (b_1 - b_3 + b_4) + \beta_2[\overline{(X^2)} + (1 - \bar{X})d_{21}]$$
$$- b_1 - b_2\frac{\sum(n_{xj}^2/n_j)}{n_x}$$
$$= b_2 - \beta_2 + \beta_2[\overline{(X^2)} + (1 - \bar{X})d_{21}] - b_2\frac{\sum(n_{xj}^2/n_j)}{n_x},$$

since $b_4 = b_2 - \beta_2$, or

(A7) Goodman bias $= \beta_2[\overline{(X^2)} + (1 - \bar{X})d_{21} - 1]$
$$+ b_2\left[1 - \frac{\sum(n_{xj}^2/n_j)}{n_x}\right].$$

Similarly, we can show for q:

$$E(\hat{q}) = E(\beta_0^*) = \beta_0 + [\overline{(X^2)} + d_{21}\bar{X}]\beta_2.$$

The actual expectation of q for the population, from equation (9) in the main text, is

(A8)
$$E(q) = b_3 + b_4 \frac{\sum(n_{xj}n_{\tilde{x}j}/n_j)}{n_{\tilde{x}}}.$$

Therefore the Goodman bias in estimating q by linear regression is

(A9)
$$E(\hat{q}) - E(q) = \beta_0 + [\overline{(X^2)} + d_{21}\bar{X}]\beta_2 - b_3 - b_4 \frac{\sum(n_{xj}n_{\tilde{x}j}/n_j)}{n\tilde{x}}$$

$$= [\overline{(X^2)} + d_{21}\bar{X}]\beta_2 - b_4 \frac{\sum(n_{xj}n_{\tilde{x}j}/n_j)}{n_{\tilde{x}}},$$

since $\beta_0 = b_3$.

PART 2: TWO LEMMAS

To make further progress, we require the following two lemmas, which concern vote proportions (or any observations whose values are bounded between zero and one).

Lemma A1. In a linear regression of X_j^2 on X_j, with $0 \le X_j \le 1$, the intercept of the regression will be less than or equal to zero.

Lemma A2. In a linear regression of X_j^2 on X_j, with $0 \le X_j \le 1$, the expected value of X_j^2 given $X_j = 1$ will be less than or equal to one.

First, note that the estimated regression line $Y = a + bX$ must intersect the quadratic curve $Y = X^2$ exactly twice. (All data points will fall on the quadratic curve; see the examples in fig. 3.) For if the line does not intersect the quadratic curve or is merely tangent to it, then it would be everywhere on or above (or everywhere on or below) the quadratic curve and the residuals would not sum to zero as the OLS calculations require. If the line intersects the curve just once, then all the residuals to one side of the intersection would be positive and all those on the other side negative, so that the residuals would not be uncorrelated with the regressor as the OLS calculations require. Finally, three or more intersections are impossible due to the strict concavity of the quadratic curve. Thus when values of the independent variable are taken from the unit interval, the estimated regression line intersects the quadratic curve exactly twice.

Let the two points of intersection be (X_1, X_1^2) and (X_2, X_2^2), $X_1 \ne X_2$. Since these two points fall on the regression line, we have from the definition of the slope b:

$$X_2^2 - X_1^2 = b(X_2 - X_1),$$

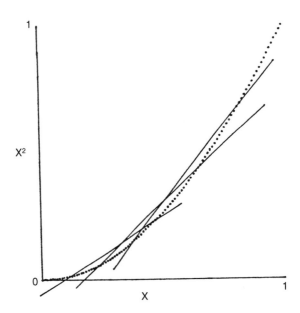

Figure 3. Examples of linear regressions of X^2 on X

or

(A10)
$$(X_2 + X_1) = b,$$

since $X_2^2 - X_1^2 = (X_2 + X_1)(X_2 - X_1)$. But, since (X_1, X_1^2) falls on the regression line,

$$X_1^2 = a + bX_1.$$

Substituting from equation (A10), we have

$$X_1^2 = a + (X_2 + X_1)X_1,$$
$$X_1^2 = a + X_1X_2 + X_1^2,$$

or,

(A11)
$$a = -X_1X_2.$$

But since $X_1X_2 \geq 0$, we have $a \leq 0$.   Q.E.D. (Lemma A1).

To prove lemma A2, we must prove that $E(X^2|X = 1) \leq 1$; that is, $a + b \leq 1$.

From equations (A10) and (A11) above,

$$a + b = -X_1X_2 + X_2 + X_1 = (1 - X_1)X_2 + X_1.$$

But, since $X_2 \leq 1, (1 - X_1) \geq 0$, and $X_1 \geq 0$, we have

$$(1 - X_1)X_2 + X_1 \leq (1 - X_1) + X_1,$$

or

$$(1 - X_1)X_2 + X_1 \leq 1.$$

Q.E.D. (Lemma A2).

PART 3: PROOF THAT IF $\beta_2 > 0$ AND b_4 IS SET TO ZERO, |GOODMAN AGGREGATION BIAS| $\geq$ |QUADRATIC AGGREGATION BIAS|

Let us compare estimates of q. This will serve as a proof for p, as well; since X_j is a linear function of $1 - X_j$, a proof for the error in one handles the other as well. The quadratic estimator of q when b_4 is assumed zero is $\hat{\beta}_0$, whose expectation is β_0, which by equation (A3) equals b_3. Since the actual expectation of q, from equation (A8), is

$$b_3 + b_4 \frac{\sum(n_{xj} n_{\bar{x}j}/n_j)}{n_{\bar{x}}},$$

then the expected quadratic aggregation bias is

$$b_3 - b_3 - b_4 \frac{\sum(n_{xj} n_{\bar{x}j}/n_j)}{n_{\bar{x}}} = -b_4 \frac{\sum(n_{xj} n_{\bar{x}j}/n_j)}{n_{\bar{x}}}.$$

From equation (A9), the expected Goodman bias is

$$[\overline{(X^2)} - d_{21}\bar{X}]\beta_2 - b_4 \frac{\sum(n_{xj} n_{\bar{x}j}/n_j)}{n_{\bar{x}}}.$$

But since d_{21} is the linear regression slope of X_j^2 on X_j, the term in brackets is the intercept in the linear regression of X_j^2 on X_j, which we proved to be nonpositive in lemma A1. Therefore, $[\overline{(X^2)} - d_{21}\bar{X}]\beta_2$ is nonpositive, since $\beta_2 > 0$. If $b_4 \geq 0$, then all the terms inside the absolute value signs are nonpositive, and hence,

$$\left| [\overline{(X^2)} - d_{21}\bar{X}]\beta_2 - b_4 \frac{\sum(n_{xj} n_{\bar{x}j}/n_j)}{n_{\bar{x}}} \right| \geq \left| -b_4 \frac{\sum(n_{xj} n_{\bar{x}j}/n_j)}{n_{\bar{x}}} \right|.$$

To avoid clutter, let us designate

$$\overline{(X^2)} - d_{21}\bar{X} = d,$$

with d therefore nonpositive, and

$$\frac{\sum(n_{xj} n_{\bar{x}j}/n_j)}{n_{\bar{x}}} = c,$$

with $c \geq 0$, since all ns are nonnegative. Then |Goodman bias| $= |\beta_2 d - b_4 c|$ and |quadratic bias| $= |-b_4 c|$, and

(A12) |Goodman bias| $-$ |quadratic bias| $= |\beta_2 d - b_4 c| - |-b_4 c|$.

Now, if $b_4 \geq 0$, then since $\beta_2 d$ and $-b_4 c$ have the same sign, this will equal $|\beta_2 d|$, which is greater than or equal to zero. That is, if we can assume $b_4 \geq 0$, and if $\beta_2 > 0$ and we set b_4 to zero, then |Goodman aggregation bias| $\geq$ |quadratic aggregation bias|. Q.E.D.

PART 4: PROOF THAT IF $\beta_2 < 0$ AND b_2 IS SET TO ZERO, |GOODMAN AGGREGATION BIAS| $\geq$ |QUADRATIC AGGREGATION BIAS|

This proof proceeds in direct parallel to the proof for $\beta_2 > 0$ and b_4 set to zero, above.

First, let us compare estimates of p. As explained in part 3 above, this will do for q as well.

The quadratic estimator of p when b_2 is set to zero is $E(\hat{\beta}_0 + \hat{\beta}_1 + \hat{\beta}_2) = \beta_0 + \beta_1 + \beta_2 = b_1 + b_2$, from equations (A3)–(A5). Since the actual expectation of p from equation (7) in the text is

$$b_1 + b_2 \frac{\sum(n_{xj}^2/n_j)}{n_x},$$

the quadratic aggregation bias is

$$b_1 + b_2 - b_1 - b_2 \frac{\sum(n_{xj}^2/n_j)}{n_x} = b_2\left[1 - \frac{\sum(n_{xj}^2/n_j)}{n_x}\right].$$

From equation (A7), the Goodman aggregation bias is

$$\beta_2[\overline{(X^2)} + (1 - \bar{X})d_{21} - 1] + b_2\left[1 - \frac{\sum(n_{xj}^2/n_j)}{n_x}\right].$$

But since $\overline{(X^2)} + (1 - \bar{X})d_{21} = \overline{(X^2)} - d_{21}\bar{X} + d_{21} \cdot 1$ is $E(X_j^2|X_j = 1)$ from a linear regression of X_j^2 on X_j, which we proved in lemma A2 to be less than or equal to one, the term in brackets which is multiplied by β_2 is nonpositive. Since β_2 is negative, the product of the two is nonnegative.

Let us designate

$$\overline{(X^2)} + (1 - \bar{X})d_{21} - 1 = d',$$

with d' therefore nonpositive, and

$$1 - \frac{\sum(n_{xj}^2/n_j)}{n_x} = c',$$

with $c' \geq 0$, since

$$\frac{\sum(n_{xj}^2/n_j)}{n_x} = \frac{\sum n_{xj}(n_{xj}/n_j)}{\sum n_{xj}}$$

and $n_{xj} \leq n_j$. Then |Goodman bias| $= |\beta_2 d' + b_2 c'|$ and |quadratic bias| $= |b_2 c'|$. That is,

(A13) |Goodman bias| $-$ |quadratic bias| $= |\beta_2 d' + b_2 c'| - |b_2 c'|$.

Now, if $b_2 \geq 0$, then since both $\beta_2 d'$ and $b_2 c'$ are nonnegative, this will equal $|\beta_2 d'|$, which is greater than or equal to zero. That is, if we can assume $b_2 \geq 0$, and if $\beta_2 < 0$ and we set b_2 to zero, then |Goodman bias| − |quadratic bias| ≥ 0. Q.E.D.

APPENDIX B

Proof that In the Expectation Aggregation Error Using the Quadratic Ecological Regression Model Is Less Than or Equal to Aggregation Error Using Linear Ecological Regression, Given the Assumptions of Equations (1) and (2) plus a Bayesian Indifference Prior

IF $\beta_2 > 0$ AND b_4 IS SET TO ZERO

We adopt the Bayesian regression model with an indifference prior, so that the mean of the posterior is the OLS estimate. Hence, we have from equation (A12) of appendix A that

$$|\text{Goodman bias}| - |\text{quadratic bias}| = |\beta_2 d - b_4 c| - |-b_4 c|,$$

with $d \leq 0$ and $c \geq 0$.

There are four possible situations with regard to the difference between biases:

1. If $b_4 \geq 0$, then $|\beta_2 d - b_4 c| - |-b_4 c| = |\beta_2 d|$, since if $b_4 \geq 0$ and $\beta_2 > 0$, $\beta_2 d$ and $-b_4 c$ have the same sign.

2. If $b_4 < 0$ and $|b_4 c| \geq |\beta_2 d|$, then $|\beta_2 d - b_4 c| \leq |-b_4 c|$, since $\beta_2 d$ and $-b_4 c$ have opposite signs, and therefore,

$$|\beta_2 d - b_4 c| - |-b_4 c| = -|\beta_2 d|.$$

3. If $b_4 < 0$ and $|2b_4 c| \geq |\beta_2 d| \geq |b_4 c|$, again $|\beta_2 d - b_4 c| \leq |-b_4 c|$, since with $|2b_4 c| \geq |\beta_2 d|$ the difference between $\beta_2 d$ and $b_4 c$ must be less than $|b_4 c|$. But now, $|\beta_2 d - b_4 c| = |\beta_2 d| - |b_4 c|$, since $|\beta_2 d| > |b_4 c|$ and the signs of $\beta_2 d$ and $-b_4 c$ are opposite; therefore,

$$|\beta_2 d - b_4 c| - |-b_4 c| = |\beta_2 d| - 2|b_4 c|$$
$$= |\beta_2 d| - |2b_4 c|.$$

But, since $|2b_4 c| \geq |\beta_2 d|$ and the signs of $\beta_2 d$ and $-2b_4 c$ are opposite, we have

$$|\beta_2 d - b_4 c| - |-b_4 c| = -|\beta_2 d - 2b_4 c|.$$

4. If $b_4 < 0$ and $|\beta_2 d| > |2b_4 c|$, now $|\beta_2 d - b_4 c| > |-b_4 c|$, because the difference between $\beta_2 d$ and $b_4 c$ is now greater than $b_4 c$; therefore,

$$|\beta_2 d - b_4 c| - |-b_4 c| = |\beta_2 d - 2b_4 c|.$$

In order to calculate the expected $|\beta_2 d - b_4 c| - |-b_4 c|$ across these four possibilities, we must sum the products of their values times the probability of each occuring. If we have no prior information about the deviation of b_4 from zero, then

$$\text{Prob}(b_4 \geq 0) = .5.$$

Let us also designate

$$\text{Prob}(b_4 < 0 \ \& \ |b_4 c| \geq |\beta_2 d|) = f,$$

$$\text{Prob}(b_4 < 0 \ \& \ |2b_4 c| \geq |\beta_2 d| > |b_4 c|) = g,$$

$$\text{Prob}(b_4 < 0 \ \& \ |\beta_2 d| > |2b_4 c|) = h,$$

and

$$f + g + h = .5.$$

To calculate the expected difference between Goodman bias and quadratic bias if $b_4 \neq 0$, we multiply each of these probabilities by its associated difference in biases, $|\beta_2 d - b_4 c| - |-b_4 c|$:

$$E(|\beta_2 d - b_4 c| - |-b_4 c|)$$
$$= .5|\beta_2 d| - f|\beta_2 d| - g|\beta_2 d - 2b_4 c| + h|\beta_2 d - 2b_4 c|.$$

Across the range of possibilities encompassed by probability g, $|2b_4 c| \geq |\beta_2 d| > |b_4 c|$. But if this is so, then

$$2b_4 c - 2b_4 c \leq \beta_2 d - 2b_4 c < b_4 c - 2b_4 c,$$

since $\beta_2 d \leq 0$ and $b_4 c \leq 0$, or

$$0 \leq \beta_2 d - 2b_4 c < -b_4 c.$$

Therefore, $|\beta_2 d - 2b_4 c| < |-b_4 c|$, but $|\beta_2 d| > |b_4 c|$, so

$$|\beta_2 d - 2b_4 c| < |\beta_2 d|.$$

Multiplying through by g, we obtain

$$g|\beta_2 d - 2b_4 c| < g|\beta_2 d|.$$

Thus,

$$E(|\text{Goodman bias}| - |\text{quadratic bias}|)$$
$$\geq .5|\beta_2 d| - f|\beta_2 d| - g|\beta_2 d| + h|\beta_2 d - 2b_4 c|.$$

But, since $h|\beta_2 d - 2b_4 c| \geq 0$ and $f + g + h = .5$, we have $(f + g)|\beta_2 d| \leq .5|\beta_2 d|$, and therefore,

$$E(|\text{Goodman bias}| - |\text{quadratic bias}|) \geq 0.$$

Q.E.D.

IF $\beta_2 < 0$ AND b_2 IS SET TO ZERO

We have from equation (A13) of appendix A that

$$|\text{Goodman bias}| - |\text{quadratic bias}| = |\beta_2 d' + b_2 c'| - |b_2 c'|,$$

with $d' \leq 0$ and $c' \geq 0$.

There are four possible situations with regard to the difference between biases:

1. If $b_2 \geq 0$, then $|\beta_2 d' + b_2 c'| - |b_2 c'| = |\beta_2 d'|$, since both $\beta_2 d'$ and $b_2 c'$ are then nonnegative.
2. If $b_2 < 0$ and $|b_2 c'| \geq |\beta_2 d'|$, then $|\beta_2 d' + b_2 c'| - |b_2 c'| = -|\beta_2 d'|$, similarly to what was shown above for $b_4 < 0$ and $|b_4 c| \geq |\beta_2 d|$.
3. If $b_2 < 0$ and $|2b_2 c'| \geq |\beta_2 d'| > |b_2 c'|$, then $|\beta_2 d' + b_2 c'| - |b_2 c'| = -|\beta_2 d' + 2b_2 c'|$, similarly to what was shown above for $b_4 < 0$ and $|2b_4 c| \geq |\beta_2 d| > |b_4 c|$.
4. If $b_2 < 0$ and $|\beta_2 d'| > |2b_2 c'|$, then $|\beta_2 d' + b_2 c'| - |b_2 c'| = |\beta_2 d' + 2b_2 c'|$, similarly to what was shown above for $b_4 < 0$ and $|\beta_2 d| > |2b_4 c|$.

If we have no prior information about the probabilities, then

$$\text{Prob}(b_2 \geq 0) = .5.$$

Let us also designate

$$\text{Prob}(b_2 < 0 \ \& \ |b_2 c'| \geq |\beta_2 d'|) = f',$$

$$\text{Prob}(b_2 < 0 \ \& \ |2b_2 c'| \geq |\beta_2 d'| > |b_2 c'|) = g',$$

$$\text{Prob}(b_2 < 0 \ \& \ |\beta_2 d'| > |2b_2 c'|) = h',$$

and

$$f' + g' + h' = .5.$$

The expected difference between Goodman bias and quadratic bias if $b_2 \neq 0$, then, is

$$E(|\beta_2 d' + b_2 c'| - |b_2 c'|)$$

$$= .5|\beta_2 d'| - f'|\beta_2 d'| - g'|\beta_2 d' + 2b_2 c'| + h'|\beta_2 d' + 2b_2 c'|.$$

Across the range of possibilities encompassed by probability g', $b_2 < 0$; and $|2b_2 c'| \geq |\beta_2 d'| > |b_2 c'|$. But if this is so, then

$$-b_2 c' < \beta_2 d' \leq -2b_2 c',$$

since $\beta_2 d' \geq 0$ and $b_2 c' \leq 0$, or

$$-b_2 c' + 2b_2 c' < \beta_2 d' + 2b_2 c' \leq -2b_2 c' + 2b_2 c',$$

or

$$b_2 c' < \beta_2 d' + 2b_2 c' \leq 0.$$

Therefore,

$$|\beta_2 d' + 2b_2 c'| \leq |b_2 c'|,$$

since both terms are nonpositive. But under the conditions spanning probability g',

$$|b_2 c'| < |\beta_2 d'|.$$

Therefore,

$$|\beta_2 d' + 2b_2 c'| \leq |\beta_2 d'|.$$

Substituting into the expectation above, we obtain

$$E(|\beta_2 d' + b_2 c'| - |b_2 c'|)$$

$$\geq .5|\beta_2 d'| - f'|\beta_2 d'| - g'|\beta_2 d'| + h'|\beta_2 d' + 2b_2 c'|.$$

But, since $(f' + g')|\beta_2 d'| \leq .5|\beta_2 d'|$ and $h'|\beta_2 d' + 2b_2 c'| \geq 0$, we have

$$E(|\text{Goodman bias}| - |\text{quadratic bias}|) \geq 0.$$

Q.E.D.

SIX

RELAXING THE GOODMAN ASSUMPTIONS

Working with Underidentified Models

We showed in chapter 5 that a quadratic model offers a form of ecological regression equal or superior to the linear model of Goodman which is in general use. The quadratic model offers an underidentified system in the parameters that are needed if we are to estimate p and q, but by assuming that one parameter (alternatively b_2 or b_4) equals zero we were able to achieve identification. Since linear ecological regression requires for identification that both equal zero, the quadratic model is superior; it requires only a subset of the Goodman assumptions and reduces aggregation bias frequently present in standard ecological regression.

Like the linear model, the quadratic model if used in this way still leaves some potential aggregation error in the estimates, covered by the rather arbitrary assumption of $b_2 = 0$ or $b_4 = 0$ (less arbitrary than Goodman's $b_2 = b_4 = 0$, but still arbitrary). It is possible, however, to use the quadratic model more flexibly, making no direct assumptions about either b_2 or b_4. Though the quadratic model is underidentified with regard to b_1, b_2, b_3, and b_4, it does offer us partial information about them. If we combine this partial information with explicit substantive assumptions about the process being studied, we may obtain narrow ranges of possible values for p and q, or even in some cases point estimates.

This general quadratic approach maximizes flexibility. Assumptions do not come off the rack, but are explicitly controlled by the researcher, whose prior knowledge and theory are involved in the analysis in a rather Bayesian spirit. While the result will probably more often be a range than a point estimate, this just reflects honestly the researcher's uncertainty about aggregation effects.

We present below examples of what are in fact a family of methods that involve incorporating into a quadratic ecological regression model the assumption that p_j and q_j are related to the aggregate independent variable. The approach is flexible, encompassing linear as well as non-linear aggregate models and allowing for the incorporation of a variety of external assumptions or parameters. As a result, there is no set procedure to present here, but rather a general concept which must be adapted by the investigator to a particular problem. However, we do present in the appendix one particular algorithm which we believe will apply to most studies of electoral stability and change.

As you will recall from chapter 5, we assumed linear relationships between p_j and q_j and the aggregate variable X_j, with p the probability that an x is y and q the probability that an $\tilde{x}$ is y in the parent population.[1] That is,

$$(1) \qquad\qquad E(p_j) = b_1 + b_2 X_j$$

and

$$(2) \qquad\qquad E(q_j) = b_3 + b_4 X_j.$$

We showed then that, in the quadratic regression equation

$$E(Y_j) = \beta_0 + \beta_1 X_j + \beta_2 X_j^2,$$

each β equals a set of the bs:

$$(3) \qquad\qquad \beta_0 = b_3,$$

$$(4) \qquad\qquad \beta_1 = b_1 - b_3 + b_4,$$

$$(5) \qquad\qquad \beta_2 = b_2 - b_4.$$

Equations (3), (4), and (5) are a set of three simultaneous equations in the four unknown b parameters, so the system is underidentified. In chapter 5 we identified the system by assuming $b_2 = 0$ or $b_4 = 0$. In this chapter we will explore the possibilities of working with the underidentified system, adding explicit theoretical or empirical assumptions in order to achieve tight estimates without relying on arbitrary assumptions.

---

1. See above, pp. 118–19, for the layout that is summarized briefly here. An earlier version of the material presented in this chapter is Shively (1987a).

THE STOKES EXAMPLE AGAIN

In chapter 5 we compared the results of quadratic and linear ecological regression using Donald Stokes's example of the 1964 and 1966 British elections.[2] Let us see what we can do with this example using the quadratic model more flexibly. As the reader will recall, the quadratic regression analysis yielded the following, where $C66$ is the Conservative proportion of the 1966 vote, and $C64$ is the Conservative proportion of the 1964 vote:

(6)
$$C66 = .010 + .783\ C64 + .239\ C64^2.$$
$$(.015)\quad (.077)\qquad (.093)$$

Standard errors are given in parentheses; $R^2 = .974$. The mean of $C64$, hereafter referred to as $\bar{X}$, is .412; the mean of $C66$ is .376. Substituting into equations (3), (4), and (5) we obtained for this case

(7)
$$b_3 = .010,$$

(8)
$$b_1 - b_3 + b_4 = .783,$$

(9)
$$b_2 - b_4 = .239.$$

Equations (7)–(9) can be manipulated so as to offer us estimates of p and q based on a variety of substantive assumptions. We shall first present the manipulation which seems to us the most useful, and then discuss other possible manipulations which could have been performed.

From equations (1) and (2), we see that for the case of $X_j = .5$, the expectations of p_j and q_j can be calculated as follows:

(10)
$$E(p|X_j = .5) = b_1 + .5b_2,$$

(11)
$$E(q|X_j = .5) = b_3 + .5b_4.$$

As it turns out, these expectations at $X_j = .5$ have some useful characteristics for us as we work with them below.

Now, by combining our estimates of β_0, β_1, and β_2 in varying ways we can construct sums which are either greater than or less than $E(p_j)$ and which may serve as bounds around the true value of $E(p_j)$.[3] Let us

---

2. See above, pp. 124–28.

3. Note that $E(p_j)$ is the expected value of p across the j units; it is *not* necessarily $\hat{p}$, the expectation of p across individuals. See above, pp. 121–23.

construct bounds of this sort involving $E(p|X_j = .5)$ and $E(q|X_j = .5)$. From equations (3)–(5), we know

$$(12) \quad 2\beta_0 + \beta_1 + \beta_2\bar{X} = 2(b_3) + (b_1 - b_3 + b_4) + (b_2 - b_4)\bar{X}$$
$$= b_1 + b_2\bar{X} + b_3 + b_4(1 - \bar{X}).$$

Now we note that, since equation (1) is linear, $E(p_j)$ equals $E(p|X_j = \bar{X})$. From equation (1) we see then that $E(p_j) = b_1 + b_2\bar{X}_j$. Substituting into equation (12), we obtain

$$2\beta_0 + \beta_1 + \beta_2\bar{X} = E(p_j) + b_3 + b_4(1 - \bar{X})$$
$$(13) \qquad = E(p_j) + b_3 + .5b_4 + b_4(1 - .5 - \bar{X})$$
$$= E(p_j) + E(q|X_j = .5) + b_4(1 - .5 - \bar{X}).$$

Now, from equation (11), rearranging terms and multiplying both sides by 2, we know that

$$(14) \qquad b_4 = 2E(q|X_j = .5) - 2b_3.$$

Substituting this for b_4 in equation (13), we see that

$$2\beta_0 + \beta_1 + \beta_2\bar{X} = E(p_j) + E(q|X_j = .5) +$$
$$[2E(q|X_j = .5) - 2b_3](1 - .5 - \bar{X})$$
$$= E(p_j) + E(q|X_j = .5) +$$
$$2E(q|X_j = .5)(1 - .5 - \bar{X}) -$$
$$2\beta_0(1 - .5 - \bar{X}),$$

since $\beta_0 = b_3$, or

$$2\beta_0 + \beta_1 + \beta_2\bar{X} + 2\beta_0(1 - .5 - \bar{X}) =$$
$$E(p_j) + E(q|X_j = .5)[1 + 2(1 - .5 - \bar{X})].$$

Substituting our estimates of $\beta_0, \beta_1,$ and β_2 and noting that $\bar{X} = .412$, we find that

$$(15) \qquad .903 = E(p_j) + 1.176E(q|X_j = .5).$$

Since $E(q|X_j = .5)$ is nonnegative, .903 is an upper bound of $E(p_j)$.

Similarly, we can establish a lower bound:

$$\beta_2(\bar{X} - .5) = (b_2 - b_4)\bar{X} - .5(b_2 - b_4)$$
$$= b_2\bar{X} - b_4\bar{X} - .5b_2 + .5b_4$$
$$= b_1 + b_2\bar{X} - b_1 - .5b_2 + .5b_4 - b_4\bar{X}$$
$$= E(p_i) - E(p|X_i = .5) + (.5 - \bar{X})b_4,$$

from equations (1) and (10);

$$\beta_2(\bar{X} - .5) = E(p_i) - E(p|X_i = .5) +$$
$$2E(q|X_i = .5)(.5 - \bar{X}) - 2b_3(.5 - \bar{X}),$$

from equation (14), or

$$\beta_2(\bar{X} - .5) + 2\beta_0(.5 - \bar{X}) =$$
$$E(p_i) - E(p|X_i = .5) + 2E(q|X_i = .5)(.5 - \bar{X}).$$

Substituting as above we find that

(16) $-.019 = E(p_i) - E(p|X_i = .5) + .176E(q|X_i = .5).$

Since $E(p|X_i = .5)$ and $E(q|X_i = .5)$ are nonnegative and since we can assume that $E(p|X_i = .5)$ is greater than $E(q|X_i = .5)$, $-.019$ provides a lower bound for $E(p_i)$.

Now, bounds of $-.019$ and $.903$ around $E(p_i)$ would be a classic example of bounds which are so wide as to be nearly useless, except that we may add substantive assumptions to narrow them. First, we have set these bounds up in terms of $E(q|X_i = .5)$ and $E(p|X_i = .5)$, quantities concerning which we may feel justified in making some assumptions. Any portion of the relationships described by equations (1) and (2) that may be due to contextual effects should be neutralized at $X_i = .5$. At $X_i = .5$ there should be no net pressure in favor of either the Labour or Conservative party; their partisans are evenly matched in such a district, so we should expect no contextual "breakage."[4]

More important, we note that 1966 was a strong Labour year; in

---

4. Under "breakage" effects, the more highly x individuals are concentrated in a district, the greater the probability that an x will be a y, and the greater the probability that an $\tilde{x}$ will be a y. This effect was first described by Berelson et al. (1954, chap. 7); two other early analyses are Miller (1956) and Putnam (1966). The assumption here is more convenient than crucial. Expectations had to be set to some value, and this eliminates some baggage.

1966, Labour received 49% of the vote nationally, compared with 45% in 1964. In such a year, in districts with contextual effects neutral, we should expect only a fairly small proportion of Labour voters to have shifted to the Conservatives. Operationally, we should be able to assume that $p|(X_j = .5)$, the loyalty rate of Conservative voters, is at least 10 times $q|(X_j = .5)$, the rate at which Labour voters defect to the Conservatives.

This assumption is based on our general knowledge of the loyalty of voters in mature democracies. As it happens, we also have available survey results which suggest that it is reasonable; Särlvik and Crewe (1983) show ratios of 10, 32, and 23.5, respectively, for the 1970 and 1974, the February 1974 and October 1974, and the 1974 and 1979 elections among British electoral panels. Since we were trying to simulate the difficulties of field and historical research, our assumption of a ratio of at least 10 was made without looking at such helpful side evidence, and we also obviously did not adjust it once we had checked our results against the Butler-Stokes panel results. In general, however, there is ample evidence and experience to suggest an assumption such as a ratio of at least 10.

Most important, we show in a robustness test below (table 1) that estimation is tolerant of a fairly wide range of assumed ratios; anything from a ratio of approximately 6 on up gives fairly similar results. As we show below, the investigator can readily test the robustness of substantive assumptions added to a general quadratic analysis. This should always be done.

Now, to blend the substantive assumption with the quadratic analysis: subtracting the right side of equation (16) from that of equation (15), we find that the range of .923 between the bounds equals $E(q|X_j = .5) + E(p|X_j = .5)$. From equation (15) we see, multiplying one term by

$$\frac{E(q|X_j = .5) + E(p|X_j = .5)}{E(q|X_j = .5) + E(p|X_j = .5)},$$

that

$$E(p_j) = .903 - \frac{1.176E(q|X_j = .5)}{E(q|X_j = .5) + E(p|X_j = .5)}$$

$$\cdot [E(q|X_j = .5) + E(p|X_j = .5)],$$

or

$$E(p_j) = .903 - \frac{1.176E(q|X_j = .5)}{E(q|X_j = .5) + E(p|X_j = .5)}(.923).$$

But if we add the substantive assumption that $E(p|X_i = .5) \geq 10E(q|X_i = .5)$, then

$$E(p_i) \geq .903 - \frac{1.176E(q|X_i = .5)}{11E(q|X_i = .5)}(.923),$$

or

(17) $$E(p_i) \geq .805.$$

Equations (15) and (17) allow us to put reasonably tight bounds of .805 and .903 around the true value of $E(p_i)$.

To put bounds around the population p, rather than $E(p_i)$, it is necessary to recover the estimates of b_1 and b_2 implicit in each bound of $E(p_i)$. Recalling (from p. 144) that $E(p_i) = b_1 + b_2\overline{X}$, we see that the upper bound of .903 implies that

$$.903 = b_1 + .412b_2.$$

Adding both sides of equations (7)–(9) gives us a second equation in b_1 and b_2: $b_1 + b_2 = 1.032$. The two equations allow us to solve for the b_1 and b_2 implied in $E(p_i) = .903$: $b_1 = .814$ and $b_2 = .218$. We then use these, as was done above (p. 120) to calculate the corresponding estimate of p:

$$\hat{p} \leq b_1 + b_2\frac{\overline{(X^2)}}{\overline{X}} = .814 + (.218)\frac{.181}{.412} = .910.$$

Similarly we calculate the lower bound of $\hat{p}$ that corresponds to an $E(p_i)$ of .805:

$$\hat{p} \geq .646 + (.386)\frac{.181}{.412} = .816.$$

Thus, we arrive at bounds of .816 and .910, or $\hat{p} = .863 \pm .047$.[5] This estimate has required only the linearity assumptions of equations (1) and (2), combined with the substantive assumption that $E(p|X_i = .5) \geq 10E(q|X_i = .5)$.

Similarly, we can estimate q and two important differences, $p - q$ and $(1 - q) - p$. The first of these differences, if we were relating

---

5. In the terms used to describe the method of bounds in chap. 8, we would take the midpoint of the bounds as our best estimate: .863, with a mean error of estimate of .024.

TABLE 1 Robustness Check for Cross-Level Estimates

Assumption	$\hat{p}$	$\hat{q}$	$\hat{p} - \hat{q}$	$(1 - \hat{q}) - \hat{p}$
$E(p\|X_j = .5) \geq 16E(q\|X_j = .5)$	$.88 \pm .03$	$.02 \pm .02$	$.86 \pm .05$	$.10 \pm .01$
$E(p\|X_j = .5) \geq 14E(q\|X_j = .5)$	$.87 \pm .03$	$.03 \pm .02$	$.85 \pm .06$	$.10 \pm .01$
$E(p\|X_j = .5) \geq 12E(q\|X_j = .5)$	$.87 \pm .04$	$.03 \pm .03$	$.84 \pm .07$	$.10 \pm .01$
$E(p\|X_j = .5) \geq 10E(q\|X_j = .5)$	$.86 \pm .05$	$.04 \pm .03$	$.83 \pm .08$	$.10 \pm .01$
$E(p\|X_j = .5) \geq 8E(q\|X_j = .5)$	$.85 \pm .06$	$.04 \pm .04$	$.81 \pm .10$	$.11 \pm .02$
$E(p\|X_j = .5) \geq 6E(q\|X_j = .5)$	$.83 \pm .07$	$.05 \pm .05$	$.78 \pm .13$	$.11 \pm .02$
$E(p\|X_j = .5) \geq 4E(q\|X_j = .5)$	$.81 \pm .10$	$.07 \pm .07$	$.73 \pm .18$	$.12 \pm .03$

social class to vote rather than relating vote at time 1 to vote at time 2, would be the "Alford index" of class voting (Alford 1963). The second difference is the difference between the loyalty rates of the two parties' voters, since $1 - q$ is the proportion of Labour voters repeating a Labour vote. We estimate q to be $.036 \pm .034$, $p - q$ to be $.827 \pm .081$, and $(1 - q) - p$ to be $.101 \pm .013$.[6]

We can assess the robustness of the four cross-level estimates relative to our substantive assumption that $E(p|X_j = .5) \geq 10E(q|X_j = .5)$ by repeating the estimation, assuming different ratios each time. Such a robustness check is presented in table 1. As the assumed ratios rise above 10, the estimates of p and q do not change greatly. As the ratios drop below 10 the estimates are reasonably stable through 6; below that level they begin to change fairly rapidly. This produces a good safety margin in our assumption, since it is highly unlikely, in the 1966 Labour landslide, that Labour defection rates would have been greater than one-sixth as high as Conservative loyalty.

We can also see in the table, as will always be true of analysis conducted in this mode, that $p - q$ is the least stable estimate. It ranges from .73 to .86, as the assumed ratio varies from 4 to 16. The estimates of p and q are each more stable than this, and $(1 - q) - p$ is remarkably stable, ranging only from .10 to .12. The reason for this is that the ranges of uncertainty in p and q accumulate in $p - q$, but cancel in $(1 - q) - p$. As a result, this technique will generally produce especially good estimates of $(1 - q) - p$, the difference in loyalty rates of the two parties.

---

6. Once bounds have been placed around q, bounds for q are most easily estimated from the equation $\bar{Y} = p\bar{X} + q(1 - \bar{X})$.

TABLE 2 Comparison of Cross-Level Estimates with
Estimates from the Butler-Stokes Panel

	Panel	Cross-Level Estimate
$\hat{p}$	.87	$.86 \pm .05$
$\hat{q}$	.03	$.04 \pm .03$
$\hat{p} - \hat{q}$	.84	$.83 \pm .08$
$(1 - \hat{q}) - \hat{p}$	.10	$.10 \pm .01$

Table 2 compares cross-level estimates based on the assumption of $E(p|X_i = .5) \geq 10E(q|X_i = .5)$, with estimates from the Butler-Stokes panel.

DISCUSSION

Note what we did here. From the nonlinear aggregate relationship, and assuming as in equations (1) and (2) that the relationships between p_i and X_i and q_i and X_i were linear, we were able to estimate b_3, $b_1 - b_3 + b_4$, and $b_2 - b_4$. We then combined these estimates in equations (15) and (17) to obtain $E(p_i)$ plus or minus expected values of p and q at $X_i = .5$, quantities about which we could make reasonable substantive assumptions. From bounds around $E(p_i)$, we finally calculated bounds around the population p and population q.

There are a considerable variety of ways in which estimates of b_3, $b_1 - b_3 + b_4$, and $b_2 - b_4$ might be combined with substantive assumptions in order to construct usable bounds around p and q. For instance, it is possible to obtain in the manner above p plus or minus expected values of p and q at X_i equal to any value from zero to one; we chose .5 because in this investigation that value lent itself best to the use of substantive assumptions, but in a different investigation a different value might have been more useful.[7]

It is also possible to cast bounds of p plus or minus functions of b_1 and b_4. It can be shown, for instance that $\beta_0 + \beta_1 + \beta_2\bar{X} = E(p) + b_4(1 - \bar{X})$, and that $(\beta_0 + \beta_1 + \beta_2)\bar{X} = E(p) - b_1(1 - \bar{X})$. This yields bounds with a range of $(b_1 + b_4)(1 - \bar{X})$, and those bounds can be narrowed in the same manner as the Stokes example if we have avail-

---

7. As an example of this, note that $2\beta_0 + \beta_1 + \beta_2\bar{X}$ equals $E(p_i) + b_3 + b_4(1 - \bar{X})$, or $E(p_i) + E(q|X_i = (1 - \bar{X}))$.

able substantive assumptions relating b_1 and b_4. Similarly, bounds can be constructed in terms of b_1 and b_2 and b_2 and b_4.

Other sorts of assumptions may also be used. Shively (1987) suggests a technique, actually a special case of the more general approach suggested here, which is appropriate if we can assume an acceleration model in which both b_2 and b_4 are nonnegative. Such would be the case, for instance, if breakage contextual effects were dominant; it would also be the case if we set up the analysis such that we can assume $p > q$ (see above, note 3, chap. 5).

The point, if it is not already clear, is that an investigator may well be able to cast bounds around p and q which are constructed so that they can readily be combined with substantive assumptions to yield narrower bounds, narrow enough to produce useful estimation. The form of the bounds will depend on the investigator's creativity and on the availability of substantive assumptions.

Whatever form is used, it is important to check for robustness of the estimates relative to one's substantive assumptions, as was done in the example.

A PARTIAL CHECK ON THE ASSUMPTION OF LINEARITY

In addition to substantive assumptions added by the investigator, the strategy described here assumes that the relationships between p_j and X_j and q_j and X_j, as described in equations (1) and (2), are linear. A rough check on this assumption is possible, as noted by Goodman (1959, pp. 624, 625), in that linear relationships of the form in equations (1) and (2) will produce an aggregate relationship which is either linear (if $b_2 = b_4$) or quadratic in form. Most kinds of nonlinearity in the (p_j, X_j) and (q_j, X_j) relationships will produce aggregate relationships of a higher-power polynomial than the quadratic.[8] If we add an X_j^3 term to the quadratic linearity, and R^2 increases statistically significantly, we will know that either the (p_j, X_j) or the (q_j, X_j) relationship is nonlinear, or that both are. Absence of an increase in R^2, however, does not conclusively demonstrate linearity, since certain forms of non-

---

8. E.g., if $E(p_j) = b_1 + b_2 X_j + b_3 X_j^2$ and $E(q_j) = b_4 + b_5 X_j + b_6 X_j^2$, then $E(Y_j) = b_4 + (b_1 - b_4 + b_5)X_j + (b_2 - b_5 + b_6)X_j^2 + (b_3 - b_6)X_j^3$. But note that it is even possible for certain nonlinear functions of p_j and q_j on X_j to produce *linear* aggregate relationships.

linearity could combine to produce a zero parameter for powers of X_j above X_j^2.

As is seen in the W. S. Robinson example at the end of this chapter, another indication of non linearity in the (p_j, X_j) and (q_j, X_j) relationships will often be that estimation using a quadratic model produces logically impossible solutions. This parallels the common situation in standard ecological regression, in which a quadratic model is indicated by the fact that linear ecological regression produces illogical estimates such as negative proportions.

ANALYSIS OF LINEAR AGGREGATE MODELS

The general strategy suggested in this chapter is appropriate even when the aggregate relationship is linear, if we have doubts about the Goodman assumptions of constant $E(q_j)$ and $E(p_j)$ or about the less-demanding assumption introduced in chapter 5 that $E(q_j)$ or $E(p_j)$ is constant.

The approach suggested above is appropriate even for such linear results, since aggregate linearity is consistent with the quadratic system of equations (3)–(5). As seen in equation (5), all that a linear aggregate result demonstrates is that $b_2 = b_4$, since $\beta_2 = 0$; that is, the slopes of p and q on X_j are equal. This might be due to $b_2 = b_4 = 0$, in which case the Goodman assumptions are met; but there are many other ways as well in which b_2 could equal b_4, even when the Goodman assumptions are false. If one is in doubt about the Goodman assumptions, linear aggregate results may be analyzed by the simultaneous equation system

$$(18) \qquad\qquad b_3 = \beta_0,$$

$$(19) \qquad\qquad b_1 - b_3 + b_4 = \beta_1,$$

$$(20) \qquad\qquad b_2 - b_4 = 0.$$

As in the examples above, there are many ways in which one could proceed using this model. One general strategy, which sets us up to introduce substantive assumptions about the relative magnitude of $E(p_j)$ and $E(q_j)$, follows:

Noting from equation (20) that $b_2 = b_4$ and recalling that $E(p_j) = b_1 + b_2\overline{X}$, we see that $b_1 = E(p_j) - b_4\overline{X}$. Summing equations (18) and (19) we obtain $\beta_0 + \beta_1 = b_1 + b_4$. Substituting, we obtain

$$\beta_0 + \beta_1 = E(p_j) - b_4\overline{X} + b_4,$$

or, rearranging terms,

(21) $$E(p_i) = (\beta_0 + \beta_1) - (1 - \bar{X})b_4.$$

From equation (21), we can solve for b_4:

(22) $$b_4 = \frac{(\beta_0 + \beta_1) - E(p_i)}{1 - \bar{X}}.$$

Recalling that $E(q_i) = b_3 + b_4\bar{X}$, noting that $b_3 = \beta_0$, and substituting from equation (22), we obtain

(23) $$E(q_i) = \beta_0 + (\beta_0 + \beta_1)\frac{\bar{X}}{1 - \bar{X}} - \frac{\bar{X}}{1 - \bar{X}}E(p_i).$$

β_0, β_1, and $\bar{X}$ will be known from the analysis; thus $E(q_i)$ is a linear function of $E(p_i)$. Equation (23) allows us to construct and use substantive assumptions about the relative sizes of $E(p_i)$ and $E(q_i)$ in order to obtain identification.

As an example, let us return to the Stokes example of chapter 5—not the quadratic model, but the flawed linear model with which Stokes originally worked. We can apply our general method to the linear model as an example, although our results should be a bit less efficient than what we got using the quadratic model, since in this case there was significant, albeit gentle, nonlinearity present.

In the Stokes example, $\bar{X}$ is .412 and the aggregate linear regression gives the following results:

$$\beta_0 = -.03 = b_3 = E(q|X_i = 0),$$

$$\beta_1 = .97 = b_1 - b_3 + b_4.$$

The estimate for β_0 is illegal since q should be nonnegative at all values of X_i, but we can work with it anyway.

Applying these values in equation (23), we obtain

$$E(q_i) = -.03 + (.95)(.701) - .701E(p_i),$$

or

(24) $$E(q_i) + .701E(p_i) = .64.$$

This is of course an underidentified system of one equation in two unknowns. But if, as above, we are in a position to add a substantive assumption about the relationship between p_i and q_i, we can achieve identification. For the purposes of this illustration, let us use an assumption similar to what we used earlier for the analysis of Stokes's data:

$$E(p_i) \geq 10E(q_i).$$

Substituting into equation (24), we obtain

$$E(q_i) + 7.01E(q_i) \leq .64,$$

or

$$E(q_i) \leq .080.$$

The corresponding bound for the population q, calculated as above (p. 150), is

$$q \leq .087.$$

Since q is also nonnegative, we now have usable bounds around q:

$$0 \leq q \leq .087,$$

or

$$q = .0435 \pm .0435.$$

Note that earlier, using the quadratic aggregate regression, we obtained the somewhat better estimate of $q = .036 \pm .034$. There is no more difference than this between the results from the two models because the nonlinearity in this case was rather slight, as seen in figure 2 of chapter 5.

Note what we have done here. Given a linear model for which we were uncertain about the validity of the Goodman assumptions, we simply treated it as a quadratic model with a zero term for β_2. This transformed it from an identified system requiring the Goodman assumptions that $b_2 = b_4 = 0$ (or the assumption required by our model introduced in chap. 5 that $b_2 = 0$ or $b_4 = 0$) to an underidentified system with none of these assumptions. Adding a substantive assumption of our own choosing, we were then able to achieve usable bounds. And the estimate so obtained compares well with the estimate of .03 from an individual-level panel survey (table 2).

W. S. ROBINSON'S EXAMPLE OF ILLITERACY AND FOREIGN BIRTH

It might be objected that the technique presented above would work well in strong, well-ordered causal systems such as the Stokes example, but would fail in the messy analyses we more typically face. A good case to explore this possibility is the horrible example by which W. S.

Robinson (1950) first demonstrated the "fallacy" of ecological correlations. Working through this example will serve also to illustrate some techniques for achieving quasi identification in difficult cases.

Using 1930 census data, Robinson showed that geographically aggregated data indicated a strong negative relationship between being born abroad and being illiterate in English, even though individual data from the census showed a modest *positive* relationship. Robinson used regional data, presumably because of the difficulty of calculating correlations by hand in 1950, but in the example below we will use state data from the 1930 census.

The basic result is the same; the simple correlation between percentage foreign-born and percentage illiterate, by state, is −.523, and standard ecological regression would indicate that .09 of native-born Americans were illiterate, compared with −.14 of foreign-born Americans; individual data, however, show that only .04 of native-born Americans, but .10 of foreign-born, were in fact illiterate. The scattergram in figure 1 reveals a relationship that is certainly messy enough for our purposes.

As the reader will see below, it turns out that even a quadratic fit is insufficient, and a third-degree polynomial model, with attendant problems of collinearity, is required. Once we had set the Robinson challenge for ourselves, we found that it was perhaps more than we had bargained for. However, in the end it yields a simple and reasonably good estimate.

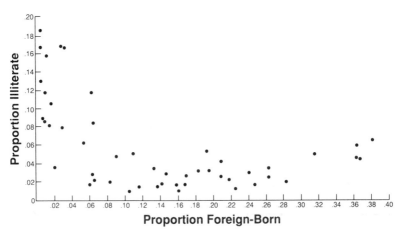

Figure 1. Illiteracy and proportion foreign-born, by state

Let us start with the abortive attempt at estimation from a quadratic model.

A quadratic regression model gives a reasonable fit to the data, with adjusted R^2 of .59.[9] Its parameters are

$$I = .126 - 1.006F + 2.264F^2,$$
$$\quad\;\; (.009) \quad (.131) \quad\;\; (.363)$$

where I is the proportion of states' populations illiterate in English and F is the proportion who are foreign-born whites. Standard errors are given in parentheses.

From equations (3), (4), and (5), we derive the three simultaneous equations

(25) $$b_3 = .126,$$

(26) $$b_1 - b_3 + b_4 = -1.006,$$

(27) $$b_2 - b_4 = 2.264.$$

Two substantive assumptions present themselves, by which we might expand this system of equations; they will also be used for the higher-order model. First, it seems reasonable to assume that p_j, the proportion of the foreign-born who are illiterate in English, is a non-negative function of the concentration of foreign-born. Where one-third or so of the population are foreign-born, it is more likely that foreign-born residents are able to read newspapers printed in their native language, do daily business in their native language, and so on, than in states where only 1% or 2% of the population are foreign-born. In the latter states, the pressures on the foreign-born to learn English are greater. Therefore, we might reasonably assume that b_2 is nonnegative.

Partly aided by this assumption, and partly by our knowledge of education and society circa 1930 in those states which have high concentrations of foreign-born, we assume further that, in states with a quarter or more of their population foreign-born, the foreign-born are at least as illiterate as natives; that is, where $F_j \geq .25$, $p_j \geq q_j$. This assumption will allow us to achieve near identification.

9. Note that we use unweighted regression even though the states varied widely in the size of their populations (see above, pp. 57–60). We also did not weight to correct for heteroscedasticity, assuming that, as in the Stokes example above, the correction would have made little difference in the results.

At $F_j = .25$, the expected value of illiteracy for the population as a whole predicted from the quadratic equation is .016, the lowest value for any $F_j \geq .25$. This, together with our assumption, implies that the illiteracy rate for natives is no greater than .016, or

$$0 \leq E(q|F_j = .25) \leq .016,$$

or

$$(28) \qquad\qquad 0 \leq (b_3 + .25b_4) \leq .016,$$

which together with equations (25)–(27) yields near-identification of the system.

However, there is a massive clinker in this system, causing large contradictions. Equations (25) and (28) yield an estimate that $-.504 \leq b_4 \leq -.440$. From equation (26) we therefore conclude that $-.440 \leq b_1 \leq -.276$. However b_1 is the expectation of p at $F_j = 0$, a figure which, as it is a proportion, must be nonnegative; since there are numerous empirical observations to anchor our model in the region of $F_j = 0$, this inconsistent result clearly faces us with a serious problem of misspecification.

Examination of the scattergram indicates a likely cause. From $F_j = 0$ to $F_j = .1$, a region in which the foreign-born are too scarce to affect illiteracy rates importantly, illiteracy declines at a rapid rate with increases in F_j. The average illiteracy rate of states from 0 to .02 F_j is .136; for states from .10 to .12 F_j it is .025. Since most of this change must result from changes in q_j, it implies such a strongly negative b_4 that the expectation of q_j would have to plunge below zero a bit farther along the graph. We therefore conclude that q_j does not vary linearly with F_j, as specified in equation (2). A test for nonlinearity confirms this, with adjusted R^2 increasing from .59 to .63 when an F_j^3 term is added.

As we noted in footnote 6, it is possible to develop a third-degree polynomial model similar to the quadratic model we used above, treating p_j and q_j as quadratic functions of X_j.

$$(29) \qquad\qquad p_j = b_1 + b_2 X_j + b_3 X_j^2 + e_{p_j}$$

and

$$(30) \qquad\qquad q_j = b_4 + b_5 X_j + b_6 X_j^2 + e_{q_j},$$

then a third-degree polynomial regression of Y_j on X_j yields a system of four equations in six unknowns:

$$b_4 = \beta_0,$$
$$b_1 - b_4 + b_5 = \beta_1,$$
$$b_2 - b_5 + b_6 = \beta_2,$$
$$b_3 - b_6 = \beta_3.$$

This model gives a distinctly improved fit on the aggregate data, compared with the quadratic model; its curve is displayed in figure 2. The parameters of the model are

$$I = .141 - 1.706F + 7.342F^2 - 9.142F^3.$$
$$\quad (.011) \quad (.322) \quad (2.181) \quad (3.878)$$

Standard errors are presented in parentheses.

Unfortunately, F, F^2, and F^3 are highly collinear. Though all four parameters of the regression equation differ significantly from zero, their standard errors are large and we choose not to put them to the rather demanding use required by the strategy presented thus far in this chapter.

However, it proves possible to proceed indirectly. While not using the unreliable parameter estimates from the regression equation, it does make sense to take predictions of $E(I_i)$ from the overall regression curve as reasonable estimates. The curve is well anchored by observa-

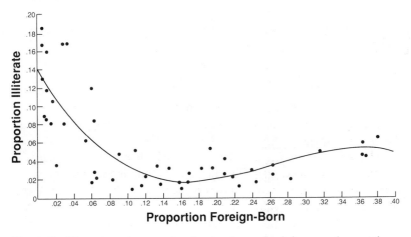

Figure 2. Illiteracy and proportion foreign-born, third-degree polynomial model

tion points, and is specified with sufficient flexibility to allow it to track them closely.

Estimates of the expected level of illiteracy at various concentrations of the foreign-born, combined with substantive assumptions, allow us to achieve near-identification of the system. Let us start with the two assumptions introduced earlier, in the discussion of the abortive attempt to use a quadratic model:

1. $E(p_j)$ does not decrease with increases in F_j.
2. At or near $F_j = .25$, $E(p_j) \geq E(q_j)$. Now, since at $F_j = .25$, $E(I_j) = .031$, therefore,
3. $0 \leq E(q|F_j = .25) \leq .031$. And, since $E(I|F_j = .25) = .75E(q|F_j = .25) + .25E(p|F_j = .25)$, therefore,
4. $.031 \leq E(p|F_j = .25) \leq .124$.

Now, p_j is nonnegative, is either constant or monotonically increasing as F_j increases, *and* falls between .031 and .124 when $F_j = .25$; *therefore*, a linear function is a reasonable specification for the relation of p_j and F_j. ($p_j \geq 0$ at $F_j = 0$ and is either constant or monotonically increasing until it reaches the range $(0.31, .124)$ at $F_j = .25$; therefore it almost surely has not done anything very fancy in between.) We noted above that q_j and F_j have a nonlinear relationship; this is why the quadratic aggregate model was unsatisfactory. So, we will specify our model as

$$(31) \qquad E(p_j) = b_1 + b_2 F_j,$$

$$(32) \qquad E(q_j) = b_3 + b_4 F_j + b_5 F_j^2,$$

$$(33) \qquad E(I_j) = E(p_j)F_j + E(q_j)(1 - F_j).$$

If we can estimate b_1 and b_2, thus estimating p_j, then that will allow us to estimate q_j indirectly through equation (33) without having identified b_3, b_4, or b_5.

The assumptions we have already stated allow us to place usefully narrow bounds around p. To calculate the minimum value of p, we note our assumption that, at every value of $F_j \geq .25$, $E(p_j) \geq E(q_j)$. The lowest possible value of $E(p_j)$ is reached in these cases when $E(p_j) = E(q_j) = E(I_j)$. We also note that $b_1 \geq 0$, so its minimum value is zero. The function of p_j on F_j which yields the minimum possible value of $E(p_j)$ will be one with an intercept of zero, which is tangent to the curve of $E(I_j)$ on F_j at the curve's highest point across the range

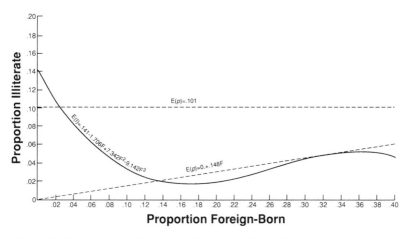

Figure 3. Maximum and minimum functions of p on F

$(.25, .38)$ in F_j. Within this range $E(I_j)$ reaches its maximum of $.053$ at $F_j = .36$, so the slope of $E(p_j)$ on F_j which will produce a minimum $E(p_j)$ is $.053/.36 = .148$ (see fig. 3). Finally, to calculate the minimum bound for p: we use $E(p_j) = 0 + .148F_j$ to calculate the expected p_j for each state; each of these $E(p_j)$ is multiplied by the number of foreign-born in the state; the results are added, and the sum is divided by the total number of foreign-born in all states, to produce $p \geq .039$.[10]

To obtain a maximum bound, we reverse the process to note that the highest possible maximum value of $E(p_j)$ for values of F_j between $.25$ and $.38$ is reached at $F_j = .38$, if $E(q|F_j = .38) = 0$. In that case, $E(p|F_j = .38) = .135$, since if $E(q_j) = 0$, $E(p_j) = E(I_j)/F_j$, or $.051/.38$. The function of $E(p_j)$ on F_j which would pass through this point and produce the maximum overall value of p is the constant function

$$E(p_j) = .135.$$

This would produce an upper bound for p, except that we must subject it to the further constraint that the function producing the upper bound must not, at any value of F_j from 0 to $.38$, produce a negative $E(q_j)$ when combined with $E(I_j)$ in equation (33). $E(p_j) = .135$ fails this

10. This is the procedure described in eq. (7) of chap. 5.

TABLE 3 Comparison of Cross-Level Estimates
with True Population Values

	True Value	Cross-Level Estimate
p	.103	$.070 \pm .031$
q	.043	$.050 \pm .007$
$p - q$	.060	$.021 \pm .038$

test, so successively lower maxima are tried until a legal upper bound is found at $p = .101$.[11]

Thus, simply assuming that $E(p_j)$ does not decrease as F_j increases and that, above $F_j = .25$, $E(p_j) \geq E(q_j)$, while noting that all proportions must be nonnegative, we have set the following bounds around p:

$$.039 \leq p \leq .101.$$

From these, we can readily calculate the following bounds around q:

$$.043 \leq q \leq .056.$$

Midpoint estimates are

(34)
$$p = .070 \pm .031,$$

$$q = .050 \pm .007.$$

No robustness check is needed here, because the bounds themselves are sufficiently narrow that we would probably not feel the need to posit constraints to narrow them further. Table 3 compares the midpoint estimates with true population values from the 1930 census.

The true population value of q is included within the estimated bounds which we have placed around q; the estimated bounds miss the true p by .002. Midpoint estimates, like the true values, show p greater than q—a positive relationship; the bounds do, however, include the possibility of a slight negative relationship, with the minimum p of .039 combined with the maximum q of .056. Thus this analysis would not eliminate the hypothesis of a negative relationship, although putting bounds around $p - q$ of

$$-.017 \leq p - q \leq .058,$$

11. Since we are dropping below the highest possible maximum, it is also necessary to compare functions with intercepts less than .135 but positive slopes. None which fit the constraint of nonnegative $E(q_j)$ produces a higher p than .101. Note that since $E(p_j)$ is a constant function, $E(p) = E(p_j)$, and we therefore do not need to calculate p_j for each state in order to calculate $\hat{p}$.

would demonstrate that the relationship is either a very slightly negative one or a still rather modestly positive one. For most purposes, this should be a satisfactory estimation; normal sample surveys, in fact, would not have produced much better.

CONCLUSION

What we have proposed in this chapter is not a precise estimation technique, but rather a strategy for bringing substantive assumptions to bear on the uncertainty inherent in cross-level inference.

That strategy is to work with a quadratic (or, rarely, a higher-degree polynomial) model at the aggregate level, specifying relationships between p_i (and q_i) and the aggregate independent variable. In the quadratic case this yields a system of three simultaneous equations in four unknowns, inviting the investigator to find a substantive assumption that will permit identification or, through a narrowed range of possibilities, near-identification of the system. The quadratic model may even be used (with a coefficient of zero for the squared term) to address a linear model for which we are suspicious about the Goodman assumptions (or about the more relaxed assumption we introduced in chap. 5). The British example might serve as a general algorithm for many analyses of electoral stability, so that investigators in that class of cases need not start from scratch. We present such an algorithm as an appendix to this chapter.

While we have only worked two examples here, they were deliberately chosen to present different kinds of challenge. The strategy presented is one that should always provide proper, though underidentified specification even when the Goodman assumptions (or our more relaxed assumption) are not met. And we believe that it will usually allow a creative investigator to find usefully close bounds of estimation.

APPENDIX

An Algorithm for Analyses of Electoral Stability

Let us review what was done in the example of British electoral change in order to lay out a general algorithm which will be applicable to many analyses of electoral change. Given a quadratic aggregate model

$$Y_i = \beta_0 + \beta_1 X_i + \beta_2 X_i^2,$$

where β_0, β_1, and β_2 are included (the model may be used for these purposes even if one or two of the terms equals zero), we assume linear relationships between p_j and X_j and between q_j and X_j:

(35) $$E(p_j) = b_1 + b_2 X_j,$$
$$E(q_j) = b_3 + b_4 X_j,$$

where p_j is the probability for a district that x individuals are y, and q_j is the probability that $\tilde{x}$ individuals are y.

As explained in the chapter, we can show that:

$$[\beta_1 + \beta_2 \bar{X} + 2\beta_0(1.5 - \bar{X})] = E(p_j) + [2 - 2\bar{X}]E(q|X_j - .5).$$

Since the terms in brackets are known or estimated, we can set $E(p_j)$ plus some multiple of $E(q|X_j = .5)$ equal to a number. If $\bar{X} > .5$, $E(p_j)$ will be greater than that number. If $\bar{X} < .5$, $E(p_j)$ will be less than that number. Thus this number forms one bound for our estimate of $E(p_j)$.

Similarly,

$$[\beta_2(\bar{X} - .5) - 2\beta_0(\bar{X} - .5)] =$$
$$E(p_j) - E(p|X_j = .5) + [1 - 2\bar{X}]E(q|X_j = .5).$$

The left-hand term (in brackets) will always be less than $E(p_j)$ if we assume $E(p|X_j = .5) > E(q|X_j = .5)$.

If $X_j < .5$, $E(p_j)$ will then fall someplace between these two bounds, whose range equals

$$E(q|X_j = .5) + E(p|X_j = .5).$$

If we can add an assumption about the relative sizes of $E(q|X_j = .5)$ and $E(p|X_j = .5)$, we can place our estimate of $E(p_j)$ within a smaller range, as was done in the example of British elections. If one does this, it is important also to test for the robustness of the estimate relative to the assumption, as was done in the example.

After bounds have been estimated for $E(p_j)$, they must be transformed into bounds for the population p, as was done in the main text (see p. 149).

If $\bar{X} > .5$, then both bounds will be lower bounds, and we will work only with the higher of the two, $\beta_1 + \beta_2 \bar{X} + 2\beta_0(1.5 - \bar{X})$. It may well be that this will be close enough to the natural upper bound of 1.0 that the investigator need do nothing more at this point since the range of bounds will be narrow, or another upper bound may need to be developed. It is also possible that a substantive assumption about $E(q|X_j = .5)$ could be added, to locate $E(p_j)$ between $\beta_1 + \beta_2 \bar{X} + 2\beta_0(1.5 - \bar{X})$ and 1.0. Also, of course, X and $\tilde{X}$ could be reversed in the analysis so that $\bar{X} \leq .5$ (if one had been regressing Labour on Labour, e.g., one could instead regress Conservative on Conservative).

This general procedure should serve well whenever reasonable assumptions about the relative sizes of $E(q|X_j = .5)$ and $E(p|X_j = .5)$ are available.

SEVEN

MODELS WITH UNOBSERVABLE VARIABLES

More Partisanship Models

PARTISANSHIP MODELS FOR AGGREGATE ELECTORAL DATA

Most studies of aggregate data have used regression analysis and its extensions as their primary statistical tool. From the beginning, however, a smaller body of work has used other methods. Factor analysis in particular has found considerable success with aggregate electoral data, and some of the most widely cited studies have relied on it in whole or in part (Gosnell 1937, app. B; Rogin 1967; MacRae and Meldrum 1969). These studies find a powerful main factor for partisanship, along with secondary factors for prominent features of the political landscape such as ideology, realignments, and so on. The results are often more persuasive than their regression counterparts, and they exhibit very little of the statistical and interpretive arbitrariness found in other factor-analytic studies of the same vintage.

In spite of its early empirical successes, ecological factor analysis is now less well regarded and much less used than ecological regression. Part of the reason is faddishness. The statistical foundations of factor analysis were laid much later than regression, and much mediocre work was published before the technique was understood theoretically. Its reputation suffered, and a generation of applied social scientists learned to avoid it. However, a chastened version eventually emerged. Renamed now as the study of "unobservable variables," factor analysis and its extensions enjoy widespread, statistically sound application in educational testing under the rubric of test score theory, in time-series analysis under the name of Kalman filtering, and in many other places. But applications to aggregate political and social data have been few.

Perhaps the strongest influence favoring regression over factor-analytic methods in aggregate data is that ecological regression possesses a clear individual-level interpretation, while ecological factor analysis does not. Since Miller (1952) and Goodman (1953), social scientists have known how to translate the coefficients of an aggregate-level regression to their individual-level counterparts. However treacherous ecological regression may be, researchers at least understand what it means. Nothing similar can be said for ecological factor analysis, whatever its empirical successes. Combined with the lingering prejudice against factor analysis generally, the missing theoretical pedigree has made ecological factor analysis the ugly stepsister.

The first part of this chapter recapitulates an individual-level interpretation of linear ecological factor analysis closely parallel to the Miller-Goodman interpretation of ecological regression. We give a simple statistical model of the voting decision, essentially formalizing the classic description of voting as partisanship plus short-term forces (Campbell 1966; Converse 1966). A simple unobservable-variable model results. The resulting "partisanship model" is, we argue, better grounded substantively than ecological regression. Examples from postwar British elections are given to illustrate the superiority of estimates to those resulting from conventional ecological regression. The final part of the chapter discusses alternative partisanship models and suggests how they might be extended.

PARTISANSHIP MODELS

It is a commonplace of electoral research that most voters act as if they had made a "standing decision" in favor of one party or another. This does not imply that they invariably vote a straight ticket; it means instead that, should they defect to the other side, they have an above-average probability of returning to their party in subsequent contests. A social-psychological version of this finding was popularized by *The American Voter* (Campbell et al. 1960), but one need not subscribe to their approach to accept the empirical finding. Voters may be behavioral partisans without being consciously identified with a party: a loyalty to their social class or their religion will produce the same effect, so long as the party is thought ordinarily to represent those interests. Indeed, even an apolitical decision to take the advice of someone else who has the appropriate beliefs will suffice. As used in this chapter, then, "party identification" will mean behavioral partisanship rather than self-conscious psychological identification with the party.

Most ecological research is concerned, not with party identification per se, but with the effects of other demographic factors on the vote—religion, ethnicity, social class, and so on. However, so powerful an influence is party identification that the effects of these other variables cannot be assessed without taking it into account. As a first step, then, the models considered in this chapter have just one explicit variable—party identification. In addition, only two-party competition will be treated. This simpler problem is of interest in its own right; more complex models with additional parties and independent variables await further research.

The simplest two-party partisanship model is that of chapter 3. Voters are either Democratic or Republican identifiers, and everyone votes. Across districts, each partisan has the same probability of voting for her party's candidate at any one election, though of course the probabilities differ across elections. Voting is independent across voters and over time.

We follow the notation of chapter 3. Let the (unobserved) proportion of Democratic identifiers in constituency j be denoted by D_j^*, so that the fraction of Republican identifiers is $1 - D_j^*$. The fraction of the vote for the Democrats in constituency j at time t is denoted by D_{tj}, and p_t^* is the fraction of Democratic identifiers who vote for the Democrats at time t. Similarly, q_t^* is the fraction of Republican identifiers who defect to the Democrats at time t.

Summing within constituencies gives, for the election at each time t,

$$(1) \qquad D_{tj} = q_t^* + (p_t^* - q_t^*)D_j^* + U_{tj}^*,$$

where U_{tj}^* is a disturbance term representing sampling error. Thus the disturbances have mean zero and are uncorrelated with D_j^*. If we regard the D_{tj} as the items, the D_j^* as the scores on the single factor, and the coefficients q_t^* and $p_t^* - q_t^*$ as the factor loadings, then with three or more elections, equation (1) may be estimated (up to the usual linear transformation) by standard unobservable-variable or factor-analytic methods.

What this simple setup shows is that unobservable-variable models may be given the same individual-level interpretation as ecological regressions. In particular, the factor loadings measure partisan loyalty and defection rates, while the factor itself represents district partisanship. Thus the partisanship model has a clear causal interpretation which is close to the standard view of voter behavior. In substantive terms, its coefficients are more meaningful numbers than the Goodman transition rates, which are purely descriptive: No one imagines that the vote at the prior period is the principal cause of the current vote. Viewed from this perspective, it is no surprise that the findings of ecological factor analyses have often been more historically and politically interesting than their regression counterparts.

One statistical difficulty remains. In most unobservable-variable models, the underlying unmeasured variable may be reading achievement, political liberalism, or von Neumann–Morgenstern utility. Such variables are interval-level measures and thus subject to a positive linear (affine) transformation, just as Fahrenheit and Celsius temperatures represent the same information on different scales. Conventional unobservable-variable models are identified only up to this transformation. Identification is typically achieved by scaling the unobserved variable to mean zero and variance unity, so that the factor scores become z-scores. No information is lost in doing so; some arbitrary scale must be chosen for interval-level variables, and the usual choice is computationally convenient.

Nearly all applications of factor analysis to aggregate electoral data have followed the standard route to identification—transforming the underlying factor to z-scores. Unfortunately, this step is entirely meaningless with electoral data. The underlying factor, partisanship, is not an interval-level scale. Each factor score is the proportion of Democratic identifiers in a particular constituency, and as a proportion, it has an absolute scale not subject to any transformations. In any given electoral system, the fraction of identifiers varies across constituencies with some true mean and variance, and its scale cannot be arbitrarily reset.

The consequence of the absolute scale for partisanship is that ecological factor analyses are unidentified. While the factor scores and loadings continue to represent partisanship and loyalty rates, respectively, they do so on unknown scales. The nature of the difficulty is illustrated in tables 1A and 1B, where two quite different sets of hypothetical parameter values are inserted into the partisanship model and are each found to fit the same data perfectly.

For some purposes, this lack of identification may make little difference. If a researcher needs only to separate more heavily Democratic districts from more heavily Republican areas, and to distinguish more strongly partisan elections from the less partisan, and if the size of the differences is truly irrelevant, then the true scale of the partisanship model is not needed. More commonly, however, large differences will be interpreted differently than small differences, so identification matters. How might it be achieved? The most reliable approach is to build

TABLE 1A Hypothetical Three-Constituency System Obeying Equations (3) and (4)

Constituency Number	D_i^*	D_{1i}	D_{2i}
1	.80	.70	.74
2	.60	.60	.58
3	.40	.50	.42

Parameters generating the vote:
$p_1^* = .80$
$q_1^* = .30$
$p_2^* = .90$
$q_2^* = .10$

Goodman transition rates:
True $p =$ .74
True $q =$ .34
$\hat{p} = 1.22$
$\hat{q} = -.38$

TABLE 1B Alternative Three-Constituency System Obeying Equations (3) and (4) and Generating Same Vote Totals as in Table 1A

Constituency Number	D_i^*	D_{1i}	D_{2i}
1	.72	.70	.74
2	.54	.60	.58
3	.36	.50	.42

Parameters generating the vote:
$p_1^* = 77/90 = .86$
$q_1^* \quad\quad = .30$
$p_2^* = 89/90 = .99$
$q_2^* \quad\quad = .10$

Goodman transition rates:
True $p =$ .78
True $q =$ .27
$\hat{p} = 1 .22$
$\hat{q} = -.38$

Variables: D_i^* = fraction of Democratic identifiers; D_{1i}, D_{2i} = Democratic vote at time 1, 2; p_1^*, p_2^* = Democratic identifier loyalty rate at time 1, 2; q_1^*, q_2^* = Republican identifier defection rate at time 1, 2; p (true) = proportion of time-1 Democratic voters who vote Democratic at time 2, q (true) = proportion of time-1 Republican voters who vote Democratic at time 2; $\hat{p}$ = ecological regression estimate of p, based on data in table above, $\hat{q}$ = ecological regression estimate of q, based on data in table above.

up from the individual level, specifying assumptions about voter behavior that identify the aggregate model.

IDENTIFICATION CONDITIONS

Continuing the framework of the last section, we now concentrate on the individual voter i in constituency j at time t. We decompose the forces influencing her vote in the same way as in an analysis of variance: We specify a grand mean over all elections, a mean deviation due to the time period, a constituency deviation from the time period, and then a residual deviation due to the individual herself. Let d_{tji} be the ith individual's vote and d_{ji}^* her partisanship, where both are dichotomous with the Democratic side scored one and the Republican side zero. Then for a Democrat, the utility of voting Democratic is given by

$$(2) \qquad \mathrm{Util}(d_{tji} = 1 | d_{ji}^* = 1) = p^* + \delta_t^* + \delta_{tj} + u_{tji}$$

$$= p_t^* + \delta_{tj} + u_{tji},$$

where, intuitively speaking, the positive number p^* is the pure utility of voting Democratic (apart from all short-term effects), δ_t^* is the mean national short-term force on Democrats at time t, p_t^* is the sum of p_t^* and δ_t^*, δ_{tj} is the mean deviation among Democrats in the jth constituency from the national Democratic short-term force, and u_{tji} is a disturbance term representing residual short-term forces on the individual. Note that δ_{tj} is not assumed fixed over time: a constituency is allowed to have atypically loyal Democrats at one time period and atypically faithless ones at another.

The typical Democrat in equation (1) votes Democratic if and only if the net utility of doing so exceeds zero, that is, if and only if

$$(3) \qquad p_t^* + \delta_{tj} + u_{tji} \geq 0.$$

Denoting by $F(x)$ the (cumulative) logistic distribution function evaluated at x, it follows from equations (1) and (2) that

$$(4) \qquad \mathrm{Prob}(d_{tji} = 1 | d_{ji}^* = 1) = F(p_t^* + \delta_{tj}) \equiv p_{tj}^*.$$

Because equations (2)–(4) are essentially an analysis-of-variance specification for dichotomous dependent variables, they are formally tautological. However, under the substantive interpretation given above, the equations have genuine political content. They imply, for example, that in the absence of any short-term force, every Democrat will vote for her party. That is, if for all j and i, $\delta_{tj} = u_{tji} = 0$, then equation (3) holds necessarily. Similarly, it may be shown that with a fixed distribution of the deviations δ_{tj}, less-partisan elections will generate larger constituency deviations from national party loyalty rates.[1] Thus this simple setup has two qualitative characteristics expected of a plausible electoral model: first, partisans are loyal in the absence of short-term forces, and second, larger deviations from partisanship at the constituency level indicate lesser partisan loyalty by individuals.

It is assumed that, at each time t, the δ_{tj} constitute a random sample from a distribution with mean zero and finite variance τ_t. Thus the mean short-term force can vary over time, and so can constituency deviations from the national mean. We also assume that u_{tji} has a standard logistic distribution for all t, j, and i. The latter postulate simply establishes the utility scale at each time period and imposes a functional form on the individual-level disturbances.

Similarly, Republicans are assumed to vote Democratic if and only if

$$-p^* + \gamma_t^* + \gamma_{tj} + \nu_{tji} \geq 0,$$

or

(5) $$q_t^* + \gamma_{tj} + \nu_{tji} \geq 0,$$

where again p^* is the pure utility of voting Democratic, γ_t^* is the mean national short-term force for Republicans, q_t^* is the sum of $-p^*$ and γ_t^*, and γ_{tj} is the Republican deviation in the jth constituency from their national short-term force, assumed to have mean zero and inter-constituency variance τ_t (the same variance as for the Democrats). Finally, ν_{tji} is a logistic disturbance. The Republican probability of voting Democratic is therefore

(6) $$\text{Prob}(d_{tji} = 1 | d_{ji}^* = 0) = F(q_t^* + \gamma_{tj}) \equiv q_{tj}^*.$$

Now the following accounting relationship necessarily holds: the votes for the first party consist entirely of loyal votes by its partisans plus defecting votes by partisans of the other party. Thus if the fraction of the vote accruing to the first party in the jth constituency at time t is

---

1. I.e., a given amount of variance in the arguments to a logistic distribution causes more variance when it occurs in the middle of the distribution than in the tails. This argument assumes that in every constituency Democrats are at least 50% loyal.

denoted by D_{tj}, and if the (typically unknown) fraction of identifiers with that party in the constituency is denoted by D_j^*, then

$$(7) \qquad D_{tj} = p_{tj}^* D_j^* + q_t^* (1 - D_j^*)$$

$$= q_{tj}^* + (p_{tj}^* - q_{tj}^*) D_j^*.$$

Taking the expectation over δ_{tj} for fixed t, set $E(p_{tj}^*) = p_t^*$ and $E(q_{tj}^*) = q_t^*$. Then

$$(8) \qquad D_{tj} = q_t^* + (p_t^* - q_t^*) D_j^* + \nu_{tj},$$

where

$$(9) \qquad \nu_{tj} = (q_{tj}^* - q_t^*) + [(p_{tj}^* - p_t^*) - (q_{tj}^* - q_t^*)] D_j^*.$$

Note that if, as usual, the constituency partisan balances are unknown, equation (8) is in factor-analytic form, with intercept q_t^*, factor loading $p_t^* - q_t^*$, and factor score D_j^*. To complete the specification, it remains only to show that the disturbance term has the appropriate properties. The first key assumption may now be stated.

Independent Constituency Effects Assumption. For fixed t and j, δ_{tj} and γ_{tj} are distributed independently of D_j^* and of each other.

Essentially, this postulate specifies that the deviation of Democrats in a particular constituency from the national short-term force on Democrats is independent of the deviation of Republicans in the same district from their national short-term force, and that both are independent of the partisan character of the district.

This assumption is strong, although perhaps not as strong as it first appears. In particular, it does *not* require that short-term forces on Democrats and Republicans be independent of each other. In general, they will not be. What is required is that *deviations* from the average short-term force be independent, so that, for example, unusually loyal Democrats are equally likely to be found in a district with either loyal or faithless Republicans. (Modifications of this assumption are considered below.)

It follows immediately from the assumption of independent constituency effects that $E(\nu_{tj}) = 0$ and $E(\nu_{tj} D_t^*) = 0$. That is, equation (8) is indeed a factor-analytic setup, with the disturbance term, ν_{tj}, having mean zero and being uncorrelated with the factor, D_j^*.

As noted above, one important difference between equation (8) and a more typical factor analysis is that the measurement scale of the factor in equation (8) is not arbitrary. The proportion of party identifiers in a constituency is a fixed quantity on an absolute scale, not the usual interval-level measure which may be transformed to a z-score with no loss of meaning. If equation (8) is estimated in the usual way, that is, by treating the factor scores as z-scores with mean zero and variance one, D_j^* is transformed to

$$(10) \qquad z_{tj} = \frac{D_j^* - m}{s},$$

where $E(D_j^*) = m$ is the mean of the constituency proportions of Democratic party identifiers and $\mathrm{var}(D_j^*) = s^2$ is the interconstituency variance in those proportions. On this standardized scale, the factor analysis carried out is

$$(11) \qquad D_{jt} = \alpha_t + \beta_t z_{tj} + \nu_{tj},$$

where $\beta_t = s(p_t^* - q_t^*)$ and $\alpha_t = q_t^* + m(p_t^* - q_t^*)$. As is well known, single-factor models like equation (8) or (11), which are related by a linear transformation of their factors, are not statistically distinguishable without further information. Both fit equally well. To identify equation (8), we need to know the parameters of the transformation (10), that is, m and s. It follows, then, that additional statistical information must be brought to bear.

Fortunately, the necessary additional information is available from the disturbances. Set $E(\nu_{tj}^2) = \omega_t^2$, and let $f(p) = p(1 - p)$ be the density of the logistic distribution as a function of the corresponding probability.[2] Then make use of the approximations, very nearly true for small τ_t, that $\mathrm{var}(p_{tj}^*) \approx \tau_t f^2(p_t^*)$ and $\mathrm{var}(q_{tj}^*) \approx \tau_t f^2(q_t^*)$. Then equation (9) implies that

$$(12) \quad \omega_t^2 \approx \tau_t \{ f^2(q_t^*) - E(D_j^*) f^2(q_t^*)$$

$$+ E(D_j^{*2})[f^2(p_t^*) + f^2(q_t^*)] \}.$$

Since $E(D_t^{*2}) = s^2 + m^2$,

$$(13) \quad \omega_t^2 \approx \tau_t \{ (s^2 + m^2) f^2(p_t^*) + [s^2 + (1 - m)^2] f^2(q_t^*) \}.$$

As it stands, equation (13) is no help in achieving identification, since it adds a parameter (τ_t) for each residual variance being ex-

---

2. E.g., at the point where the probability (area to the left on a logistic curve) is .25, the density is .25(.75) = .1875. That is, f maps the cumulative distribution function into the density.

plained. However, the τ_t represent unexplained variation across constituencies. If we take these variations as representing random local deviations in short-term forces, then in a stable electoral system, we might expect them to have nearly the same variance over time. In that spirit, we make the second key assumption:

Identifying Condition. For all t, $\tau_t = \tau$, a fixed constant.

This condition suffices to identify the model. From equation (13), we have

$$(14) \quad \omega_t^2 \approx \tau\{(s^2 + m^2)f^2(p_t^*) + [s^2 + (1 - m)^2]f^2(q_t^*)\}.$$

This approximate condition on the disturbance variances, estimated jointly with the basic factor-analytic specification in equation (8), implies an estimate for each of the parameters with a minimal set of assumptions. For example, by specifying the exact distributional form of the τ_t, one could compute the variance (eq. [13]) exactly. And given, in addition, the distribution of mean partisanship across constituencies, one could perform full MLE, exploiting the central limit theorem to guarantee Gaussian disturbances for ν_{tj}.

In this chapter, we adopt a consistent but less than fully statistically efficient estimation procedure for two reasons. First, distributional assumptions are always doubtful, particularly so when describing unobservables, so that initial explorations of any model "inefficiently" and part by part lays bare its strong points and weak spots, while full-scale MLE or minimum χ^2 estimation, by estimating all the parameters simultaneously, tends to blur the successes and failures of the component parts. Our goal in studying a simplistic model of this kind is not to estimate it with minimum variance under idealistic assumptions; that is a task for a well-tested and more sophisticated model at a later stage. Instead, we want to learn which aspects of the model are promising, and for the others, how they might best be modified. We proceed with those objectives in mind.

The first step is to assess how well the basic reduced-form factor-analytic model (1) fits the data. This initial estimation can be done without imposing the identification condition. While this approach produces loading and factor-score estimates identified only up to a linear transformation, the disturbance variances are identified, and they allow us to compare the fit of the factor-analytic model with its regression counterpart applied to the same data.

Ecological regression and ecological factor analysis were applied to British elections in the immediate postwar period, 1950–66. This sample was chosen because the British have relatively strong party loyalties, because no realignments occurred, and because the final two elections have been studied before with both ecological regression and a panel survey (Stokes 1969; see also our use of the example in chaps. 5 and 6). Election returns were coded from *The Times* (1950, 1951, 1955, 1959, 1964, 1966) *House of Commons* series. As in Stokes, only constituencies with straight fights (no Liberal) in 1964 and 1966 were selected. Unlike Stokes, this study dropped Northern Ireland constituencies, with their atypical politics and distinctive parties, along with those constituencies heavily redistricted during 1950–66. This left 147 districts for the analysis. The set of districts is very similar to, but not identical with, the set we used in chapters 5 and 6.

Table 2 shows the partisan nature of the sample that results. Since Liberal candidates are largely a phenomenon of Conservative areas, deleting their districts gives a Labour-leaning cast to the sample, just as it did for Stokes. The losses due to redistricting did not alter the partisan or geographic balance.

The resulting data set exhibits all the usual recalcitrance when ecological regression is applied, just as we saw for its sibling in chapter 5. With all vote outcomes expressed as Conservative fractions of the two-party vote, ecological regressions were estimated for each pair of adjacent years. The results are given in table 3. The fits are excellent: R^2 is invariably above .95, and the standard errors are infinitesimal—rarely more than a percentage point. But the estimates are not credible:

TABLE 2 Partisan Character of the Ecological Sample: British Districts with Straight Fights in Both 1964 and 1966

Year	National Conservative Fraction of Two-Party Vote (%)	Ecological Sample Conservative Fraction of Two-Party Vote[a] (%)
1966	46.7	35.5
1964	49.6	38.8
1959	53.0	42.0
1955	51.8	41.1
1951	49.6	40.0
1950	47.3	38.5

[a]Northern Ireland and seats heavily redistricted during 1950–66 excluded. $N = 147$ seats.

TABLE 3 Ecological Regression Results: British Districts with Straight Fights in Both 1964 and 1966

Year Regressed on Year	Conservative Loyalty (%)	Labour Defection (%)	R^2	$\hat{\sigma}$ (percentage points)
1966 on 1964	95.7 (.81)	−2.8 (.53)	.98	3.0
1964 on 1959	92.3 (1.02)	0.2 (.75)	.95	5.9
1959 on 1955	98.5 (1.08)	2.4 (.77)	.95	6.6
1955 on 1951	100.6 (.90)	1.5 (.61)	.97	4.3
1951 on 1950	99.6 (.82)	2.6 (.53)	.97	3.5

Note: Northern Ireland and seats heavily redistricted during 1950–66 excluded. $N = 147$ seats. Numbers in parentheses are standard errors.

they show extremely little defection (less than 5% in every case but one), and two of the estimates are out of bounds. In particular, the first Labour defection estimate is −2.8%, with a standard error of about half a percentage point. Thus this meaningless number is no sampling fluke; it is more than five standard deviations from zero.

The Butler-Stokes panel study of Britain may be used to find the corresponding survey estimates for the 1964 to 1966 transition, and these in turn may be translated into a line with the slope and intercept which ecological regression should produce. Stokes (1969) does so, with results familiar from chapter 5 and given below in table 7. The ecological estimate of the Labour defection rate falls below that of the survey by 6 percentage points; the Conservative loyalty rate estimate is fully 9 points above.

As Stokes cautions, the survey estimates are not infallible. In addition to sampling error, the educative effect of being in a panel survey and the selection effect of the attrition of less-interested respondents will cause the panel estimates to deviate from the true values. However, the main consequence of these panel design effects would be to produce more sophisticated and consistent respondents, thereby exaggerating the survey loyalty rates and depressing the defection rates. Unfortunately, a bias in this direction hurts the ecological estimates rather than helps them. Thus, if design effects of this kind have happened, the ecological results are even more wrong than they appear. In any event, there is no statistical adjustment to the survey results which would

TABLE 4 Ecological Factor Analysis: British Districts with Straight
Fights in Both 1964 and 1966

Year	Intercept α_t	Factor Loading β_t	R^2 [$\hat{\omega}_t$]
1966	.3546	.1046	.994
	(.0090)	(.0066)	[3.0]
1964	.3882	.1049	.995
	(.0090)	(.0066)	[3.0]
1959	.4195	.1133	.997
	(.0096)	(.0069)	[2.3]
1955	.4111	.1161	.999
	(.0097)	(.0069)	[1.6]
1951	.3995	.1154	.999
	(.0096)	(.0069)	[1.5]
1950	.3847	.1163	.997
	(.0098)	(.0071)	[2.3]

Note: Northern Ireland and seats heavily redistricted during 1950–66 excluded. The
single factor is standardized to mean zero and variance one. $N = 147$ seats. ω_t^2 is the
variance of the disturbance term ("unique variance"); $\hat{\omega}_t$ above is expressed in percentage points and is directly comparable to $\hat{\sigma}$ in table 3. Numbers in parentheses are
standard errors.

justify the ecological estimate of the Labour defection rate, which is
hopelessly negative.

By contrast, the ecological factor analysis is displayed in table 4. The
estimates fit the data extremely well, with standard errors of fit considerably smaller than those of the corresponding ecological regression.
Not surprisingly, using partisanship as a causal variable is superior to
working with the purely descriptive ecological regressions. This result
is one more confirmation that taking account of unobserved partisanship is often critical to substantively meaningful ecological inference
about voting.

No identification condition was imposed in table 4, so that the factor scores and loadings are identified only up to a linear transformation. Thus the excellent fit tells us only that some one version of the
partisanship model is successful, but not which one. Since many different identification conditions are possible and none has the credibility
of the reduced-form model in equation (1), we have estimated the
reduced-form version of the model first before adding less reliable conditions. Once the model passes the initial test, however, further testing
is in order, and identification conditions are needed. For at this stage,
without knowing the scale of the parameters, we are unable to give

them the clear substantive interpretation that permits assessment. The next step, therefore, is to impose the identification condition.

With the addition of a disturbance term, the relationship (14) can be used as a nonlinear regression equation to estimate m and s, the mean and variance of constituency-level partisanship. First, use the definitions of α_t and β_t in equation (11) to solve for p_t^* and q_t^*:

$$(15) \qquad\qquad p_t^* = \alpha_t + \beta_t(1 - m)/s$$

and

$$(16) \qquad\qquad q_t^* = \alpha_t - \beta_t m/s$$

Then, since estimates of ω_t^2 do not depend on the scale of D_j^*, they can be obtained from a factor analysis with an arbitrary scaling such as in equation (11) and then inserted into equation (14) as the dependent variable. With the substitutions (15) and (16) and the estimates α_t and β_t inserted as independent variables, equation (14) becomes a nonlinear regression equation with coefficients τ, m, and s. Those estimates in turn may be used to solve for the true scale of the factor, and hence for the party loyalty and defection rates.

In summary, then, the exploratory analysis set out here proceeds as follows:

1. Carry out a factor analysis like equation (11), with an intercept and a single factor standardized to mean zero and variance one. This is easily done with standard software, for example, LISREL.
2. Insert the residual variances from step 1 into equation (14) as the dependent variable, and make the substitutions (15) and (16). Enter the estimates of α_t and β_t as independent variables. Then carry out a nonlinear regression to estimate τ, m, and s.
3. Use the estimates of α_t, β_t, m, and s to estimate the first-party loyalty rate, p_t^*, and the second-party defection rate, q_t^*. The formulas are given by equations (15) and (16).

Table 5 gives the estimates from the nonlinear regression that estimates m, s, and τ (we used the nonlinear OLS estimation routine in the software package TSP, ignoring the small amount of heteroscedasticity due to the slightly different standard errors for the estimated dependent-variable scores). In MLE or minimum χ^2 estimation, an identifying relationship of this kind would be assumed to fit perfectly, apart from sampling error. To the degree that fit can be assessed with just six observations, we see that the fit is indeed excellent, though a

TABLE 5 Nonlinear Regression Estimates of Mean (m) and Interconstituency Standard Deviation (s) of Proportion of Conservative Identifiers in British Districts with Straight Fights in Both 1964 and 1966

Parameter	Estimate	Nominal Standard Error
m	.424	.025
s	.132	.0044
τ	.077	.025
R^2	.885	
$\bar{R}^2$	.808	
$\bar{y}$	.000548	
$\hat{\sigma}$	.000126	
N	6	

Equation: $\hat{\omega}_i^2 = \tau\{(s^2 + m^2)f^2(p_i^*) + [s^2 + (1 - m)^2]f^2(q_i^*)\}$, where $p_i^* = \hat{\alpha}_i + \hat{\beta}_i(1 - m)/s$, $q_i^* = \hat{\alpha}_i - \hat{\beta}_i m/s$, and $f(\cdot)$ is the logistic density. y-bar denotes the mean of the dependent variable.

combination of specification error and sampling noise leaves it well short of perfection.

Substantively, the estimates of m and s mean that the districts in the sample average 42% Conservative (with a standard error of 2.5 percentage points) and that, across districts, the standard deviation of the Conservative fraction of the electorate is 13 percentage points. Both estimates are quite reasonable. In fact, if Liberal identifiers in straight-fight constituencies are grouped with Conservatives to create a two-party categorization matching the factor-analytic model, the off-year (1963) partisan division in the Butler-Stokes survey is 42.9% Conservative.

Finally, table 6 supplies the final partisan loyalty estimates and contrasts them with the corresponding estimates from the panel survey. Again Liberal identifiers are grouped with Conservatives to make two-party comparisons possible. The match of the ecological results to the 1964 and 1966 survey data is more than satisfactory, with none of the differences reaching 3 percentage points. Moreover, the estimates are substantively reasonable in other respects as well. The year 1959 shows a strong trend to the Conservatives by both parties; 1966 exhibits just the same pattern but in the direction of Labour. As tables 1A and 1B show, these two elections were high-water marks for their respective victors. The estimates also show that while the 1950 and 1964 campaigns led to virtually identical outcomes in these districts, the forces

TABLE 6 Ecological Factor Analysis and Panel Survey Estimates of British Voter Transition Rates in Districts with Straight Fights in Both 1964 and 1966

Year	Behavioral Party Identification Ecological Estimates[a] (%)		Self-Reported Party Identification Survey Panel Estimates[b] (%)	
	Conservative Loyalty	Labour Defection	Conservative Loyalty	Labour Defection
1966	80.0	1.9	81.6	4.0
1964	84.5	5.2	87.1	5.3
1959	91.3	5.6		
1955	91.6	3.9		
1951	90.2	3.0		
1950	89.1	1.2		

[a]Northern Ireland and seats heavily redistricted during 1950–66 excluded. $N = 147$ seats.
[b]From the Butler-Stokes (1969) panel respondents in seats with straight fights. Total $N = 524$. Liberal identifiers are grouped with Conservatives. Party identification is taken from the 1963 (off-year) response.

fashioning them were rather different. As the first referendum on the Atlee government, the 1950 contest was relatively partisan. By contrast, 1964 exhibited less loyalty, with the new Labour government getting into office more by virtue of greater Conservative faithlessness than by any increase in the fervor of its own partisans.[3]

A variety of data-analytic checks were carried out to validate the estimates in table 6. Each involved an alteration or weakening of the assumptions in the underlying model. First, the logistic distribution assumption was dropped in favor of a normal distribution. As would be expected, the fit was virtually identical. Second, the assumption that the interconstituency variance in short-term forces (τ) was identical for Conservatives and Labour was dropped. Doing so improved the fit of the nonlinear regression considerably. The Conservatives were estimated to have the larger variance, probably because the fraction of Liberal identifiers implicitly grouped with them varies from place to place, causing their loyalty rates to be more variable than Labour's.

Third, the assumption that within each constituency, short-term

---

3. This was the conclusion drawn by at least one contemporary observer, based on the fact that while the total Labour vote in 1964 was virtually identical to that five years earlier, the total Conservative vote was down (*The Times* 1964, p. 240, in an article authored by Richard Rose). However, inferences of this sort are quite slippery, as a few moments' calculations with artificial examples will demonstrate.

forces on Conservatives and Labour are uncorrelated was changed to the postulate that those two forces are perfectly correlated. In effect, this version substitutes a pure constituency effect for the original two uncorrelated forces. This model fit slightly less well than the corresponding model with uncorrelatedness, but it also improved substantially when Conservatives were allowed to have a larger variance in their (still perfectly correlated) short-term force.

The partisanship model was quite robust under these modifications. None of these alterations changed the ecological estimates of the loyalty or defection rates by more than 3 percentage points, and most made less difference than that. Thus the basic model with the current identification performs well under a variety of modest modifications.

A more difficult test for a model designed to estimate *partisanship* transition rates is the estimation of the *voter* transition rates. Among the voters who chose the Tories at time 1, how many chose them again at time 2? And among those who voted Labour at time 1, how many defected to the Conservatives at time 2? Since survey estimates of these two proportions, denoted p and q, respectively, are available for the transitions from 1964 to 1966, we focus on them.

The partisanship model just estimated yields voter transition rates as a function of the partisanship loyalty rates. For example, the voter loyalty rate p is given by

$$(17) \qquad p = \frac{\text{Prob(voting twice for Tories)}}{\text{Prob(voting for Tories at time 1)}}.$$

Now the numerator is a weighted average of the probabilities that a Tory partisan and that a Labour partisan would vote Tory twice, with the weights being their proportions in the population of sampled constituencies (namely, m and $1 - m$). The denominator is simply the Tory vote proportion at time 1 in the same constituencies. Since, conditional on partisanship, vote choices are assumed independent over time, all the quantities needed to compute the loyalty rate p are readily obtained from tables 2, 5, and 6. For the 1964 to 1966 transition, we have

$$(18) \qquad p = \frac{.424(.845)(.8) + .576(.052)(.019)}{.388}$$

$$= .740.$$

Similar calculations yield the voter defection rate, q.

The voter transition rates for 1964–66 implied by the partisanship

TABLE 7 Three Estimates of 1964–66 British Voter Transition Rates

	Loyal to 1964 Tory Vote (%)	Defect from 1964 Labour Vote (%)
Ecological regression	95	−3
Linear Partisanship model	74	10
Thomsen model	86	4
Survey estimate	87	3

Note: Ecological regression estimates computed from prior tables. Survey results from Stokes (1969).

model are given in table 7, along with the corresponding ecological regression estimates and the survey values. Simply put, while ecological regression finds too much stability, this particular partisanship model finds too little. The assumption that a Tory who defects in 1964 is no more likely to defect in 1966 than any other Tory is undoubtedly the culprit.

The notion of an underlying dichotomous partisanship is too discrete. Some partisans are highly partisan, others barely so. This matters little in estimating partisanship transition rates: Differences among voters may be averaged to produce the good partisanship loyalty estimates found in table 6. Unfortunately, averaging will not work with voter transition rates computed from partisanship transition rates, since quadratic terms are involved. Consider first a constituency in which every Tory partisan is likely to be loyal to partisanship with a probability of .7 at each of two elections. Thus the probability of a Tory voting Tory twice is .49. Now imagine another district, also with an average .70 probability that a Tory will vote Tory at each election. Suppose, however, that in the latter district Tory partisans are heterogeneous, with half being hardcore loyalists certain to choose the Tories at each time period and the other half perennial defectors with probability .4 of doing so. In this district, the probability of a Tory partisan voting Tory twice is $(1^2 + .4^2)/2 = .58$, which differs substantially from the .49 in the first district. The simple partisan model estimated above would ignore the heterogeneity and treat the second district as if it were the first one. Hence it underestimates the stability of vote choice.

What the simple partisanship model teaches is that unobservable-variable methods have an important place in studies of aggregate voting behavior. Their statistical estimates rest on firmer causal foundations than the usual ecological regressions, and they often result in better-fitting models with deeper substantive insights. Even in their simplest form, they may reproduce partisanship loyalty and defection rates very well. However, the dichotomous version of partisanship shows statistical signs of misspecification when used to estimate voter transitions. Unless partisanship models make explicit allowance for different strengths of partisanship, they will not be able to reproduce the observed over-time stability in vote choices.

In recent years, ecological models incorporating heterogeneity in partisan strength have become available. They are discussed in the following section.

CONTINUOUS PARTISANSHIP MODELS

The most prominent expositor of aggregate electoral models which allow for heterogeneous intensity of partisanship is Thomsen (1987). (Earlier versions by Thomsen appeared in several unpublished papers from the 1970s and 1980s cited in Thomsen 1987; a sketch of the same model was set out independently in Achen 1983a.) To lay out Thomsen's framework, suppose that there are just two parties, so that party identification may be expressed as a position on a unidimensional scale. In district j, let p_{ji} be the (long-term) party identification of person i, and let $f_j(\cdot)$ be its density within the district. The latter distribution is assumed to be normal or Gaussian, so that within each district party identification is distributed as a Gaussian with mean p_j and variance σ^2:

$$(19) \qquad f_j(p_{ji}) = \phi(p_{ji}|p_j, \sigma^2),$$

where $\phi(p_{ji}|p_j, \sigma^2)$ is the density of a normal distribution with mean p_j and variance σ^2. Thus the variance is assumed constant over districts, but the mean varies.

Next, the voter's decision at each time period t is modeled as it would be in psychometric scaling theory: Each election is treated as if it were an "item" on a psychological test. Thus every election has its own response curve, a function that gives the probability of choosing the Democrats, say, as a function of partisanship. In accordance with Gaussian scaling models, the curve is assumed to be a normal ogive whose argument is linear in partisanship. Denote by $\Phi(\cdot)$ the cumulative distribution function of the standard normal distribution and by d_{tji} the vote of the ith voter in constituency j at time t ($d_{tji} = 1$ for a Democratic vote, 0 otherwise). Then the response curve for the relationship of vote to partisanship takes the form

(20) $$\text{Prob}(d_{tji} = 1|p_{ji}) = \Phi(\alpha_t + \beta_t p_{ji}),$$

where α_t and β_t are parameters unique to each election.

To derive the vote in constituency j, the individual probabilities must be averaged over the distribution of p_{ji} within each constituency j:

(21) $$E(d_{tji}) = \int_{-\infty}^{\infty} \Phi(\alpha + \beta p_{ji})\phi(p_{ji}|p_j, \sigma^2)dp_{ji}.$$

The integral may be evaluated by completing the square: A mixture of normal ogives with normally distributed means and common variances is itself a normal ogive (e.g., Lord and Novick 1968, pp. 376–77). Hence the previous equation may be written as

(22) $$E(d_{tji}) = \Phi\left[\frac{\alpha_t + \beta_t p_j}{(1 + \beta_t^2 \sigma^2)^{1/2}}\right].$$

Apart from sampling error, the left-hand side is just D_{tj}, the vote for Democrats at time t in constituency j. If we ignore the sampling error for a moment, we can transform both sides by the inverse Gaussian cumulative distribution function, which puts the vote proportions on the scale familiar from probit analysis:

(23) $$\Phi^{-1}(D_{tj}) = \alpha_t' + \beta_t' p_j,$$

where $\alpha_t' = \alpha_t/(1 + \beta_t^2\sigma^2)^{1/2}$ and $\beta_t' = \beta_t/(1 + \beta_t^2\sigma^2)^{1/2}$. That is, Thomsen's result is that, on this transformed scale, the constituency vote is linear in mean constituency partisanship.

Since an equation like this holds for each election, it follows that, under these assumptions, the regression of one election on another is not linear in the vote proportions, as so much prior work has assumed. Instead, the regression will be linear only after the vote proportions have been transformed to the probit scale. Transformations of that kind have been used from time to time in ecological regression, since they automatically force the resulting transition probability estimates into the bounded range (e.g., Brown, 1982). But Thomsen was the first to give the specification a meaningful substantive interpretation.

Since the probit transformation is nearly linear in the middle ranges, Thomsen's nonlinearity will be almost invisible in most two-party systems. (However, it may make an important difference in the estimates: see chap. 5.) But in systems with small parties, the model implies substantial nonlinearity in Goodman-style regressions. Thomsen (1987, chap. 2) gives several empirical examples in which the curvilinearity is obvious and consequential, and others in which it is less visible, including the 1964–66 Stokes data. In short, Thomsen's considerable achievement is to demonstrate clearly that linear ecological models are at best only approximations to the actual functional forms found in the data. And he shows theoretically why nonlinearity is to be expected.

Identification of Thomsen's model is far more difficult. Indeed, the identification problem blocks the path just as it did in the simpler dichotomous partisanship version. Examination of equation (22) shows, for example, that if β is doubled while p_j and σ are halved, the probability of a vote for the Democrats is unchanged and the statistical fit will be identical. But of course the substantive interpretation is radically different in the two cases.

Thomsen's actual estimation method is very simple and very clever. Since his primary interest is in estimating voter transition rates, he uses the partisanship model as a means to that end. Under his model, the distribution of the probability of voting Democratic is normal within each district at each time period. The underlying partisanship model creates a correlation between these two normal distributions within each district. Now the observed vote is just a dichotomization of each of these normal distributions. Thomsen's observation is that pairs of dichotomized, correlated normal distributions have long been studied in statistical theory under the topic of tetrachoric correlation, and he exploits this theory to create his estimator.

Thomsen's approach to estimating the transition rates across a pair of elections is given by the following four steps (Thomsen 1987, pp. 55–64):

1. Transform the (two-party) vote proportions at each time period to the probit scale.

   For example, if the vote proportion for the Democrats is .60, the transformed vote is the value of a standard normal variable such that 60% of the area under the density is to its left. Thus, in this case, the transformed vote is .253, since $\Phi^{-1}(.60) = .253$, where again $\Phi^{-1}(\cdot)$ is the inverse (cumulative) distribution function of a standard normal distribution.[4]

2. Next, using the transformed vote proportions, compute the Pearson correlation r between the votes at the two time periods.

The following step employs Yule's Q as an approximation to the tetrachoric correlation in order to transform the Pearson r into the corresponding correlation between the individual-level dichotomous vote variables. Denote the national Democratic vote at time 1 by D_1 and the corresponding fraction at time 2 by D_2. Thus:

3. Estimate D_{12}, the fraction of the voting population who select the Democrats both times:

(24) $$\hat{D}_{12} = (1 + 2rD_1 + 2rD_2 - r - k)/4r,$$

where $k = [(1 + 2rD_1 + 2rD_2 - 4)^2 - 8r(1 + r)D_1D_2]^{1/2}$.

Now recall that the Goodman loyalty rate is the proportion of time-1 Democratic voters who support them again at time 2. This fraction may be written as the ratio of those who voted Democratic twice to the Democratic vote at time 1. Similarly, the Goodman defection rate is the proportion of time-1 Republican voters who switch to the Democrats at time 2. The latter fraction is the ratio of those who voted Democratic at time 2 but not at time 1 to the Republican vote at time 1. The final step of Thomsen's procedure estimates the two transition rates in this fashion, using the estimate of D_{12} from step 3.

4. Estimate the Goodman loyalty rate as $\hat{p} = \hat{D}_{12}/D_1$. Similarly, estimate the Goodman defection rate $\hat{q} = (D_2 - \hat{D}_{12})/(1 - D_1)$.

Standard errors for these estimates have not been worked out, although asymptotic solutions appear to be susceptible to straightforward, somewhat tedious computation.

In Thomsen's technique, the identification problem is handled by assuming that the ecological correlation between the transformed vote proportions is the same as the individual-level correlation between transformed vote probabilities. Thomsen gives a sufficient condition for this identity to hold, namely, that all districts have normally distributed partisanship with the same mean and variance. Thus Thomsen's model succeeds when districts are perfectly homogeneous in their

---

4. Thomsen suggests using the logit transformation instead of the probit, so that a vote proportion of .60 would be transformed to ln[.60/(1 − .60)]. This function is somewhat easier to compute, and as Thomsen points out, probits and logits are so similar that the choice is presumably unimportant.

partisanship distribution, a condition that he believes is nearly true for the Danish electoral districts that are the focus of his empirical applications. Indeed, his empirical results seem to show reasonably good accord with the corresponding survey values, certainly much better than the usual Goodman ecological regression results. Thomsen's method has also enjoyed some success in other contexts (Berglund and Thomsen 1990), and it works well in the Stokes problem of British voting transitions between 1964 and 1966 (see table 7). Oddly, in most of these instances, the electoral districts are quite different from each other, so that Thomsen's sufficient condition for identification fails decisively. Yet Thomsen's method seems to work plausibly well. This raises the possibility that his method is justified under weaker conditions than he gives.

At present, however, it is fair to say that Thomsen's identification condition is troubling. Empirically, it is at best an approximation, and theoretically, it raises serious problems. For, on the one hand, if districts are not all alike, identification fails. On the other, if they are all alike, then ecological correlations cannot be computed, since there is no variance apart from sampling error. One cannot have it both ways; to ignore the contradiction is essentially to assume the aggregation problem away. Nor is the difficulty a minor technical matter. It is not immediately obvious how Thomsen's model can be identified in another way. In short, Thomsen's largest contribution is perhaps in identifying the class of model required, rather than in developing the particular version of it that will ultimately prevail.

Partisanship models face additional difficulties as well. Few political systems have only two parties, and even those with two-party systems allow voters the option of abstention, so that citizens always have a minimum of three choices. Even with ecological regression, which deals flexibly (if not often successfully) with multiple parties, researchers often turn multiple choices into dichotomies by collapsing parties into two broad groupings. Alternatively, they sometimes ignore all but two parties and work with two-party fractions. The same two tricks are used in partisanship models, as in the dichotomous partisanship model applied to Britain's three-party system above and in Thomsen's (1987, chaps. 4.2–4.3) studies of choice among pairs of parties. However, both approaches distort the situation by essentially denying that more than two choices exist, or by assuming that the voters for minor parties would always split their votes among the major parties in the same proportion as the rest of the population. It is not hard to show that in realistic circumstances, serious biases can occur under either approach.

Yet serious modeling of multiple choices is not easy either. With k alternatives, partisanship models require $k - 1$ correlated unobservable variables, thereby posing sticky problems of specification, identification, computation, data analysis, and substantive credibility. Apart from versions that assume away the correlations, to our knowledge not a single example is in print.

Partisanship models also face the challenge of assessing relationships between other demographic variables and the vote. One approach is to treat the regression of vote on, say, social class as closely akin to the regression of one vote on another vote and simply to apply the same partisanship model as in Thomsen (1987, chap. 4). This approach requires reinterpretation of the model, since no underlying variable like partisanship generates both the social class distribution and the vote preferences. More important, when the demographic variable is a discrete characteristic such as race or gender or religious denomination, there is the substantive problem of interpreting the supposed Gaussian distribution that underlies it. Without that special underlying structure, the estimating procedure is difficult to defend. Again, progress on this topic awaits further research. Achen (1994) takes some initial steps toward generalizing Thomsen's model and justifying its identification conditions.

CONCLUSION

Much remains to be done before partisanship models become equal competitors with ecological regression. Extensions must be developed to cope with abstention and multiple parties. Variables other than partisanship must be incorporated. Normality assumptions must be tested and weakened if necessary (Achen 1993). And most important, substantively credible identification conditions must be developed.

In spite of their elementary state, however, the class of partisanship models shows considerable promise. Such models have a stronger substantive interpretation than ecological regression and a better record of producing plausible estimates. Thomsen's method in particular, though not yet fully characterized theoretically, is easily applied and has a record of producing sensible results. With the steady development of identification conditions suited to different groups of electoral systems, these models should take their place among the repertoire of statistical tools available to students of aggregate data.

In the meantime, researchers sensitive to the central role of partisanship in electoral behavior will want to take it into account in everyday work with aggregate electoral data, that is, in ecological regressions. How might that be done? The insight provided by partisanship models is that voter transition rates are not constant across districts, but instead vary with district partisanship. Thus the simple Goodman model is inadequate, even with demographic factors added as controls. Instead, ecological regressions should be specified with transition rates that are functions of district partisanship.

In practice, partisanship will nearly always be unobservable.[5] However, past votes, which are a direct measure of partisan preference, may be used to proxy for partisanship. Intuitively, no other measure is likely to be nearly so good, an hypothesis confirmed in aggregate empirical work: Voter transition rates covary with prior votes far more closely than with demographic variables (Upton 1978).

Thus perhaps the best practical advice for coping with aggregation bias in electoral data is to specify ecological regressions with transition rates dependent on prior votes. We explored models of this kind in detail in chapter 5, and we demonstrated their ability to dramatically reduce aggregation bias in electoral data. Thomsen's model is essentially another version of the same idea. Both approaches outperform Goodman regression. This chapter gives an explanation for their success: Partisanship is the key variable in voter transition rates, prior votes are usually the best available proxy for partisanship, and thus transition rates should be specified as functions of prior votes.

---

5. For the American case, voters in many states register by political party, so that registration rolls might be used to construct an aggregate measure of partisanship. Votes might then be regressed on this variable directly, to measure partisan loyalty and defection rates. In addition, Goodman-type regressions might be constructed in which transition rates depend on the partisanship measure, in the manner discussed in chap. 2. In practice, however, this approach is usually unsuccessful. Party registration is often a poor index of behavioral partisanship, and odd statistical results seem to occur when "party of registration" is substituted for "party identification." In effect, partisanship remains unobserved even in the presence of party registration data. See also p. 93, no. 10.

EIGHT

TABULAR APPROACHES

The Method of Bounds and the Method of Differences

Chapters 5–7 have proposed alternative statistical models that may be used to extract estimates of individual transition probabilities from covariances of aggregated variables. In this chapter we will go back to the simple, basic information about transition probabilities contained in the aggregated data themselves. We will discuss ways in which this information may be combined with substantive assumptions directly, rather than via covariance models, to produce cross-level inferences.

For any aggregated group, the known aggregate frequencies of individuals' characteristics impose constraints on the possible combinations of those characteristics at the individual level. For instance, in figure 1, since .4 of the population are Republican and .1 are middle class, it is impossible that the individual-level combination "middle-class Republican" occurs among more than .1 of the population. A class of tabular approaches takes advantage of these constraints to make inferences from aggregated data to individuals. These are simple—almost primitive—methods, but they have not been used widely in the past; in their basic form, they usually proved too imprecise to be useful. Recent advances have made them somewhat more usable, however. They have three important advantages as compared with the covariance-based methods presented in the rest of this book: (1) they do not require the demanding assumptions of Goodman ecological regression and related methods; (2) all assumptions are made explicitly, and we see directly which are doing the work of estimation; and (3) because they are based on each single unit rather than on covariance across units, they yield a separate estimate of the individual-level relationship for each unit.

	Working Class	Middle Class	
Democrat	a	b	.6
Republican	c	d	.4
	.9	.1	

Figure 1. Example of the method of bounds

We shall first present the basic method of bounds of Duncan and Davis (1953) and then three more recently developed tabular approaches: (1) the method of bounds with external evidence and assumptions added, (2) the method of bounds with an approximated informative prior, and (3) the method of differences.

THE DUNCAN-DAVIS METHOD OF BOUNDS

The first description of the method of bounds was by Duncan and Davis (1953) who noted that, for any geographic unit, the average values of variables at the aggregate level may render impossible certain combinations of those variables at the individual level.[1] Thus we may be able, simply by observing aggregate proportions, to eliminate some possible individual-level relationships and put maximum and minimum bounds around the true individual-level relationship. In the example in figure 1, .9 of the district's population are working class, and .6 of its vote is Democratic. This means that it is impossible that less than .3 of the population are working-class Republicans (since .9 of the population are working class, but only .6 of the population voted Democratic). It is also impossible that more than .4 of the population are working-class Republicans, since only .4 of the population voted Republican at all. Therefore, though potentially from 0% to 100% of working-class individuals could have voted Republican, the aggregate proportions limit the possibilities to between .3/.9 and .4/.9, or between 33% and 44%. And, if between .3 and .4 of the population are working-class Republicans (c), then between 0 and .1 of the population

1. An early forerunner, which however was not picked up on by others, was proposed by R. Blank (1905).

are middle-class Republicans (d), between .5 and .6 are working-class Democrats (a), and between 0 and .1 are middle-class Democrats (b).

A serious problem with the Duncan-Davis technique is that it usually yields a much broader possible range than in the example here. In general, the more evenly scores are distributed in an aggregate unit, the wider the range of possible individual-level relationships will be. If in figure 1 the district had been 50% working class and 50% middle-class, for instance, the Duncan-Davis techniques would tell us that between 0% and 80% of working-class voters had voted Republican. This would not help us much. For this reason, the Duncan-Davis variant on cross-level inference has long remained primarily a curiosity, without much application.

The Midpoint of the Bounds

In general, the Duncan-Davis bounds have simply been treated as what they are, aggregate-based logical limits to the possible parameters of the individual-level relationship; as such, they have focused investigators' attention on the extreme possibilities of the individual-level relationship.

If instead we focus on the midpoint of the bounds, we find a somewhat more useful analytic tool. The bounds present us with a range, for which we may postulate an "ignorance prior" or "indifference prior," in Bayesian terms. That is, we regard any of the possible values within the bounds as having an equal probability of being the true value. The midpoint is then the best estimate according to the criterion of "mean square error"; on the average, the square of the difference between the midpoint and the true value is less than the square of the difference between any other point and the true value.

We can also calculate for the midpoint a measure of the error we can expect in using it as our estimate. The "mean error of estimate" is the average difference in absolute value between the midpoint of the bounds and all other points within the bounds. That is, it is the error we may expect to make in using the midpoint of Duncan-Davis bounds as our estimate.

Like mean square error, the mean error of estimate is minimized at the midpoint, as compared with other points which might be used as estimators; the average absolute value of errors is minimized around the median, and in the uniform distributions we are dealing with here, the midpoint is the median as well as the mean. The mean error of estimate for Duncan-Davis bounds equals one-fourth of the range of the bounds. This is an error of estimate averaged over our prior belief, not a conventional standard error such as those associated with non-Bayesian analysis.

THE METHOD OF BOUNDS WITH EXTERNAL EVIDENCE AND ASSUMPTIONS ADDED

As noted, the Duncan-Davis technique was little used for many years. More recently, however, a number of scholars have begun to adapt the Duncan-Davis technique by adding substantive assumptions to narrow the bounds beyond the strictly logical limits that are placed on them by the Duncan-Davis technique.[2] This strategy was first proposed in Shively (1974); recent elaborations or work in this mode include Claggett (1985), Claggett and Van Wingen (1988), Flanigan and Zingale (1985), Sigelman (1991). Let us set up the situation illustrated in figure 1 more generally in figure 2: X, $\tilde{X}$, Y, and $\tilde{Y}$ are the known aggregate proportions for a district, with $X + \tilde{X} = 1.0$ and $Y + \tilde{Y} = 1.0$. Let a, b, c, and d be the proportions having various combinations of x, $\tilde{x}$, y, and $\tilde{y}$. Thus a is the proportion of the population who are simultaneously x and y, and so on: $a + b + c + d = 1.0$, $a + b = Y$, and so forth. Let

$$p = \text{proportion of those having } x \text{ that also have } y, \quad \text{or} \quad \frac{a}{X},$$

$$q = \text{proportion of those having } \tilde{x} \text{ that also have } y, \quad \text{or} \quad \frac{b}{\tilde{X}},$$

$$r = \text{proportion of those having } y \text{ that also have } x, \quad \text{or} \quad \frac{a}{Y},$$

$$s = \text{proportion of those having } \tilde{y} \text{ that also have } x, \quad \text{or} \quad \frac{c}{\tilde{Y}}.$$

In any tabular ecological inference we will be trying either to estimate a, b, c, and d from the known X, $\tilde{X}$, Y, $\tilde{Y}$, or to estimate p, q, r, and s from the known X, $\tilde{X}$, Y, and $\tilde{Y}$.

The augmented Duncan-Davis approach is best presented by setting up the situation portrayed in figure 2 as an underidentified system of simultaneous equations and inequalities. We know that the

---

2. This section is adapted from Shively (1974).

	X	X
Y	a	b
Y	c	d

Figure 2. Tabular cross-level inference

following relationships hold for the total population or for any jth subpopulation:

(1) $$Y_j = p_j X_j + q_j \tilde{X}_j,$$

(2) $$X_j = r_j Y_j + s_j \tilde{Y}_j,$$

(3) $$p_j X_j = r_j Y_j,$$

(4) $$0.0 \leq p_j, q_j, r_j, s_j \leq 1.0.$$

Equation (3) holds because each side of the equation represents the proportion of individuals having both attributes x and y.

This system of three equations and one inequality in four unknowns yields a family of possible solutions for p_j, q_j, r_j, and s_j. Boundaries for this general solution are the Duncan-Davis limits. If a further equation could be added in a particular study, then the system could be solved. If further inequalities could be added, then the family of possible solutions might be reduced, and its boundaries narrowed.

Such additional equations or inequalities might come from external evidence, judgments based on past experience, and so forth. The investigator's success in narrowing the Duncan-Davis limits will depend on her background and on her ingenuity in devising supplementary equations or inequalities which satisfy her and her readers.

An Example: Social Democratic Voting in Imperial Germany

To explore the potential of this technique, we have attempted to estimate the class basis of the German Social Democratic party (SPD) in 1912. It was the SPD at this period which led Michels to propose his "iron law of oligarchy." It is of some interest to determine how exclusively the SPD's appeal was directed to the working class at that time.

The database for this example consists of the 41 largest cities of the German Empire, plus the 40 provinces, duchies, and the like, of the Empire with the cities' population removed. Thus, the German population is divided for purposes of this analysis into 81 exhaustive and mutually exclusive subsets, 41 of which are urban. For each of these

TABLE 1 Estimated Conditional Probabilities under Successive Additions to the Duncan-Davis Model

System	Estimated Probability That Workers Voted SPD	Estimated Probability That Middle Class Voted SPD
A. Basic Duncan-Davis model	.384	.240
	(.181)	(.113)
B. Above, plus assumption that working-class turnout ≤ .97 times middle-class turnout	.352 (.166)	.259 (.103)
C. Above, plus assumption that workers are at least as likely as middle class to vote SPD	.502 (.091)	.166 (.057)

Note: Numbers in parentheses are mean errors of estimate.

aggregate units, we obtained the number of working class and of middle class in the electorate, and the number of socialist votes cast in the 1912 election.[3]

The basic Duncan-Davis analysis does not yield sufficiently narrow limits in the case to be useful for many purposes. As shown on the first line of table 1, this analysis yields an estimate of .24 of the middle-class electorate voted for the SPD, with a mean error of estimate of .113. That is, on the average, using this method our error would have an absolute value of .113.

In succeeding rows of table 1, we have added further inequalities to the basic system of equations (1)–(4). First, we added for each district an assumption that working-class turnout in the election was no greater than .97 times the middle-class turnout, a ratio derived from an early survey conducted in Dresden (Wurzbürger 1907). Applying this assumption serially to the districts yielded the modest improvement of estimation shown in row B of table 1.

Next, as shown in row C of the table, we added the assumption that the probability of a worker voting socialist was greater than or equal to the probability of a member of the middle class doing so. This gave

3. The data are drawn from appropriate volumes of *Statistik des Deutschen Reichs,* the official German statistical series. "Workers" are defined as all those identified as *Arbeiter,* in industry and commerce. The proportion of workers in the electorate is estimated by taking the proportion of men over the age of 25 (the age and gender limits for suffrage) who were workers. This is an approximation to the registered electorate, but a pretty close one.

more usable estimates, with an average error of estimate for the middle-class proportion of .057; this is still substantial, but is getting into the region of what should be usable.

Details of each of these applications are given in the appendix.

In an earlier version of this example, Shively (1974) included a further assumption, that "breakage" effects (see above, chap. 6, n. 4; cf. Berelson et al. 1954, pp. 98–101) operated across the districts, with socialist voting by workers, for instance, increasing in an assumed manner with increasing concentrations of workers in districts. While this is a reasonable hypothesis, the added wisdom (or caution) of years makes us less anxious to include it as a postulate for estimation. Had it been added to the assumptions in rows A–C of table 1, it would have yielded estimated probabilities for workers and the middle class of .521 and .153, respectively, with mean errors of estimate of .047 and .029. The breakage assumption is also described in the appendix, for those wishing to see how it would work.

It is perhaps surprising to see from row C how low the electoral polarization of Germany was in 1912. Our best estimate of the polarization is a difference of .336 between working-class and middle-class support for the socialists, with .166 of the middle-class electorate voting socialist. Even if we corrected for the possibility that our average expected errors were in the direction of overestimating middle-class support and underestimating workers' support, we would still get a difference of only .484, with .109 of the middle-class electorate voting socialist. These estimates, which required only fairly easy, nonheroic assumptions, seem to bear out Michels's view that the SPD was already "bourgeoisified" in 1912.

We must reiterate, however, that the mean error of estimate is not to be compared with the standard error of estimate in non-Bayesian regression analysis. The mean error of estimate means just what it says: on the average, using these procedures, we should expect to make an error of .057 in estimating the middle-class probability. Though this would seem to us to be within the range of usability, it is also error not to be taken lightly.

One advantage of the method of bounds is that it allows us readily to compare subsets of the the aggregate units. Since the bounds are calculated for the full population by summing the maximum and minimum possible frequencies for the aggregate units, it is simple to sum these frequencies for only a selected portion of the aggregate units, such as a region, or even to look at a particular aggregate unit by itself. For the city of Berlin, for instance, the assumptions in row C of table 1 would yield an estimate that .492, or roughly half, of the middle class voted SPD in 1912; the mean error of estimate is .059.

The method of bounds as illustrated here may be useful as a technique in its own right, or as a supplement to other techniques. Its usefulness in any particular problem will depend on the geographic distribution of the variables, and on the number of plausible assumptions the investigator can bring to bear.

THE METHOD OF BOUNDS WITH AN APPROXIMATED INFORMATIVE PRIOR

Either in its original form or with external assumptions added as in the example above, the method of bounds suffers from the fact that it produces logical bounds, which do not imply any variation in the probability density for the true parameter within the bounds. Given no further information, we therefore treat the density as uniform, with a point near the extremes of the bounds having the same probability of equaling the true value as a point near the middle.

In the preceding section we treated this equiprobable distribution as an indifference prior and were thus able to develop the midpoint of the distribution as a best estimate. In this section we will introduce the strategy of approximating an "informative prior"—a prior density which gives more weight to some possibilities than to others. This will allow us to develop an estimator for which one can expect, on the average, to incur errors that are less than the mean error of estimate; the latter is based on the indifference prior, so by further restricting the underlying probability density to approximate an informative prior, we should reduce our uncertainty and thus reduce the size of errors.[4]

The approach below posits a single substantive assumption (direction of the relationship) which will frequently be usable in a wide variety of studies. It will in general allow us to narrow the Duncan-Davis bounds substantially, and perhaps more important, it allows analysis of the place of the true parameter within the bounds.

Returning to the setup presented in connection with figure 2, and

4. John Wanat (1979, 1982) has developed a "maximum possibility" technique for generating the underlying probability density. Noting that some cell entries occur more frequently than others among the set of all possible combinations of internal entries that are consistent with the marginals, he chooses the cell entries that show up most frequently among possible solutions as the best ("most possible") estimates. We do not believe, however, that frequent occurrence among logically possible solutions makes a cell entry more likely to be the true value.

without loss of generality, let us assume for either the whole population or any jth subpopulation that

$$p_j \geq q_j.$$

That is, we assume one of the probabilities everywhere greater than or equal to the other; in a voting study, for instance, we might feel justified in assuming loyalty rates to be greater than or equal to defection rates. We can interpret Y_j as a weighted average of p_j and q_j, noting that since Y_j is the proportion of all cases that are y, then since p_j is the proportion of a subset of the cases (i.e., the x) that are y and $p_j \geq q_j$, then $p_j \geq Y_j$ and $q_j \leq Y_j$. Therefore, multiplying through by X_j,

$$p_j X_j \geq Y_j X_j,$$

but since $p_j X_j = a_j$,

$$a_j \geq Y_j X_j.$$

Thus we have established a new lower bound for a_j, which will be equal to or greater than the basic Duncan-Davis bound. In the example of figure 1, for instance, if we could have assumed $p_j \geq q_j$, the lower bound for a_j would have been $X_j Y_j = .54$, rather than .5.

Beyond allowing us to narrow the bounds, using this assumption yields an interpretation of the true location of a within the bounds. The upper bound of a_j is the lesser of X_j and Y_j; that is, it is the lesser of $a_j + b_j$ and $a_j + c_j$. Subtracting a_j from the upper bound, then, yields the lesser of b_j and c_j. That is, the distance between the true parameter a_j and its upper bound is $\min(b_j, c_j)$:

$$\min(X_j, Y_j) - a_j = \min(b_j, c_j)$$

Working from the other end, subtracting its lower bound from a, we obtain

$$a_j - X_j Y_j = a_j - (a_j + b_j)(a_j + c_j)$$

$$= a_j - (a_j^2 + a_j c_j + a_j b_j + b_j c_j)$$

$$= a_j(1 - a_j - c_j) - b_j(a_j + c_j)$$

$$= a_j(b_j + d_j) - b_j(a_j + c_j),$$

since $a_j + b_j + c_j + d_j = 1$. Thus,

$$a_j - X_j Y_j = a_j \tilde{X}_j - b_j X_j$$

$$= X_j \tilde{X}_j \left(\frac{a_j}{X_j} - \frac{b_j}{\tilde{X}_j} \right),$$

or

$$a_i - X_i Y_i = X_i \tilde{X}_i (p_i - q_i).$$

The distance between its lower bound and the true parameter a_i is thus $X_i \tilde{X}_i (p_i - q_i)$.

We have shown by this analysis that the distance down from the upper bound to a_i is the lesser of b_i and c_i and the distance up from the lower bound to a_i is $X_i \tilde{X}_i (p_i - q_i)$. Graphically,

$$
\left.
\begin{array}{c}
\min(X_i, \ Y_i) \\[3em]
a_i \\[3em]
X_i Y_i
\end{array}
\right\}
\begin{array}{l}
\min(b_i, \ c_i) \\[3em]
X_i \tilde{X}_i (p_i - q_i)
\end{array}
$$

The smaller $\min(b_i, c_i)$ is, and the larger $X_i \tilde{X}_i (p_i - q_i)$ is, the higher a_i will be located within the bounds.

It is not uncommon that we can assume the direction of a relationship we are studying. In studies of intergenerational mobility, of relationships between social class and behavior, of electoral transitions, and in many other cases we can confidently predict the direction of relationships. Doing so allows us to narrow the Duncan-Davis bounds appreciably, and it also allows us to approximate the probability density of the parameter within the bounds if it is possible to make further assumptions about $\min(b_i, c_i)$ or $X_i \tilde{X}_i (p_i - q_i)$.

Shively (1991) develops this technique in detail for the case of electoral transition, where we can generally assume that $\min(b_i, c_i)$ is low and $p_i - q_i$ is high. He tests the method from the marginals of several panel studies of British and American elections by calculating point estimates of the proportions in each cell of the diagonal of the transition matrix. When these estimates are compared to the cells of the observed transition matrices based on the surveys, the average error is only .012. The following example is adapted from that study.

An Example: The New Deal Election of 1932

In general, in analyzing interparty electoral transition, we expect that either b or c will be fairly small, because electoral change usually favors one party or another. In a Democratic year, for instance, we would expect the cell for Democrats defecting to the Republicans to be fairly small, although we certainly would not expect it to be zero. Similarly, in a Republican year the cell for Republicans defecting to the Democrats should be fairly small. Therefore, we probably should expect $\min(b, c)$ to be rather small in studies of electoral transition.

Also, we should expect $p - q$ to be fairly substantial in such studies because the voters of a party are in general much more likely to repeat a vote for that party than are voters of the other party likely to switch to it. We should be able to assume $\min(b, c)$ to be low and $p - q$ to be high in widely varying electoral situations. These assumptions should be true even in realignment elections where there would typically be a large movement in one direction, but still considerable stability exhibited within the realignment. The assumptions will not apply so well to young electorates, such as those of Eastern Europe in the 1990s, whose behavior is still rather unstructured.

Accordingly, since for established electorates $\min(b, c)$ may be expected to be low and $p - q$ high, if we can correct for the known $X\tilde{X}$ in $X\tilde{X}(p - q)$, we should expect the true value of a to fall in the upper range of its bounds. We can proceed by using a conservative estimate of the relative sizes of $\min(b, c)$ and $p - q$ to reset the lower bound of a. This will take into account the size of $X\tilde{X}$ as well. We now have an adjusted set of bounds for which a is unlikely to fall near the lower bound (because we have deliberately set the bound conservatively) and also unlikely to fall near the upper bound (because, while we expect $\min(b, c)$ to be fairly small, we do not expect it to approach zero.) Because a is unlikely to fall near either tail of the bounds, if we assume that the probability density of a within the bounds is single-peaked, the midpoint of the bounds becomes our best estimate, with an expected error of something less than the mean error of estimate.

Note that this approximation is rough indeed. All we have been able to assume is that the true value of a falls toward the middle of the adjusted bounds, since we have a good basis for assuming that it is less likely to lie at the extremities. Still, this gives us a better basis than we had with a uniform distribution for taking the midpoint as our esti-

| | ELECTION 1 | | |
	Party$_1$	Party$_2$	
Party$_1$	.42	.08	.5
Party$_2$	.18	.32	.5
	.6	.4	

ELECTION 2 (vertical label on left)

Figure 3. Example of interparty electoral transition

mate. Here the midpoint is the best estimate of *a*, in more than just the sense that it minimizes square error loss.

To proceed with the example, let us assume $\min(b, c) \le .67(p - q)$. This is conservative because $p - q$ will in general be fairly large. For example, figure 3 depicts a typical situation of electoral change. In this figure, $p - q = .42/.6 - .08/.4 = .50$, but $\min(b, c)$ is only .08. Obviously, the assumption that $\min(b, c) \le .67(p - q)$ is very conservative here, as it will be in general. The ratio of .67 is deliberately set so high that we imagine that $\min(b, c)$ will rarely approach that level. (If $p - q = .5$, e.g., $\min(b, c)$ would have to be greater than .33 to violate the assumption!) This allows us to regard the midpoint of bounds adjusted on this assumption as the best estimate, because either tail of the bounds will appear unlikely to include the true parameter.

The figure of .67, while it is not arbitrary, is certainly subjective. It is reassuring, however, to find that the analysis appears to be remarkably robust relative to the ratio we choose. (See table 2 and its discussion, below.)

Having made a conservative assumption, we proceed to adjust the lower bound in accordance. If $\min(b, c) \le .67(p - q)$, the lower bound of *a* can be set to

$$XY + \frac{X\tilde{X}}{X\tilde{X} + .67}[\min(X, Y) - XY].$$

This lower bound is consistent with the assumed ratio and also adjusts for the known value of $X\tilde{X}$.[5] The region just above this new lower bound is an unlikely region for *a*, since *a* would occur in this region only if $\min(b, c)$ approached $.67(p - q)$.

We can now estimate *a*, and if we were working with a 2×2 table we could proceed readily. Since a 2×2 table has only one degree of freedom, we could calculate the remaining internal proportions from *a* together with the observed marginals. However, our example—like all electoral studies—requires at least a 3×3 table, to take into account the option of abstention as well as the options of voting Demo-

---

5. To derive the lower bound from $\min(b, c) \le .67(p - q)$, note that if $\min(b, c) \le .67(p - q)$, then $0 \ge \min(b, c) - .67(p - q)$, or $X\tilde{X}(p - q) \ge X\tilde{X}(p - q) + \min(b, c) - .67(p - q)$, or $a - XY \ge X\tilde{X}(p - q) + \min(b, c) - .67(p - q)$. The term on the right-hand side reduces to $[X\tilde{X}/(X\tilde{X} + .67)][\min(X, Y) - XY]$. For a full proof, see Shively (1991, p. 90).

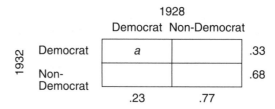

Figure 4. First New Deal election

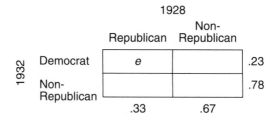

Figure 5. 2 × 2 Table for first New Deal election: Democrats

1928

	Republican	Non-Republican	
Democrat 1932	e		.23
Non-Republican			.78
	.33	.67	

Figure 6. 2 × 2 table for First New Deal election: Republicans

cratic or Republican. To analyze the 3 × 3 table for electoral transition from 1928 to 1932 shown in figure 4, we proceed as follows:

1. To estimate *a*, we set up a dichotomous table of Democrats and non-Democrats, as in figure 5. The *a* for this table will be the proportion of the electorate who voted Democratic at both elections, and it can therefore be transferred directly to cell *a* of figure 4.
2. Similarly, dichotomous tables for Republicans (fig. 6) and abstention are analyzed to estimate *e* and *i* and to insert them in figure 4. The diagonal for the 3 × 3 table has now been estimated.
3. A number of potentially interesting figures involving diagonal and

off-diagonal cells may now be calculated from the estimates of a, e, and i, in combination with the marginals.

Let us proceed first to estimate the diagonal. Working from figure 5, the basic bounds around a, from an assumption that $p - q \geq 0$, are

$$XY = (.23)(.33) = .08 \leq a \leq .23 = \min(X,Y);$$

$X\tilde{X}$ equals .177. Adding the conservative assumption that $\min(b, c) \leq .67(p - q)$, we adjust the lower bound upward by

$$\frac{X\tilde{X}}{X\tilde{X} + .67}[\min(X, Y) - XY] = \frac{.177}{.844}(.23 - .08) = .03.$$

Adding .03 to the old lower bound of .08, we obtain new bounds:

$$.11 \leq a \leq .23.$$

Assuming that the true a is unlikely to occur within either tail of this range and that its probability distribution is unimodal, we choose as our best estimate the midpoint of the range, .17. Note that we cannot assign a measure of error to this estimate since the probability distribution within the bounds is only very roughly identified. The error is lower, in any case, than the mean error of estimation for an equiprobable distribution with bounds of this width.

Repeating the analysis for cells e (using fig. 6) and i (not illustrated), we estimate

$$e = .17,$$

$$i = .35.$$

We have thus estimated the diagonal, as shown in figure 7. Before we proceed to consider the off-diagonal cells, we note that a number of potentially interesting figures can be calculated, simply from the diagonal estimates together with the marginals. For example:

1. The Republican rate of desertion

   $$= (.33 - .17)/.33 = .48,$$

2. The Democratic desertion rate

   $$= (.23 - .17)/.23 = .26,$$

3. Gross movement between the parties

   $$= (.33 - .17) + (.23 - .17) - (.44 - .35)$$
   $$= (b + c) + (d + f) - (c + f) = b + d = .13,$$

1928

	Democrat	Republican	Abstention + minor parties	
Democrat	.17	.115 (.023)	.06 (.015)	.33
Republican	.03 (.015)	.17	.03 (.015)	.23
Abstention + minor parties	.03 (.015)	.07 (.015)	.35	.45
	.23	.33	.44	

(Left margin label: 1932)

Gross movement between parties	.13
Gross movement in/out of abstention	.19
Stable party votes	.34
Republican desertion rate	48%
Democratic desertion rate	26%
Rate of movement to Republicans by non-Republicans	9%
Rate of movement to Democrats by non-Democrats	21%
Rate of movement to abstention by previous voters	18%
Rate of movement to voting by previous abstentions	26%

* mean errors of estimate in parentheses

Figure 7. First New Deal election with all cells estimated. *Note:* Numbers in parentheses are mean errors of estimate.

4. Gross movement in and out of abstention

$$= (.44 - .35) + (.45 - .35) = .19,$$

5. Movement by Democrats and nonvoters to the Republicans

$$= (.23 - .17)/(.23 + .44) = .09,$$

and so on. These are calculated directly from the marginals, plus the diagonal.

We cannot use this method to estimate off-diagonal cells, as we did for the diagonal, because we cannot set up dichotomous tables such as those in figures 5 or 6 for off-diagonal cells. More precisely, we could set them up, but we could not confidently make the sorts of assumptions about them regarding $\min(b, c)$ and $p - q$ that we need to approximate a probability density for the resulting bounds. Instead, we will use the marginals and our estimates of the diagonal cells to set normal Duncan-Davis bounds for each off-diagonal cell, estimating the entry for the cell by the midpoint of the bounds, with an associated mean error of estimate.

To estimate bounds for the off-diagonal cells, let us first note a number of sums:

$$b + c = .33 - .17 = .16,$$

$$d + f = .23 - .17 = .06,$$

$$g + h = .45 - .35 = .10,$$

$$d + g = .23 - .17 = .06,$$

$$b + h = .33 - .17 = .16,$$

$$c + f = .44 - .35 = .09.$$

It is possible to use these sums and the differences derived from them to estimate bounds around the off-diagonal proportions. Note that for these bounds we do not have any way to predict the probability that the true value will occur in varying regions within the bounds; therefore, we cannot choose a best point estimate based on them. Unlike the diagonal, the bounds for these cells must remain as bounds.

From the sums, we also calculate the following differences:

$$c - h = (b + c) - (b + h) = 0,$$

$$b - f = (b + c) - (c + f) = .07,$$

$$f - g = (d + f) - (d + g) = 0,$$

$$d - c = (d + f) - (c + f) = -.03,$$

$$h - d = (g + h) - (d + g) = .04,$$

$$g - b = (g + h) - (b + h) = -.06.$$

Now, working with the sums and differences, we can develop a set of bounds for the off-diagonal proportions. For b, we note that $b + c = .16$ (the smaller of the two sums involving b) offers an upper bound. From the differences, we see that $b - f = .07$, so $b \geq .07$. Thus,

$$.07 \leq b \leq .16.$$

Since these bounds enclose an equiprobable distribution, we follow the procedure described in the first section of this chapter and take as our best estimate the midpoint .115, with a mean error of estimate of .0225. The smaller sum involving c is $c + f = .09$. From the differences, we see that $d - c = -.03$, so c must be greater than or equal to .03. Thus, $.03 \le c \le .09$, for an estimate of .06 with mean error of estimate of .015. Our upper bound for d is the lower of its sums, .06; neither difference involving d yields a nonnegative lower bound, so the highest possible lower bound is zero. Thus, $0 \le d \le .06$, for an estimate of .03 with mean error of estimate of .015. Similarly, we can estimate: $f = .03$, $g = .03$, and $h = .07$, with mean errors of estimate of .015, .015, and .015, respectively. We thus complete our estimation of the internal proportions as in figure 7. Although the equiprobable bounds in the off-diagonal cells are reasonably narrow, breaking down the sums and differences to individual cells has added considerable uncertainty to our estimation. Working directly with figures, such as $b + d$ (gross exchange between parties), $(b + h)/.33$ (the rate of Republican desertion), and so on, will generally be more useful than working with bounds estimates for individual off-diagonal cells; which will be more useful, however, obviously depends on the investigator's purposes.

One obvious question about this method is, How much does the choice of the ratio .67 in the assumption $\min(b, c) \le .67(p - q)$ affect the estimates? A rough test of the robustness of the method relative to this assumption may be performed simply by inserting other ratios and observing how much this changes the estimates. Table 2 presents such a test for the estimates in the 1928–1932 example. Raising the ratio to 1 or lowering it to .33 does not appear to greatly change the estimation. A ratio of greater than 1 would be almost absurd, and using a ratio of less than .33 as a *conservative* assumption would begin to be questionable; this indicates that the method is quite robust relative to the assumed ratio.[6] We have not tested for robustness in this way on more than a few cases, however, and robustness will presumably depend on the distribution of marginals, so we would suggest that users test for it on at least a sample of their analyses.

Apparently, the choice of ratio does not affect the estimates greatly. The only other assumptions used in this analysis are (1) that probability densities within bounds are single-peaked and (2) the basic assumption that $p \ge q$ for each subsidiary 2×2 table; that is, the probability of Democrats repeating a Democratic vote is greater than the probability of non-Democrats shifting to the Democrats, and the probability of Republicans repeating a Republican vote is greater than the probability of non-Republicans shifting to the Republicans, and the probability of abstainers repeating abstention is greater than the probability of voters

---

6. The ratio can be reduced even further to .17 without changing the results greatly.

TABLE 2 Estimates for 1928–32 with Varying Ratios of $(p - q)$ to min (b, c)

Estimates	Ratio		
	.33	.67	1
a	.18	.17	.17
b	.12	.12	.11
c	.05	.06	.07
d	.03	.03	.03
e	.18	.17	.16
f	.03	.03	.03
g	.03	.03	.04
h	.05	.07	.08
i	.37	.35	.34
Gross movement between parties	.12	.13	.13
Gross movement in/out of abstention	.15	.19	.21
Rate of Republican desertion	.46	.48	.50
Movement by Democrats and nonvoters to Republicans	.07	.09	.09

switching to abstention. If we are confident of these assumptions, then, given the robustness of our estimates relative to the ratio that we chose, we can be confident that the true values that we seek are very close to the estimate displayed in figure 7.

Relationship of the Method(s) of Bounds to Ecological Regression

The methods presented above appear quite different from the regression- and correlation-based methods which occupied chapters 2–7. And, historically they have developed independently of the other methods. But it is clear that there must be some connection between the two approaches. What is it?

We can see the connection most easily by returning to the basic truism of ecological regression, equation (1) of chapter 1:

$$Y_i = p_i X_i + q_i(1 - X_i).$$

We can restate this, still as a truism, by rearranging and dividing through by $(1 - X_i)$:

$$(5) \qquad q_i = \frac{Y_i}{1 - X_i} - \left(\frac{X_i}{1 - X_i}\right) p_i.$$

That is, for each jth district, q is a linear function of p, with parameters that are determined by the marginals. Each district will have its own equation.

For instance, for a district with $X = .7$ and $Y = .6$,

$$q_j = \frac{.6}{.3} - \frac{.7}{.3}p_j = 2 - 2.33p_j.$$

Note that across the potential range of p_j from 0.0 to 1.0, q_j would at some points take on impossible values (e.g., if $p_j = 0$, $q_j = 2$). The value of p_j for which $q_j = 1.0$ is therefore the lowest possible value of p_j; any lower value would correspond to an impossible q_j. In this example, $p_j = .42857$ corresponds to $q_j = 1.0$. Thus, $p_j \geq .42857$, or $a_j/X_j \geq .42857$; therefore, $a_j \geq .3$, which is of course exactly the "basic" Duncan-Davis lower limit of a when $X = .7$ and $Y = .6$. The Duncan-Davis upper bound for a can be similarly calculated from equation (5). Thus the truism in equation (5) can produce for each district the Duncan-Davis limits. This is illustrated in figure 8.

Now, what of Goodman ecological regression? Each district has its own line similar to that of figure 8, with its intercept and slope determined by the marginal X, $\tilde{X}$, Y, and $\tilde{Y}$. If p and q were constant across all districts, these lines (which still would vary because X and Y vary across the districts) would all intersect at a single point, the solution space for the set of simultaneous equations, and p and q would be identified by that point.

In ecological regression, we assume that p and q vary randomly across the districts around their true values; if the assumption is true, this allows us to solve for the true values by the method of least squares, even though—because of the random element—the lines do not intersect at a single point.

The basic Duncan-Davis limits, aggregated across all the districts' equations, define the outer limits of any possible solution space. When we add external evidence or assumptions to narrow the Duncan-Davis limits, we are doing the same thing that we do in ecological regression—we are using external assumptions to reduce the size of the solution space of the m lines relating p_j and q_j. In the case of Duncan-Davis limits, however, we do this by eliminating segments of the lines, rather than by generating a least squares solution.

Note that, since this is done district by district, rather than by assuming a model for covariance across the districts as we do in regression, it is possible to extend analysis by the method of bounds down to individual districts.

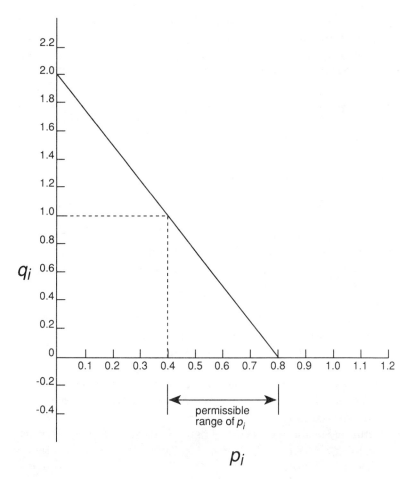

Figure 8. Graphical presentation of bounds for the example of $q_i = 2 - 2.33p_i$

How useful is the method of bounds, compared with regression and other covariance techniques? Estimates from the method of bounds appear rather crude compared with covariance-based estimates, and the range of error indicated in the mean error of estimate, for instance, is generally large compared with what we would expect from covariance-based estimates. Finally—and this is probably the most troubling aspect of bounds methods to users—bounds estimates are not embedded in a structure of statistical theory that allows us to assess them against probability distributions.

There is an irony here, though. A Duncan-Davis bounds estimate extracts all the information present in the marginals of the districts. Every bit of added precision in regression or other estimates, every connection to statistical theory, is a result solely of assumptions the investigator has imposed on the data. Perhaps the moral we should draw in comparing the two is not that the method of bounds is a less exact cousin of covariance techniques, but that it shows exactly what the evidential base of those techniques is.

THE METHOD OF DIFFERENCES

The method of differences is related to the Duncan-Davis technique but is not an extension of it as are the two other approaches presented so far. Rather than estimating internal cells from the known marginals, as the method of bounds does, this method produces an exact measure of certain *differences* between internal cells. Most important, at least for the 2×2 case, the method requires no constraining assumptions whatsoever.

We will first present the argument for the case of the 2×2 table, and then in order to provide an example, we extend it to the 4×4 table for use in studies of electoral change and stability.[7] An auxiliary assumption is required for the 4×4 extension, so its use here is limited to the study of electoral change. However, it should be possible to extend the model in a similar way to other substantive questions, if the investigator is creative in developing auxiliary assumptions.

Returning again to the setup of figure 2 (illustrated in fig. 9), where $X_j = a_j + c_j$, $\tilde{X}_j = b_j + d_j$, $Y_j = a_j + b_j$, and $\tilde{Y}_j = c_j + d_j$, it is easy to see that certain differences among the unknown a_j, b_j, c_j, and d_j may be calculated directly from the known X_j, $\tilde{X}_j$, Y_j, and $\tilde{Y}_j$. Specifically, $X_j - \tilde{Y}_j = (a_j + c_j) - (c_j + d_j) = a_j - d_j$, and similarly $\tilde{X}_j - \tilde{Y}_j = b_j = c_j$.

These are not estimates, but direct measures based on the aggregate values. They can be calculated for any given aggregate unit from that unit's values of X_j, $\tilde{X}_j$, Y_j, and $\tilde{Y}_j$. These identities can be useful in many contexts, including, as in the example below, studies of electoral stability and change. If the marginals are the party votes at two successive elections so that, say, X_j is the Democratic vote at time 1 and $\tilde{X}_j$ is the Republican vote at time 1, Y_j the Democratic vote at time 2 and $\tilde{Y}_j$ the Republican vote at time 2, then $a_j - d_j$ is the difference between

7. This section is adapted from Shively (1982).

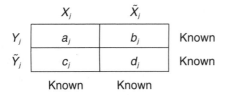

Figure 9. Tabular cross-level inference

two blocs of stable supporters (the bloc of voters who voted Democratic twice minus the bloc who voted Republican twice) and $b_i - c_i$ is the difference between the two parties' recruitment success (the bloc of voters who shifted to the Democrats minus the bloc who shifted to the Republicans).

However, electoral change and stability involve not only parties' votes but also movement into and out of abstention. To use these identities to study electoral change we must move beyond the 2 × 2 table.[8]

Measuring the Impact of Partisan Blocs and the Floating Vote in the American Case: Extension to 4 × 4 Tables

For ease of introducing our example, we will make the extension to a 4 × 4 case in terms of Democrats, Republicans, "other," and nonvoters. The model would apply to any electoral transition, however, as long as one felt confident of the substantive assumption we introduce below.

To devise measures for the impact of partisan blocs and the floating vote in American elections, it seems reasonable to treat the result of an election (on which they have "impact") simply as the margin of the Democratic vote over (or under) the Republican vote. This margin consists of four factors:

S_{D_j}, the bloc of stable voters who repeat a previous Democratic vote,

S_{R_j}, the bloc of stable voters who repeat a previous Republican vote,

8. In most tabular methods, including the Duncan-Davis–based approaches above, dealing with tables of greater rank than 2 × 2 involves further assumptions or uncertainties because of the greater number of degrees of freedom involved. Since electoral transition always involves at a minimum a 3 × 3 table (two parties plus abstention), applications to it of tabular methods always require some ingenuity. In addition to the example here, see Claggett and Van Wingen (1988) and Shively (1991).

M_{D_j}, the bloc of voters recruited to the Democrats from among previous nonvoters, previous supporters of the Republican Party, and previous supporters of minor parties, and

M_{R_j}, the bloc of voters recruited to the Republicans from among previous nonvoters, previous supporters of Democrats, and previous supporters of minor parties.

The margin $D_j - R_j$ is the sum of two differences:

$$D_j - R_j = (S_{D_j} + M_{D_j}) - (S_{R_j} + M_{R_j}),$$

or by rearranging terms,

$$(6) \qquad D_j - R_j = (S_{D_j} - S_{R_j}) + (M_{D_j} - M_{R_j}).$$

The first of these differences $(S_{D_j} - S_{R_j})$ is the contribution of blocs of stable partisan voters to the margin; the second difference $(M_{D_j} - M_{R_j})$ is the contribution to the margin of all sorts of voters recruited by the two parties. If we could measure $S_{D_j} - S_{R_j}$ and $M_{D_j} - M_{R_j}$ over a pair of elections, then we could assess the relative contribution of partisan blocs in the electorate to the outcome of the second election, compared with the contribution of those who have shifted their votes.

There are 16 possible combinations of a Democratic, Republican, or "other" vote or abstention at the first of two elections with a Democratic, Republican, or "other" vote or abstention at the second election. These combinations are indicated as lowercase letters in figure 10. Here $S_{D_j} - S_{R_j} = a_j - f_j$ and $M_{D_j} - M_{R_j} = (b_j + c_j + d_j) - (e_j + g_j + h_j)$.

To extend the technique beyond the simple 2×2 case we presented above, it is necessary to work with successive dichotomizations. For instance, dichotomizing electors into Democrats and non-Democrats allows us to measure the differences between the stable Democratic vote and the stable non-Democratic "vote" (including abstention as a "vote"), that is,

$$a_j - (f_j + g_j + h_j + j_j + k_j + l_j + n_j + o_j + p_j).$$

This would be measured by $D_{2j} - R_{1j} - O_{1j} - A_{1j}$. Similarly, $R_{2j} - D_{1j} - O_{1j} - A_{1j}$ will equal

$$f_j - (a_j + c_j + d_j + i_j + k_j + l_j + m_j + o_j + p_j).$$

Other dichotomizations are possible, and might be used for other purposes, but these two will give us what we need. The difference between

TIME 1

	D$_{1j}$	R$_{1j}$	O$_{1j}$	A$_{1j}$
D$_{2j}$	a$_j$	b$_j$	c$_j$	d$_j$
R$_{2j}$	e$_j$	f$_j$	g$_j$	h$_j$
O$_{2j}$	i$_j$	j$_j$	k$_j$	l$_j$
A$_{2j}$	m$_j$	n$_j$	o$_j$	p$_j$

(left label: TIME 2)

D_{tj} is the proportion of the electorate voting Democratic at time t in the jth district.

R_{tj} is the proportion of the electorate voting Republican at time t in the jth district.

O_{tj} is the proportion of the electorate voting for other parties at time t in the jth district.

A_{tj} is the proportion of the electorate abstaining at time t in the jth district.

$D_{1j} = a_j + e_j + i_j + m_j$

etc.

Figure 10. Components of electoral transition

(stable D_j minus stable rest) and (stable R_j minus stable rest) intuitively has something to do with the difference between a_j and f_j, and in fact if we subtract the second of these differences from the first we find that

$$D_{2j} - R_{1j} - O_{1j} - A_{1j} - (R_{2j} - D_{1j} - O_{1j} - A_{1j})$$

$$= (a_j - f_j - g_j - h_j - j_j - k_j - l_j - n_j - o_j - p_j)$$

$$- (f_j - a_j - c_j - d_j - i_j - k_j - l_j - m_j - o_j - p_j)$$

$$= 2(a_j - f_j) - (g_j + h_j + j_j + n_j) + (c_j + d_j + i_j + m_j).$$

That is,

$$(a_j - f_j) = \tfrac{1}{2}[(D_{2j} - R_{1j} - O_{1j} - A_{1j}) - (R_{2j} - D_{1j} - O_{1j} - A_{1j})]$$

$$+ \tfrac{1}{2}[(g_j + h_j + j_j + n_j) - (c_j + d_j + i_j + m_j)].$$

In other words, we can measure $a_j - f_j$ from the observed marginals with an error of $\tfrac{1}{2}[(g_j + h_j + j_j + n_j) - (c_j + d_j + i_j + m_j)]$. The first half of this error is the total gross exchange between the Republican party and abstention or "others," whereas the second half of the error is the total gross exchange between the Democratic party and abstention or "others." If the gross exchange rates of the two parties are equal, the error will be zero.

This is a condition which often is approximated closely; and even when it is not met the error which is produced is generally small, because it consists of half the *difference* between the two gross rates. To measure $a_i - f_i$ from the aggregate results, we must assume that the difference is zero and accept that some error will result. Shively (1982) presents estimates of the magnitude of such error, which appears to be fairly small in a number of cases.

Once we have measured $S_{D_j} - S_{R_j}$, that is, $a_i - f_i$, it is simple to calculate $M_{D_j} - M_{R_j}$ from equation (6). Since our measure of $M_{D_j} - M_{R_j}$ is simply the difference between the election margin and our measure of $a_i - f_i$, it will include an error of exactly the same magnitude as the error in our measure of $a_i - f_i$, but with the sign reversed. Thus, to evaluate error in the one measure is to evaluate it in the other as well.

An Example: American Elections, 1868–1988

Table 3 displays values of $S_{D_j} - S_{R_j}$ and $M_{D_j} - M_{R_j}$ for American presidential elections from 1868 to 1988. Sets of voters are expressed here as proportions of the potential electorate. Thus $S_{D_j} - S_{R_j}$ equals the proportion of all eligible who voted Democratic both at this and the preceding election, minus the proportion who voted Republican both at this and the preceding election.[9] The term $M_{D_j} - M_{R_j}$ equals the proportion who abstained or voted for the Republicans or a minor party at the first election and voted Democratic at the second, minus the proportion who abstained or voted for the Democrats or a minor party and then voted Republican.

The third column of Table 3 displays the proportional contribution of the difference between solid blocs of votes to the election outcome. We have seen in equation (6) that $D_j - R_j$, the election margin, equals the sum of $S_{D_j} - S_{R_j}$ and $M_{D_j} - M_{R_j}$. We can therefore calculate the

9. The "eligible" population consists of the population legally qualified by age, gender, and citizenship to vote. Data for this analysis were drawn from U.S. Bureau of the Census, *Historical Statistics of the United States: Colonial Times to 1970*, 1071–1072 and 1079–1080; U.S. Bureau of the Census, various editions of the *Statistical Abstract of the United States*.

TABLE 3 American Presidential Elections: 1868–1988

Year	Net Democratic Advantage in Blocs of Stable Votes[a]	Net Democratic Advantage in Recruitment[b]	Proportional Contribution of Blocs to Electoral Margin[c]
1868	−.058	.016	.784
1872	−.062	−.020	.756
1876	−.029	.053	.354
1880	.010	−.014	.417
1884	−.001	.003	.250
1888	.004	.002	.667
1892	.015	.008	.652
1896	−.006	−.029	.171
1900	−.040	−.005	.889
1904	−.084	−.039	.683
1908	−.089	.034	.724
1912	.008	.097	.076
1916	.46	−.026	.639
1920[d]	...	...	...
1924	−.126	.003	.977
1928	−.111	.012	.902
1932	.001	.100	.010
1936	.124	.023	.844
1940	.105	−.043	.709
1944	.052	−.010	.839
1948	.033	−.009	.786
1952	−.022	−.046	.324
1956	−.081	−.013	.862
1960	−.046	.047	.495
1964	.070	.069	.504
1968	.068	−.072	.486
1972	−.066	−.062	.516
1976	−.059	.070	.457
1980	−.020	−.031	.392
1984	−.103	−.053	.660
1988	−.053	.014	.791

Source: For data sources, see n. 9.

[a] $S_{Di} - S_{Ri}$.

[b] $M_{Di} - M_{Ri}$.

[c] $|S_{Di} - S_{Ri}| / (|S_{Di} - S_{Ri}| + |M_{Di} - M_{Ri}|)$.

[d] No measurements were made for the 1920 election because of the massive expansion of the electorate between 1916 and 1920, due to the enfranchisement of women.

proportional contribution of blocs to the overall outcome by dividing the absolute value of $S_{D_j} - S_{R_j}$ by the sum of absolute values of $S_{D_j} - S_{R_j}$ and $M_{D_j} - M_{R_j}$.

Perhaps the most interesting substantive finding is the changed role of party blocs in election outcomes since 1960. From 1868 through 1956 the pattern is consistent. Differences between party blocs dominate decisions, with proportional contributions of two-thirds or more, punctuated by elections of change (1952, 1932, 1912, 1896, and possibly 1884) in which differential recruitment erupted, with bloc differences contributing one-third or less.

Through 1956, only 4 of 22 elections show proportional contribution scores between .333 and .667. From 1960 through 1988, by contrast, 7 of the 8 elections fall in the middling range between .333 and .667. This suggests a sea change in the role of party voting in determining election outcomes.[10]

CONCLUSION

Neither the method of bounds nor the method of differences require any assumptions at all in their simple form. As such, they are undemanding methods. Both, however, will in general require the addition of assumptions or contextual evidence by the investigator if they are to yield useful results. In the case of the method of bounds, the basic Duncan-Davis limits will frequently be too broad to add much to the analysis; additional inequalities or an added equation are needed. In the method of differences, the 2 × 2 case is fully identified, but most analyses will require more degrees of freedom, hence the extension to a 4 × 4 table to study electoral stability and change. Such extensions require added assumptions.

The trade-off, as compared with ecological regression, is that the investigator loses the neat identification of inference from regression, but is freed from adherence to restrictive and sometimes ill-examined assumptions. Instead, the investigator must create explicit assumptions to achieve reasonable estimation. This places the emphasis on investigative creativity and on the acquisition of contextual knowledge— squarely where the emphasis should be.

---

10. The return in 1984 and 1988 to the earlier pattern might be a result of the strong candidate presence of Reagan in 1984, with carryover to Bush in 1988 (cf. the 1956 Eisenhower election).

APPENDIX

Applying Assumptions to Shrink Duncan-Davis Bounds: The Social Democratic Example

The narrowing of bounds in table 1 was accomplished in the following manner. To add the assumption of row B, we added the inequality

(A1)
$$p_j \le \frac{.97 f_j}{.97 + .03 M_j},$$

where f_j is the proportion of registered electors voting in the jth aggregate, and M_j is the proportion of the registered electorate that is middle-class. Thus p_j is the proportion of workers voting socialist in the jth aggregate.

The right-hand side of the inequality is an estimate of the proportion of working-class electors turning out to vote. A survey of nonvoters, conducted in Dresden after the 1907 election, indicates that the ratio of workers' participation to middle-class participation in the election was .97 (Wurzbürger 1907). The ratio of .97 is recalculated from Wurzbürger's table (p. 388), and from census data on Dresden. Based on that ratio, the estimated turnout among workers can be calculated from overall turnout and from the proportion of middle class in the electorate by the formula on the right-hand side of the inequality. Thus, the inequality states that the proportion of workers voting socialist was not more than the estimated proportion of workers voting. Inequality (A1) depends on the assumption that the ratio of working-class turnout to middle-class turnout in all districts of Germany was less than or equal to the 1907 Dresden ratio. This is probably a safe assumption, since Dresden was a heavily working-class, socialist city; the inequality is if anything conservative. We see in table 1 of the text that a slight narrowing of the Duncan-Davis limits is accomplished by adding inequality (A1) to the system.

The calculation of conditional probabilities for the population, based on the addition of this inequality, proceeded in the following way: For each of the 81 aggregate units, we estimated the proportions of the working class voting in the election by the formula on the right-hand side of inequality (A1). Multiplying this proportion by the number of workers, we estimated the number of workers voting in the district. If this figure was lower than the previous upper limit of the possible number of working-class socialist voters, it was substituted for that limit. In this case, we also raised the lower limit of the possible number of middle-class socialist voters by the same amount, since the total number of socialist voters minus the maximum possible number of working-class socialist votes must equal the minimum possible number of middle-class socialist votes. We then summed the maximum numbers of working-class socialist votes across the 81 units, dividing this sum by the number of workers in the population to calculate the conditional probability, as in the usual Duncan-Davis analysis. We calculated the other three conditional probabilities in the same way. The calculations for the effects of adding the two inequalities below proceeded in a similar manner.

At row C, a further inequality was added:

(A2) $$p_i \geq q_i;$$

that is, the proportion of workers voting socialist is greater than or equal to the proportion of middle-class electors voting socialist. The addition of inequalities (A1) and (A2), both apparently safe assumptions, narrows the Duncan-Davis limits appreciably.

Finally, as noted in the text, one might also add a somewhat more risky assumption. The extensive documentation of breakage effects in voting suggests that the proportion of workers voting socialist might have been lower in areas where workers were not numerous than in heavily working-class areas (see Berelson *et al.* 1954, pp. 98–101; Putnam 1966; Butler and Stokes 1969, pp. 144–150; Butler and Stokes provide a particularly strong example of breakage using class and vote). Thus, we might expect that in predominantly middle-class areas, the true probability that a worker voted socialist would tend to have been closer to the minimum possible value than the maximum possible value, while in heavily working-class areas, the reverse should be true. One could operationalize this expectation in the following manner, which is admittedly arbitrary. As a district approaches zero proportion working class, the maximum probability that a worker votes socialist is dropped to the midpoint between the maximum and minimum, while the minimum remains unchanged. As a district approaches 1.0 working class, the maximum probability remains unchanged, while the minimum is raised to the midpoint between the maximum and minimum. At any point between 0.0 and 1.0 working class, the maximum drops toward this midpoint in inverse proportion to the proportion working class, and the minimum rises toward this midpoint in direct proportion. Hence, the gap between the minimum and maximum values is reduced by half for each district. How much of this reduction comes from the top, and how much from the bottom, depends on the proportion of working class in the district. As the proportion of working class approaches zero, we could assume that the true value falls in the lower half of the preexisting range, because of the breakage effect, and that as the proportion working class approaches one, the true value rises to somewhere in the upper half of the preexisting range.

The assumption adds to the system the following inequality:

(A3) $$p_{\min,j} + .5\,W_j(p_{\max,j} - p_{\min,j}) \leq p_j$$

$$\leq p_{\max,j} - .5(1.0 - W_j)(p_{\max,j} - p_{\min,j}),$$

where $p_{\min,j}$ is the estimate of the minimum value based on equations (1)–(4) and inequalities (A1) and (A2), $p_{\max,j}$ is the estimate of the maximum value based on equations (1)–(4) and inequalities (A1) and (A2), and W_j is the proportion of the registered electorate working class in the jth aggregate.

NINE

CONTEXTUAL STUDIES AND AGGREGATION

A major development of social research over the last few decades is "contextual analysis," research which describes the effect of characteristics of individuals' environments on their behavior. Examples include Bodman (1983), Butler and Stokes (1969, pp. 144–50), Huckfeldt (1986), Huckfeldt and Sprague (1987, 1988, 1991), MacKuen and Brown (1987), Miller (1956), Putnam (1966), and Wright (1977); Prysby and Books (1991) review the field. Although sometimes confused with the "group mind" or "holistic" viewpoint discussed in chapter 1, contextual arguments are quite different. All explanation occurs at the level of the individual. Individuals interact, but they do not coalesce into a single actor.

From the outset, let us state clearly what we mean by "contextual effects." To begin, we set aside the nearly trivial definition in which every variable whose definition requires a social context is said to be a contextual effect. The problem with this definition is not so much that it is mistaken as that it is useless. Even descriptive features of an individual such as "registered Democrat," "middle income," or "practicing Catholic" are definable only by reference to a social context, and their social and political consequences will vary from place to place. They are not variables applicable to Robinson Crusoe, and in that sense they are contextual. But if we call any impact of these variables a "contextual effect," regardless of whether the causal effect was mediated or influenced by other people, then few social effects will be anything but contextual. With this definition, the category of contextual effects would deserve no special statistical attention.

A more meaningful definition of contextual effects, and the standard one in the literature, requires that group properties actually influence behavior in some social domain. The principal mechanism is usually thought to be communication among individuals in a group. For that reason, it might appear that the obvious place to study contextual effects is the group or aggregate level, where the effects are said to take place. Indeed, as early as 1970, Hauser (1970, 1974) suggested a relationship between social contextual analysis and cross-level inference, and Firebaugh (1978) later demonstrated a connection between the two.

The nature of the connection between contextual effects and cross-level inference is easily spelled out. Begin by recalling the basic assumption needed for regression with aggregated variables to yield unbiased estimates of the corresponding micromodel parameters: Parameter variation across districts must be uncorrelated in a certain sense with the measured district-level independent variables (see chap. 4, pp. 104–7, for a precise definition of "uncorrelated"). But when contextual effects are present and imperfectly modeled, they are likely to cause a violation of this condition. Most obviously, if the independent variables are prior vote totals subject to the same contextual effects as the current votes being explained, troublesome correlation with parameter variation is virtually certain. In short, unmodeled (or imperfectly modeled) contextual effects usually imply aggregation error.

As Hauser (1970, 1974) points out, however, the converse is not necessarily true: aggregation error need not imply the presence of contextual effects. Indeed, we have seen repeatedly in previous chapters that aggregation itself, without any contextual influences, is sufficient to induce distortions in macrorelations. And as will be seen below, even individual-level data, if they are used to measure networks of interaction, may readily involve "selection" bias that is a close cousin of bias due to selection into districts.

The central difficulty in studying contextual effects is to separate these selection effects from possible contextual influences. This is an identification problem directly parallel to the problem of cross-level inference with which we have dealt throughout this book: the data do not contain sufficient information to distinguish genuine effects from selection effects. To produce identification we must add further constraints rooted in theory or experience. Unfortunately, this difficulty has been too little appreciated by practitioners of contextual analysis.

In what follows, we will spell out the nature of the problem and propose some partial solutions. The next four sections take up issues involved in the use of aggregate data as proxies for context, and in the final section we will look at some more hopeful possibilities in the use of sophisticated individual-level data sets.

HOLISM, CONTEXT, AND AGGREGATION

Common practice in contextual analysis has been to use as proxies for "context" the same sort of accidental geographic aggregations with which we have dealt in our discussions of cross-level inference. The principal difficulty in using aggregate data to study contextual effects is that models employing statistical aggregates are often subject to aggregation bias even in the absence of contextual effects of any sort. A typical individual-level model will have its functional form distorted at the macrolevel, tempting the researcher to imagine that contextual forces of one sort or another are at work, when nothing of the kind is true. Some researchers have thought that if Goodman ecological regression failed in any way, or if the relationship was nonlinear, then contextual effects must be present.

The fallacy is most often visible in the sociological literature, where the Durkheimian beauties of emergent properties have often bedazzled researchers. Too much of the sociological literature on contextual effects has consisted of singing the theoretical praises of holistic effects, arguing the substantive plausibility of contextual effects, and then showing statistical biases due to aggregation effects, without noticing that meanings have shifted along the way.

The mistake occurs because any social process which behaves differently at the aggregate level is thought to give evidence of contextual or emergent influences. But this view has long been indefensible (e.g., Theil 1955). Functional differences at the aggregate level are often due to pure aggregation effects quite distinct from contextual processes. Purely reductionist, entirely individualistic behavioral models with no social communication and no group effects need not aggregate to the same functional form as their individual-level counterparts. Thus the oft-repeated empirical finding that aggregate models have different forms than their corresponding micromodels proves nothing about the existence of group or contextual influences, to say nothing of emergent group properties. No matter how plausible contextual or emergent models may be in the abstract, no amount of evidence consistent with simple aggregation bias will establish their importance.

In prior chapters, we have discussed two paths by which pseudo-contextual effects may arise. In chapter 3, we demonstrated that heterogeneity in a population (e.g., Democratic and Republican identifiers or middle-class and working-class citizens) may cause ecological regressions to indicate more voting stability than actually exists. Highly Democratic districts will appear unusually loyal to the Democrats; highly Republican districts will seem unusually fond of the Republicans. But the cause was not context. In that model, social communication and group mind effects were assumed away: Any Democratic identifier behaved the same way everywhere, as did any Republican. Pure aggregation produced the classic signs of contextual effects, but no contextual effects were present.

In a similar way, in chapter 5 we discussed the varying-coefficients version of the Goodman model (quadratic regression) and applied it to the Stokes data. Again we showed that nonfixed coefficients were sufficient to account for the apparent contextual effects in the data, even if the coefficients varied for reasons unrelated to contextual influences or emergent group properties.

In this chapter, we treat the issue from a third perspective, namely selection effects. From this viewpoint, the problem is particularly transparent, and a simple simulation illustrates our argument.

PSEUDOCONTEXTUAL EFFECTS IN AGGREGATE DATA

Following Blalock (1964), we imagine that the observed population is sorted into districts in accordance with the "urn model" introduced in chapter 1. According to that model, the basic assumption for cross-level inference from aggregate-level regression will be met if all individuals, conditional on their scores on the independent variables, have probabilities of being located in districts (or other contextual groups, such as clubs, schools, or neighborhoods) by historical aggregation processes in a way that is uncorrelated with their values on the dependent variable. (In the language we introduced on p. 16, history's assignment of individuals is conditionally independent.) Otherwise, a classic selection bias results, and the macroregression is biased.

This model could be expanded in a realistic way by allowing individuals, once they have come to be located in districts, to act on each other and change their values on the dependent variable. This is precisely a "contextual" process, and it would produce further systematic variation across districts in the probability that individuals of a given type on the independent variable will be of a given type on the dependent variable. (I.e., Goodman's transition probabilities p_j and q_j, as defined in equation (4) of chapter 1, will covary with the independent variable.)

Both parts of the process—the original location in districts and subsequent interaction among individuals—might contribute to the variation in probabilities across districts. And it is important to note that either might produce systematic variation without the other contributing at all. That is, if individuals have been aggregated independently of the dependent variable, "contextual" interaction if it is present will still be free to produce systematic variations in probabilities across districts. On the other hand, even if there are no effects from "contextual" interaction, if individuals have been aggregated according to their values on the dependent variable, then probabilities will still vary systematically across the districts.

Thus the two possible sources of variation are confounded in the aggregated data. There is no way to distinguish by observation of the data whether one, or the other, or both simultaneously, are at work.

A SIMULATED EXAMPLE

An example illustrates how a process of aggregation in which individuals are grouped according to their values on a dependent variable can produce what appears to be a result of contextual interaction among individuals. From a simulated pool of 3,000 individuals with a modest bivariate relationship between social class and support for school expenditures (table 1), we constructed 10 aggregated districts in the following manner. Conditional probabilities were set, for each category of "support for school expenditures," of the likelihood of settling in each of the 10 districts; the probabilities used are presented in table 2. The 3,000 individuals were then randomly assigned to districts solely according to these probabilities. Thus they were assigned to districts on

TABLE 1 Bivariate Distribution of Class and Support for School Expenditure in the Simulation Pool

Attitude	Social Class		Total
	Middle	Working	
Support higher school expenditure	900	450	1,350
Do not support	600	1,050	1,650
Total	1,500	1,500	

TABLE 2 Conditional Probabilities of Location in
Districts

District	Probability	
	Given Support for Expenditures	Given Nonsupport
A	.01	.25
B	.03	.20
C	.05	.16
D	.07	.13
E	.09	.10
F	.11	.07
G	.13	.05
H	.15	.02
I	.17	.01
J	.19	.01
	1.00	1.00

the basis of their attitude on school expenditure, and independent of their social class; that is, they were aggregated along the dependent variable. Social class varied considerably across the resultant districts, but only as a residue of the bivariate individual-level relationship between attitude and class.

Note that what happens in this simulation is that, regardless of what the individual-level process is, *at the aggregate level* attitudes toward school expenditure are correlated with the social-class makeup of districts. Districts are constructed (by migration, historical processes of socialization, institutional history, etc.) by selecting people on the basis of their attitude toward school expenditure, and the class makeup of the districts is simply a result of this process. The process has been simplified for this example by eliminating any direct relationship between location and class, but it is quite realistic in its central process; people do choose which district to live in, in part, because of the schools and property taxes in the district.

Table 3 and figure 1 display the results of this little simulation. A strong apparent "contextual" effect appears in these districts, with the proportion of middle-class individuals supporting school expenditures strongly and positively related to the proportion middle class in the district. This occurs even though none of the processes of diffusion, reinforcement, and so forth, which are posited in contextual models were present. No analysis of the resulting data could determine whether

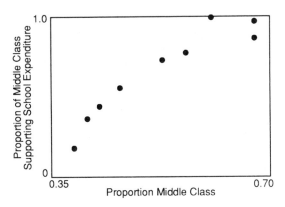

Figure 1. Phantom "contextual" effects in the simulation

TABLE 3 Simulation Results

District	Proportion of Population Middle Class	Proportion of Middle-Class Individuals Supporting Higher Expenditure on Schools
B	.39	.18
A	.41	.02
C	.41	.36
D	.43	.44
E	.46	.55
F	.53	.72
G	.57	.76
I	.61	.98
H	.68	.86
J	.68	.96

contextual processes were or were not present. An analyst looking at figure 1 would have to say that the relationship there could be due either to contextual processes, or to aggregation effects, or to a combination of the two.

CURRENT STATUS OF THE PROBLEM

Many scholars studying contextual effects with macrolevel variables appear not to have appreciated the significance of the confounding effect of selection effects due to geographic aggregation. When they have addressed the problem, they have dismissed it a bit casually:

> Concern for the selection problem in contextual analysis is well advised. Awareness is essential to avoid incorrect inferences about the existence of group effects. However, the problem of determining the direction of causal effects is not unique to models of behavior containing group variables. In the study of socio-economic class and mental illness, one theory is that lower socio-economic status increases the probability of mental illness. On the other hand, it could be that mental illness leads to lower socio-economic status. In these situations, arguments generally are based on such things as the temporal ordering of observations and substantive knowledge. Methods for estimating reciprocal causal paths do exist and are becoming more widely used in fields like economics, sociology, and political science (cf. Asher 1974; Duncan 1970).
> —(Boyd and Iversen 1979, pp. 194–195)

> If the contextual analyst thinks the dependent variable may have a substantial simultaneous effect on a contextual independent variable, perhaps as a result of individuals' locational decisions, then the analyst must use a simultaneous equation model rather than a single-equation regression model.　　—(Stipak and Hensler, 1982, p. 163)

But this does not do much for us. Establishing a simultaneous equation model of this kind is not a simple exercise; in practice, we are not aware of any contextual analysis in which an attempt has been made to use such a model. The appeal to simultaneous equation estimation has served more as an evasion than an answer. Indeed, it would not be an answer in any case. Such estimation would still be subject to the aggregation biases that affect all aggregated data analysis; the biases would just operate in two directions rather than one. Even if this theoretic difficulty were surmounted, a further problem would be posed by the very large measurement error involved in using accidental aggregate variables as proxies for local context. (See below, pp. 230–32 for discussion of sophisticated individual-level data sets that involve less measurement error.)

Confounding of aggregation processes and contextual interactions must occur frequently. In studying political behavior, for example, the relationship between "life-style" and many political attitudes and behaviors must often lead individuals to locate themselves in geographic districts at least partly because of factors that will correlate with variables we wish to treat as dependent in contextual analyses. Our simulated example was of this sort; it is well understood that individuals may settle in varying parts of a metropolitan area, depending on their attitude toward school expenditures. Similarly, people who like to hunt will tend to cluster together, as will those who like chamber music, those who oppose abortion, those who like to do yard work, and so on. Any of these may correlate with political choices; at one point early in the postwar period, public opinion pollsters in West Germany found that their best single predictor of voting behavior was whether people had little statues of dwarves in their gardens! It is not necessary that people's location in a geographic area be solely a function of the variable in question, as was the case in the simulation; if there are *any* direct effects of the dependent variable or its correlates on geographic location—effects not mediated by the independent variable(s)—then phantom "contextual" effects will be created to confound analysis in aggregate data.

WHAT IS TO BE DONE?

Contextual analysis is potentially very powerful. It has already enriched our theories of political behavior by drawing them across levels of analysis. It has also made those theories more realistic. It is crashingly obvious now, but was not "obvious" until contextual theorists pointed it out, that a middle-class voter behaves differently in a West Virginia coal town than in suburban Philadelphia.[1]

However, contextual analysis is caught in a problem of *empirical* estimation. In conventional "contextual" data, aggregation effects are hopelessly confounded with contextual processes. The problem is serious enough that we do not believe contextual processes can be satisfactorily evaluated using aggregated, group-level variables. Individual-level data are needed. How might they be used?

Erbring and Young (1979) have set up the problem in a particularly helpful way. They consider the case of contextual effects due to communication networks, and specify their model unambiguously at the individual level. In that case, the social-context variables are given by the scores on the dependent variable of other individuals with whom a

---

1. For all this, in the dead of night we would admit to a certain continuing agnosticism on the whole question of contextual effects. Certainly, a member of the middle class acts differently in suburban Philadelphia than in a West Virginia coal town. But does "middle class" mean the same in both places? And why did these two members of the "middle class" end up (and stay) in such disparate places? If they act differently, can we really say this is due to differences in their surroundings? It is still the case, after decades of serious work by smart people, that contextual theories are ill articulated—the dramatic exception is Erbring and Young (1979)—and the empirical evidence maculate.

given person is in contact. Everyone who communicates with a given person exerts some influence, and the effect may be reciprocal. Thus, if relationships are linear, we may write with Erbring and Young

(1) $$y = \rho W y + X \beta + u,$$

where y is the vector of observations on the dependent variable, W is a matrix of interconnections (so that w_{ij} is positive if i is influenced by j and i and j are distinct), X is a matrix of observations on the exogenous variables, u is a disturbance vector, ρ is a scalar parameter, and β is the vector of regression coefficients on the exogenous variables.

In equation (1), the vector y is the list of the opinions of everyone in the network, while W measures the network's interconnections. The effect of premultiplying y by the matrix W is to create a vector whose elements are the group influences on each person—a weighted average of the opinions of those who influence the individual. Thus the full equation says that opinions are a linear function of both the net influence of others and of exogenous variables. (Notice that the exogenous variables themselves may be demographic variables which proxy for additional communication networks, e.g., "Catholic" or "Asian-American.") All relationships are based on the individual as the unit of observation.

The Erbring-Young model is a powerful instrument for thinking about context. By demonstrating that contextual effects have their natural theoretical formulation at the individual level, the model clears away confusions that have bedeviled too much thinking on the subject. The dangers of using aggregate data to estimate contextual effects become obvious. And unlike so much of the "network" literature in sociology, this model makes clear both its causal structure and the statistical foundation on which it rests.

However, the model also makes clear why the estimation of contextual influence is not statistically routine even with individual-level data. Equation (1) is simultaneous in its causal effects: everyone may influence everyone else. Hence the conventional statistical methods used in contextual studies are inappropriate. Cross-tabulations or ordinary regressions which relate people's opinions to those of their friends are biased as statistical methods.

The bias is typically toward finding contextual effects even when they do not exist. Due to occupational, residential, and geographic segregation along many dimensions, people with preexisting similar opinions would tend to wind up as friends and neighbors, even if they never spoke to one another and knew nothing of each other's views. Do their subsequent conversations make them even more similar? These two causes of opinion clustering are quite different: The first is the grouping into neighborhoods or conversational networks that causes selection bias, while the second is genuinely contextual. Unfortunately, conventional cross-tabulation and regression methods cannot tell the difference. Genuine effects are indistinguishable from the artifactual clustering of opinions that is always present.

The Erbring-Young model shows that statistical methods which assume unidirectional causation are inadequate. Structural equation techniques ("simultaneous equations") are needed to assess contextual effects. This is yet another contribution of Erbring and Young—placing the study of context squarely within a statistical tradition whose estimation methods are adequate to the task.

Even with structural equation methods, however, estimating a contextual relationship like equation (1) is no simple matter, as Erbring and Young themselves point out. First, the number of equations may be enormous—as many equations as there are individuals in the network. Even if purely computational issues can be overcome, the data demands quickly become intimidating. In a conventional survey sample of a thousand persons from a town, the matrix W of influence connections will have one million entries, most of them zero, no doubt, but many thousands of others nonzero. The specification assumes that all these entries are known to the investigator in advance. Filling in the entries requires detailed knowledge of the communication network, which will rarely be available. Yet if, as is customary in contextual studies, the opinions of neighbors and friends are approximated by more conveniently acquired data, measurement error results.

A second difficulty is present as well. Erbring and Young treat the matrix of network connections, W, as fixed. In practice, of course, it is endogenous (cf. p. 226 above). That is, to a substantial degree people can choose the people they talk to, and they will often choose to talk to people similar to themselves. Even if friends are chosen for nonpolitical reasons (say, common hobbies or church membership), similarities in opinions are likely to occur. Thus even if assignment to districts were perfectly random or conditionally independent, and even if no one's opinions ever influenced anyone else, contextual studies would still find that people's opinions were correlated with those of the people with whom they interact. Again, conventional statistical methods will always find a contextual correlation, but nothing follows about the reciprocal influence of opinions.

A trustworthy assessment of contextual effects therefore requires that network connections be treated as endogenous. The theoretical foundations for doing so exist. Unlike the case with aggregate data, structural equation methods applied to survey data offer more than a pious hope. Nonlinear simultaneous equation techniques are designed for cases like equation (1) with an endogenous W. However, as we have said, the practical challenges of carrying out the task are formidable, and econometric progress would seem to depend on creative but credible simplification of the task. The subject awaits further inspiration.

In summary, then, contextual studies aim to demonstrate that friends' and neighbors' opinions cause one's own opinions. Indeed, the correlations are always strong. To be persuasive about contextual causation of opinions, however, the correlation must be shown to be neither (1) the effects of measurement error, nor (2) selection effects due to geographic clustering, nor (3) selection effects due to choice of partners for interaction. Thus any study claiming to have found contextual effects in individual-level data must pass three tests to attain credibility:

1. Statistical noise: Is the contextual variable in use a genuine measure of the average opinion in one's social network? If not, how have the measurement errors been dealt with?
2. Selection due to geographic clustering: How confident can we be that an apparent effect of one's neighborhood on one's opinions is not due to one's opinions determining one's neighborhood? To the extent that simultaneity is present, how has its impact been minimized?
3. Selection due to choice of partners for interaction: How confident can we be that an apparent effect of one's conversation partners on one's opinions is not due to one's opinions determining one's conversational partners? How has the impact of this kind of simultaneity been minimized?

We know of no contextual studies which fully meet these criteria. Certainly the usual efforts, which regress individual opinions on demographic variables plus countywide averages in the hope that the county averages are statistically significant, cannot expect to be very persuasive. However, some investigators such as Putnam (1966) and Huckfeldt and Sprague (1987, 1988, 1991), among others, have made significant progress, using sophisticated data sets that measure both individual opinions and those of others who influence the individual. (Sprague 1982, is also relevant.)

Huckfeldt and Sprague, for instance, conducted a three-wave survey of 1,500 residents of 16 neighborhoods in South Bend, Indiana. They characterized the 16 neighborhoods with regard to opinion and behavior by the mean response of those interviewed in each neighborhood. This created 16 aggregate districts that are more finely delineated than the usual accidental aggregations used in contextual studies.

Huckfeldt and Sprague also asked respondents to identify the three people they "talked with most about the events of the past election year," and in a fourth wave they interviewed 900 of these discussants. Thus they obtained information on conversational network contexts as well as the aggregated neighborhood contexts. In analyzing the data set, they use as independent variables combinations of respondents' demographic characteristics, neighborhood characteristics, and discussants' characteristics. A good example is table 3 of Huckfeldt and Sprague (1991, p. 134), where they predict each respondent's vote from party identification, union membership, age, and other demographic characteristics, plus the union membership in the respondent's neighborhood and the main discussant's candidate preference. Thus in terms of Erbring and Young's model, Huckfeldt and Sprague approximate the influence vector Wy by measuring the principal influence path directly for each respondent and then adding a simple average of the neighborhood to stand in for other influences.

Such studies have not provided a way to eliminate selection biases due either to neighborhood clustering or to the reciprocal impact of opinions on friendship choices. The Huckfeldt and Sprague "neighborhood" measures, for instance, are just as surely geographic aggregates as if the Census Bureau had done the estimation rather than the investigators, and are thus fully subject to selection effects through geographic aggregation. However, these data do offer the advantage that distortions due to measurement error (problem 1 above) are minimized by careful delineation of neighborhoods. Moreover, interviewing both respondents and their discussants is a sophisticated study design greatly superior to earlier studies which relied on respondent recall for all information about discussants. If simultaneous equation models were to be tried in contextual studies, these data sets provide something like the detailed observations that would be required.

Last, if one is dealing with dichotomous opinions or behaviors, such data sets also offer an opportunity for at least a negative test of contextual effects. Since these data include rates of interaction with others who share one's opinions or behaviors, they allow us to compare the amount of dyadic agreement in the population with a baseline suggested by Przeworski (1974, pp. 35–36). Przeworski's baseline is the relative frequency of interaction between two group members that would be produced by random mixing of individuals in a district, given the proportion of group members in that area. For a network of any size, the baseline distribution of group members within it is calculated easily from the binomial theorem. If, on average, interaction makes opinions more similar to the majority view, then surveys will show that interacting pairs are more similar than chance would predict. Thus if reported interactions between people with shared opinions are no higher than the baseline, then we can say with assurance that there are no contextual effects due to majority influence.[2] When this is the case, any apparent "neighborhood" effect ordinarily should be ascribed to selection effects. Thus suppose that the proportion of working-class socialists interacting with other working-class socialists is no more than chance. Then the fact that the proportion of the working class voting socialist rises with the percentage working class in the district must be due to selection bias rather than majoritarian contextual influence.

This approach provides a negative test, but of course it cannot prove a positive result. If interaction rates among those with shared opinions are above the random-mixing baseline, we cannot know whether conversations are producing opinions or opinions producing conversation. And if apparent neighborhood effects are also present, then the positive result is useless for deciding whether those effects are due to selection into neighborhoods or to genuine contextual processes.

CONCLUSION

Crude measures of contextual influence, such as districtwide opinions, are typically used in aggregate studies. Their measurement errors are substantial. More importantly, pseudocontextual effects may appear at the aggregate level for reasons having nothing to do with social interactions, as in the simulation discussed in this chapter. In aggregate data, no statistical evidence exists by which to distinguish the real from

---

2. Under the assumption that individuals adopt the view of the majority of their discussants with some probability p, we have proved for interacting networks of size three that if interactions between people with shared opinions are no higher than Przeworski's baseline, then this implies no majority influence (i.e., $p = 0$). We believe the proof should generalize readily except in the degenerate case in which all networks are of size two; we offer the generalization here as a conjecture.

the apparent. By their nature, then, aggregate data are virtually useless for studying contextual effects.

Individual-level studies offer the only real hope of teasing out genuine contextual effects. Even with individual data, however, the task is not easy, and much of the theoretical and methodological foundation remains unbuilt. Traditional sociological theorizing has often been muddled, and contemporary sociological studies of networks commonly employ ad hoc measures and methods with little connection to statistical theory. Fortunately, recent improved individual-level data sets take us an important step forward in reducing measurement error and in offering the opportunity for at least a negative test of contextual effects. They also hold out the hope that structural equation methods may ultimately provide full statistical tests of contextual influence.

The theoretical and statistical complexities of individual-level contextual models remain daunting. More sophisticated modeling of context is the principal current challenge facing students of contextual effects. Attempting this will force the investigator back to the development of richly articulated theory, which lets contextual analysis play to what in any case should be its greatest strength.

REFERENCES

Achen, Christopher H. 1983a. If Party ID Influences the Vote, Goodman's Ecological Regression Is Biased. Paper presented at meetings of the American Political Science Association, Chicago, September 1–4.

———. 1983b. Toward Theories of Data. In *The State of Political Science,* ed. Ada Finifter. Washington, D.C.: American Political Science Association.

———. 1986a. Necessary and Sufficient Conditions for Unbiased Aggregation of Cross-Sectional Regressions. Paper presented at meetings of the American Political Science Association, Washington, D.C., August 28–31.

———. 1986b. *Statistical Methods for Quasi-Experiments.* Berkeley and Los Angeles: University of California Press.

———. 1992. Social Psychology, Demographic Variables, and Linear Regression. *Political Behavior* 14, 3:195–211.

———. 1993. MLE, Aggregate Data, and the Montana Test. Paper presented at meetings of the American Political Science Association, Washington, D.C., September 1–5.

———. 1994. Electoral Volatility and Dimensional Models for Historical Data Analysis. Paper presented at meetings of the Midwest Political Science Association, Chicago, April 14–16.

Alford, Robert R. 1963. *Party and Society.* Chicago: Rand McNally.

Alker, Hayward R., Jr. 1969. A Typology of Ecological Fallacies. In *Quantitative Ecological Analysis in the Social Sciences,* ed. M. Dogan and S. Rokkan, 69–86. Cambridge, Mass.: MIT Press.

Anselin, Luc. 1988. *Spatial Econometrics.* Boston: Kluwer.

Ansolabehere, Stephen, and Douglas Rivers. 1992a. Bias in Ecological Regression Estimates. Manuscript.

———. 1992b. Using Aggregate Data to Correct for Nonresponse and Misreporting in Surveys. Paper presented at meetings of the Political Methodology Group, Harvard University, July 15–18.

Asher, Herbert B. 1974. Some Consequences of Measurement Error in Survey Data. *American Journal of Political Science* 18:469–85.

Bentley, Arthur F. 1908. *The Process of Government: A Study of Social Pressures.* Chicago: University of Chicago Press.

Berelson, Bernard, Paul F. Lazarsfeld, and William N. McPhee. 1954. *Voting.* Chicago: University of Chicago Press.

Berglund, Sten, and Søren Risbjerg Thomsen. 1990. *Modern Political Ecological Analysis.* Abo, Denmark: Abo Academy Press.

Bernstein, F. 1932. Über eine Methode, die Soziologische und Bevölkerungsstatistische Gliederung von Abstimmungen bei Geheimem Wahlverfahren Statistisch zu Ermitteln. *Allgemeines Statistisches Archiv* 22:253–56.

Blalock, Hubert M. 1964. *Causal Inferences in Nonexperimental Research.* Chapel Hill: University of North Carolina Press.

Blank, R. 1905. Die Soziale Zusammensetzung der Sozialdemokratischen Wählerschaft Deutschlands. *Archiv für Sozialwissenschaft und Sozialpolitik* 20:507–53.

Bodman, A. R. 1983. The Neighborhood Effect: A Test of the Butler-Stokes Model. *British Journal of Political Science* 11:427–47.

Boudon, Raymond. 1963. Propriétés Individuelles et Propriétés Collectives: Un Problème d'Analyse Écologique. *Revue Française de Sociologie* 4: 275–99.

Bowers, William J. 1974. *Executions in America.* Lexington, Mass.: Lexington Books.

Boyd, Lawrence H., Jr., and Gudmund R. Iversen. 1979. *Contextual Analysis: Concepts and Statistical Techniques.* Belmont, Calif.: Wadsworth.

Brown, Courtney. 1982. The Nazi Vote: A National Ecological Study. *American Political Science Review* 76:285–302.

———. 1988. Mass Dynamics of U.S. Presidential Competitions, 1928–36. *American Political Science Review* 82:1153–81.

———. 1991. *Ballots of Tumult.* Ann Arbor: University of Michigan Press.

Brown, Philip J., and Clive D. Payne. 1986. Aggregate Data, Ecological Regression, and Voting Transitions. *Journal of the American Statistical Association* 81:452–60.

Butler, David, and Donald Stokes. 1969. *Political Change in Britain.* New York: St. Martin's.

Campbell, Angus. 1966. Surge and Decline: A Study of Electoral Change. In *Elections and the Political Order,* ed. Angus Campbell, Philip Converse, Warren Miller, and Donald Stokes, 40–62. New York: Wiley.

Campbell, Angus, Philip Converse, Warren Miller, and Donald Stokes. 1960. *The American Voter.* New York: Wiley.

Childer, Thomas. 1983. *The Nazi Voter: The Social Foundations of Fascism in Germany, 1919–1933.* Chapel Hill: University of North Carolina Press.

Claggett, William. 1985. Conversion, Recruitment, Mobilization and Realignments. Paper presented at meetings of the American Political Science Association, New Orleans, August 29–September 1.

Claggett, William, and John Van Wingen. 1988. Ecological Inference: An Extension of an Old Procedure. Paper presented at meetings of the Southern Political Science Association, Atlanta, November 4–6.

Cliff, A. D., and J. K. Ord. 1973. *Spatial Autocorrelation.* London: Pion.

Converse, Philip. 1966. The Concept of a Normal Vote. In *Elections and the Political Order,* ed. Angus Campbell, Philip Converse, Warren Miller, and Donald Stokes, 9–39. New York: Wiley.

———. 1969. Survey Research and the Decoding of Patterns in Ecological Data. In *Quantitative Ecological Analysis in the Social Sciences,* ed. M. Dogan and S. Rokkan, 459–85. Cambridge, Mass.: MIT Press.

Crewe, Ivor, and Clive Payne. 1976. Another Game with Nature: An Ecological Regression Model of the British Two-Party Vote Ratio in 1970. *British Journal of Political Science* 6:43–81.

Deaton, Angus, and John Muellbauer. 1980. *Economics and Consumer Behavior.* New York: Cambridge University Press.

Duncan, O. Dudley. 1970. Partials, Partitions, and Paths. In *Sociological Methodology,* ed. E. F. Borgatta and G. W. Bohrnstedt, 38–47. San Francisco: Jossey-Bass.

Duncan, O. Dudley, and Beverly Davis. 1953. An Alternative to Ecological Correlation. *American Sociological Review* 18:665–66.

Durkheim, Emile. 1897. *Le Suicide.* Paris: F. Alcan.

Erbring, Lutz. 1990. Individuals Writ Large: An Epilogue on the "Ecological Fallacy." *Political Analysis* 1:235–69.

Erbring, Lutz, and Alice A. Young. 1979. Individuals and Social Structure: Contextual Effects as Endogenous Feedback. *Sociological Methods and Research* 7:396–430.

Falter, Jürgen W. 1991. *Hitler's Wähler.* Munich: Beck.

Fiorina, Morris. 1981. *Retrospective Voting in American Elections.* New Haven, Conn.: Yale University Press.

Firebaugh, Glenn. 1978. A Rule For Inferring Individual-Level Relationships from Aggregate Data. *American Sociological Review* 43:557–72.

Flanigan, William H., and Nancy Zingale. 1985. Alchemist's Gold: Inferring Individual Relationships from Aggregate Data. *Social Science History* 9: 71–92.

Freedman, David A., Stephen P. Klein, Jerome Sacks, C. Smythe, and C. Everett. 1991. Ecological Regression and Voting Rights *Evaluation Review* 25: 673–711.

Friedman, Gerald. 1990. Capitalism, Republicanism, Socialism, and the State: France, 1871–1914. *Social Science History* 14:151–74.

Gehlke, C. E., and Katherine Biehl. 1934. Certain Effects of Grouping upon the Size of the Correlation Coefficient in Census Tract Material. *Journal of the American Statistical Association,* Proceedings Supplement 29 (March): 169–70.

Gienapp, William E. 1987. *The Origins of the Republican Party, 1952–1856.* New York: Oxford University Press.

Goguel, François. 1951. *Géographie des Élections Française de 1870 à 1951.* Paris: A. Colin.

Goodman, Leo. 1953. Ecological Regression and the Behavior of Individuals. *American Sociological Review* 18:663–64.

———. 1959. Some Alternatives to Ecological Correlation. *American Journal of Sociology* 64:610–25.

Goodman, Paul. 1988. *Towards a Christian Republic: Antimasonry and the Great Transition in New England, 1826–1836.* New York: Oxford University Press.

Gosnell, Harold. 1937. *Machine Politics: Chicago Model.* Chicago: University of Chicago Press.

———. 1942. *Grass Roots Politics.* Washington, D.C.: American Council on Public Affairs.

Gow, David John. 1985. Quantification and Statistics in the Early Years of American Political Science, 1880–1922. *Political Methodology* 11 (1–2): 1–18.

Green, J. A. John. 1964. *Aggregation in Economic Analysis.* Princeton, N.J.: Princeton University Press.

Grofman, Bernard. 1991. Statistics without Substance. *Evaluation Review* 15: 659–72.

Haitovsky, Yoel. 1973. *Regression Estimation from Grouped Observations.* New York: Hafner.

Hamilton, Richard F. 1982. *Who Voted for Hitler?* Princeton, N.J.: Princeton University Press.

Hannan, Michael T. 1991. *Aggregation and Disaggregation in the Social Sciences,* rev. ed. Lexington, Mass.: Lexington Books.

Hanushek, Eric A., John E. Jackson, and John F. Kain. 1974. Model Specification, Use of Aggregate Data, and the Ecological Correlation Fallacy. *Political Methodology* 1:89–107.

Hauser, Robert M. 1970. Context and Consex: A Cautionary Tale. *American Journal of Sociology* 75:645–64.

———. 1974. Contextual Analysis Revisited. *Sociological Methods and Research* 2:365–75.

Hawkes, A. G. 1969. An approach to the Analysis of Electoral Swing. *Journal of the Royal Statistical Society,* Ser. A 132:68–79.

Hedayat, A. S., and Bikas K. Sinha. 1991. *Design and Inference in Finite Population Sampling.* New York: Wiley.

Hildreth, C., and J. P. Houck. 1968. Some Estimators for a Linear Model with Random Coefficients. *Journal of the American Statistical Association* 63: 584–95.

Huckfeldt, Robert. 1986. *Politics in Context: Assimilation and Conflict in Urban Neighborhoods.* New York: Agathon.

Huckfeldt, Robert, and John Sprague. 1987. Networks in Context: The Social Flow of Political Information. *American Political Science Review* 81:1197–1216.

———. 1988. Choice, Social Structure, and Political Information: The Informational Coercion of Minorities. *American Journal of Political Science* 32: 467–82.

———. 1991. Discussant Effects on Vote Choice: Intimacy, Structure, and Interdependence. *Journal of Politics* 53:122–58.

Ijiri, Yuji. 1971. Fundamental Queries in Aggregation Theory. *Journal of the American Statistical Association* 66:766–82.

Irwin, Galen, and Duane A. Meeter. 1969. Building Voter Transition Models from Aggregate Data. *Midwest Journal of Political Science* 13:545–66.

Iversen, Gudmund. 1981. Group Data and Individual Behavior. In *Analyzing Electoral History*, ed. Jerome M. Clubb, William H. Flanigan, and Nancy H. Zingale, 267–302. Beverly Hills: Sage.

Jackson, John E. 1975. Issues, Party Choices, and Presidential Votes. *American Journal of Political Science* 19:161–85.

Jones, E. Terrence. 1972. Ecological Inference and Electoral Analysis. *Journal of Interdisciplinary History* 2:249–62.

Judge, George G., W. E. Griffiths, R. Carter Hill, Helmut Lutkepohl, and Tsoung-Chao Lee. 1985. *The Theory and Practice of Econometrics*, 2d ed. New York: Wiley.

Kalbfleisch, J. D., and J. F. Lawless. 1984. Least-Squares Estimation of Transition Probabilities from Aggregate Data. *Canadian Journal of Statistics* 12:169–82.

Key, V. O., Jr. 1949. *Southern Politics in State and Nation*. New York: Knopf.

———. 1955. A Theory of Critical Elections. *Journal of Politics* 17:3–18.

———. 1959. Secular Realignment and the Party System. *Journal of Politics* 21:198–210.

King, Gary. 1990. On Political Methodology. *Political Analysis* 2:1–29.

Klein, L. R. 1946. Remarks on the Theory of Aggregation. *Econometrica* 14 (October):285–98.

Klein, Stephen P., and David A. Freedman. 1993. Ecological Regression in Voting Rights Cases. *Chance* 6:38–43.

Klein, Stephen P., Jerome Sacks, and David A. Freedman. 1991. Ecological Regression vs. the Secret Ballot. *Jurimetrics* 31:393–413.

Kmenta, Jan. 1971. *Elements of Econometrics*. New York: Macmillan.

Kousser, J. Morgan. 1973. Ecological Regression and the Analysis of Past Politics. *Journal of Interdisciplinary History* 4:237–62.

———. 1974. *The Shaping of Southern Politics*. New Haven, Conn.: Yale University Press.

Langbein, Laura Irwin, and Allan J. Lichtman. 1976. *Ecological Inference*. Beverly Hills, Calif.: Sage.

Lave, Lester B., and Eugene P. Seskin. 1977. *Air Pollution and Human Health*. Baltimore: Johns Hopkins University Press.

Le Bon, Gustave. 1897. *The Crowd*. London: T. Fisher Unwin.

Lee, T. C., G. G. Judge, and A. Zellner. 1970. *Estimating the Parameters of the Markov Probability Model from Aggregate Time Series Data*. Amsterdam: North-Holland.

Lewis-Beck, Michael S. 1988. *Economics and Elections*. Ann Arbor: University of Michigan Press.

Lichtman, Allan. 1991. Passing the Test. *Evaluation Review* 15:770–99.

Lord, Frederick M., and Melvin R. Novick. 1968. *Statistical Theories of Mental Test Scores*. Reading, Mass.: Addison-Wesley.

Lupia, Arthur, and Kenneth McCue. 1990. Why the 1980s' Measures of Racially Polarized Voting Are Inadequate for the 1990s. *Law & Policy* 12: 353–387.

McCarthy, Colm, and Terence Ryan. 1977. Estimates of Voter Transition Probabilities from the British General Election of 1974. *Journal of the Royal Statistical Society,* Ser. A 140, pt. 1: 78–85.

McCarthy, John L., and John W. Tukey. 1978. Exploratory Analysis of Aggregate Voting Behavior: Presidential Elections in New Hampshire, 1896–1972. *Social Science History* 2:292–331.

McCrary, Peyton. 1990. Racially Polarized Voting in the South: Quantitative Evidence from the Courtroom. *Social Science History* 14:507–31.

McCue, Kenneth F. 1992. The Inference of Individual Probabilities from Aggregate Data. Paper presented at meetings of the Political Methodology Group, Harvard University, July 15–18.

MacKinnon, James G., and Halbert White. 1985. Some Heteroskedasticity-Consistent Covariance Matrix Estimators with Improved Finite-Sample Properties. *Journal of Econometrics* 29:305–25.

MacKuen, Michael, and Courtney Brown. 1987. Political Context and Attitude Change. *American Political Science Review* 81:42–56.

MacRae, Duncan, Jr., and James A. Meldrum. 1969. Factor Analysis of Aggregate Voting Statistics. In *Quantitative Ecological Analysis in the Social Sciences,* ed. M. Dogan and S. Rokkan, 487–506. Cambridge, Mass.: MIT Press.

MacRae, Elizabeth Chase. 1977. Estimation of Time-Varying Markov Processes with Aggregate Data. *Econometrica* 45:183–198.

Madansky, A. 1959. Least Squares Estimation in Finite Markov Processes. *Psychometrika* 24:137–44.

Maritz, J. S. 1970. *Empirical Bayes Methods.* London: Methuen.

Marks, Gary, and Matthew Burbank. 1990. Immigrant Support for the American Socialist Party, 1912 and 1920. *Social Science History* 14 (Summer): 175–202.

May, Kenneth O. 1946. The Aggregation Problem for a One-Industry Model. *Econometrica* 14 (October): 285–98.

Meckstroth, Theodore W. 1974. Some Problems in Cross-Level Inference. *American Journal of Political Science* 18:45–66.

Michels, Robert. 1949. *Political Parties.* Glencoe, Ill.: Free Press.

Miller, G. A. 1952. Finite Markov Processes in Psychology. *Psychometrika* 17: 149–67.

Miller, Warren E. 1956. One-Party Politics and the Voter. *American Political Science Review* 50:707–25.

Miller, W. L. 1972. Measures of Electoral Change Using Aggregate Data. *Journal of the Royal Statistical Society,* Ser. A 135, pt. 1: 122–42.

Miller, W. L., Gillian Raab, and K. Britto. 1974. Voting Research and the Population Census 1918–71: Surrogate Data for Constituency Analyses. *Journal of the Royal Statistical Society,* Ser. A 137, pt. 3: 384–411.

Muncaster, Robert, and Dina Zinnes. 1984. The Dynamics of Hostile Activity and the Prediction of War. *Journal of Conflict Resolution* 28 (June): 187–229.

Ogburn, William F., and Delvin Peterson. 1916. The Political Thought of Social Classes. *Political Science Quarterly* 31 (June): 300–317.

Orwell, George. 1946. *Animal Farm.* New York: Harcourt, Brace.

Powell, James L., and Thomas M. Stoker. 1985. The Estimation of Complete Aggregation Structures. *Journal of Econometrics* 30:317–44.

Prysby, Charles L., and John W. Books. 1991. *Political Behavior and the Local Context.* New York: Praeger.

Przeworski, Adam. 1974. Contextual Models of Political Behavior. *Political Methodology* 1:27–60.

Putnam, Robert D. 1966. Political Attitudes and the Local Community. *American Political Science Review* 60:640–54.

Reynolds, John F. 1988. *Testing Democracy: Electoral Behavior and Progressive Reform in New Jersey, 1880–1920.* Chapel Hill: University of North Carolina Press.

Richardson, Lewis F. 1960. *Arms and Insecurity.* Chicago: Quadrangle Books.

Richmond, J. 1976. Aggregation and Identification. *International Economic Review* 17:47–56.

Ripley, Brian D. 1981. *Spatial Statistics.* New York: Wiley.

Robinson, W. S. 1950. Ecological Correlations and the Behavior of Individuals. *American Sociological Review* 15:351–57.

Rogin, Michael P. 1967. *The Intellectuals and McCarthy: The Radical Specter.* Cambridge, Mass.: MIT Press.

Roth, Randolph A. 1987. *The Democratic Dilemma: Religion, Reform, and the Social Order in the Connecticut River Valley of Vermont, 1791–1850.* New York: Cambridge University Press.

Rubinfeld, Daniel J. 1991. Statistical and Demographic Issues Underlying Voting Rights Cases. *Evaluation Review* 15:659–72.

Särlvik, Bo, and Ivor Crewe. 1983. *Decade of Dealignment: The Conservative Victory of 1979 and Electoral Trends in the 1970s.* Cambridge: Cambridge University Press.

Schlicht, Ekkehart. 1985. *Isolation and Aggregation in Economics.* Berlin: Springer.

Schmidt, Peter. 1976. *Econometrics.* New York: Marcel Dekker.

Schumpeter, Joseph A. (1942) 1976. *Capitalism, Socialism and Democracy.* New York: Harper and Row.

Shafer, W., and Hugo Sonnenschein. 1982. Market Demand and Excess Demand Functions. In *Handbook of Mathematical Economics,* vol. 2. Ed. K. J. Arrow and M. D. Intriligator, chap. 15. Amsterdam: North-Holland.

Shively, W. Phillips. 1969. "Ecological" Inference: The Use of Aggregate Data to Study Individuals. *American Political Science Review* 63:1183–96.

———. 1974. Utilizing External Evidence in Cross-Level Inference. *Political Methodology* 1:61–74.

———. 1982. The Electoral Impact of Party Loyalists and the "Floating Vote": A New Measure and a New Perspective. *Journal of Politics* 44:679–91.

————. 1987a. Cross-Level Inference as an Identification Problem. Paper presented at meetings of the Midwest Political Science Association, Chicago, April 8–11.

————. 1987b. A Strategy for Cross-Level Inference under an Assumption of Breakage Effects. *Political Methodology* 11:167–79.

————. 1991. A General Extension of the Method of Bounds, with Special Application to Studies of Electoral Transition. *Historical Methods* 24:81–94.

————. 1992. From Differential Abstention to Conversion: A Change in Electoral Change, 1864–1988. *American Journal of Political Science* 36:309–30.

Siegfried, Andre. 1913. *Tableau Politique de la France de l'Ouest Sous la Troisième République.* Paris: A. Colin.

Sigelman, Lee. 1991. Turning Cross Sections into a Panel: A Simple Procedure for Ecological Inference. *Social Science Research* 20:150–70.

Silbey, Joel H., Allan G. Bogue, and William H. Flanigan. 1978. Introduction. In *The History of American Electoral Behavior,* ed. J. H. Silbey, A. G. Bogue, and W. H. Flanigan. Princeton, N.J.: Princeton University Press.

Silva, Ruth C. 1962. *Rum, Religion, and Votes: 1928 Re-Examined.* University Park: Pennsylvania State University Press.

Sprague, John. 1976. Estimating a Boudon Type Contextual Model: Some Practical and Theoretical Problems of Measurement. *Political Methodology* 3:333–53.

————. 1982. Is There A Micro Theory Consistent with Contextual Analysis? In *Strategies of Political Inquiry,* ed. Elinor Ostrom. Beverly Hills, Calif.: Sage.

Stipak, Brian, and Carl Henster. 1982. Statistical Inference in Contextual Analysis. *American Journal of Political Science* 26:151–75.

Stoker, Thomas M. 1984. Completeness, Distribution Restrictions, and the Form of Aggregate Functions. *Econometrica* 52:887–907.

————. 1985. Aggregation, Structural Change, and Cross-section Estimation. *Journal of the American Statistical Association* 80:720–29.

————. 1986. Aggregation, Efficiency and Cross-Section Regression. *Econometrica* 54:171–88.

Stokes, Donald E. 1969. Cross-Level Inference as a Game against Nature. In *Mathematical Applications in Political Science IV,* ed. Joseph L. Bernd, 62–83. Charlottesville: University Press of Virginia.

Theil, Henri. 1955. *Linear Aggregation of Economic Relations.* Amsterdam: North-Holland.

Thomsen, Søren Risbjerg. 1987. *Danish Elections 1920–1979: A Logit Approach to Ecological Analysis and Inference.* Aarhus, Denmark: Politica.

The Times. 1950, 1951, 1955, 1959, 1964, 1966. *House of Commons.* London: The Times Office.

Tönnies, Ferdinand. 1924. Korrelation der Parteien in Statistik der Kieler Reichstagswahlen. *Jahrbücher für Nationalökonomie und Statistik* 122:663–72.

Upton, Graham J. 1978. A Note on the Estimation of Voter Transition Probabilities. *Journal of the Royal Statistical Society,* Ser. A 141, pt. 4: 507–12.

Wanat, John. 1979. The Application of a Non-Analytic, Most Possible Estimation Technique: The Relative Impact of Mobilization and Conversion of Votes in the New Deal. *Political Methodology* 6:357–374.

———. 1982. Most Possible Estimates and Maximum Likelihood Estimates. *Sociological Methods and Research* 10:453–62.

White, Halbert. 1980. A Heteroskedasticity-Consistent Covariance Matrix Estimator and a Direct Test for Heteroskedasticity. *Econometrica* 48: 817–38.

Wright, Gerald C. 1977. Contextual Models of Electoral Behavior: The Wallace Vote. *American Political Science Review* 71:497–508.

Würzburger, Eugen. 1907. Die "Partei der Nichtwähler." *Jahrbücher für Nationalökonomie and Statistik* 88:381–89.

Zellner, Arnold. 1969. On the Aggregation Problem: A New Approach to a Troublesome Problem. In *Economic Models, Estimation and Risk Programming,* ed. K. A. Fox et al., 365–74. Berlin: Springer.

INDEX